SUCCESSFUL
RESTAURANT
DESIGN

SUCCESSFUL RESTAURANT DESIGN

Regina S. Baraban
Joseph F. Durocher, Ph.D.

VNR Van Nostrand Reinhold
New York

Library of Congress Catalog Card Number 88-14149

ISBN 0-442-21839-7

Printed in the United States of America

Designed by Monika Grejniec

Van Nostrand Reinhold
115 Fifth Avenue
New York, New York 10003

Van Nostrand Reinhold International Company Limited
11 New Fetter Lane
London EC4P 4EE, England

Van Nostrand Reinhold
480 La Trobe Street
Melbourne, Victoria 3000, Australia

Nelson Canada
1120 Birchmount Road
Scarborough, Ontario M1K 5G4, Canada

16 15 14 13 12 11 10 9 8 7 6 5 4 3 2

Library of Congress Cataloging-in-Publication Data
Baraban, Regina S.
   Successful restaurant design/Regina S. Baraban, Joseph F. Durocher.
      p.   cm.
   Includes index.
   ISBN 0-442-21839-7
   1. Restaurants, lunch rooms, etc.—Design and construction.
I. Durocher, Joseph F., 1948–   . II. Title.
TX945.B36   1988
647'.95'0682—dc19   88-14149
                                                         CIP

CONTENTS

PREFACE

The story goes like this: One day we compared libraries. One of us had books on design and architecture, some of which focused on front-of-the-house spaces in restaurants; the other had a multitude of texts on restaurant management and back-of-the-house design. The books that covered the back of the house said nothing about the front, and vice versa. As we began to review each other's books—now in a combined library—we realized that one set of books looked at the restaurant only from the front door to the kitchen entrance. The other books started at the receiving dock and stopped at the same kitchen door. None of them clearly showed how the front and back of the house worked together.

The rest, as they say, is history. We'd like to note, however, that *Successful Restaurant Design* is not a technical manual. Rather, it is a guide to help the reader understand how a restaurant works, back and front, because we believe this understanding is essential to good restaurant design. It also reveals the thinking of leading designers and restaurateurs—not just what they did but why they did it. We chose to focus not just on million-dollar extravaganzas but also on more modest places as well, places that represent the heart of the restaurant industry. We selected examples from all types of food-service establishments, from hospital cafeterias to the hottest new gathering places.

This is a book of philosophy and ideas as well as practical applications. Our thesis is that restaurant design is a process; a set of interactive steps that can't be reduced to fail-safe formulas. By the same token, good design can't guarantee business success. We refer to all the restaurants in the present tense, even though some of them will already have closed their doors.

By looking at the restaurant as a whole, front and back, from the point of view of customer, chef, manager, owner, and designer, we offer a new perspective. Our hope is that this book will help to bridge communication gaps between people as well as between libraries.

ACKNOWLEDGMENTS

Throughout this project a host of designers, architects, restaurateurs, and photographers generously contributed their time and expertise. To all of them, we are forever grateful.

Special thanks go to Ron Bergeron, Yvette Croteau, and Eileen McGahey from the Department of Media Services at the University of New Hampshire; to Ann Stanley; to *Food Management* magazine; to *Metropolis* magazine; and to *Restaurant Business* magazine. In particular, we are grateful to *Metropolis* for allowing us to share information gathered for "Best Dressed Restaurants" reviews of America, Extra! Extra!, Alo Alo, Zig Zag Bar & Grill, Twenty:Twenty, Batons, Shun Lee West, Nishi Noho, McDonald's Rockefeller Center, and Remi. To

Food Management magazine, we give acknowledgments for the information first published in the May 1987 issue, pages 200–205, regarding The Greenery at St. Vincent Medical Center. To Mitch Schechter and Donna Boss of *Food Management* and Susan Szenasy of *Metropolis*, thanks for your kind support during this effort.

To our family and friends, who for too long had to hear "Sorry, we have to work on the book," thanks for standing by us then and being there now, especially Gladys and Harry Scheckman, Regina's parents, and Carolyn W. Durocher. Dad would be proud. To Debra, Lori, and Gail Durocher: Summers will be a lot more fun without us glued to our computers.

1

THE PROCESS OF FOODSERVICE DESIGN

WHERE DESIGN BEGINS

The restaurant can be compared to any complex system that depends on all of its parts to function correctly. Metaphorically speaking, it is comparable to an old-fashioned pocket watch. What people see is the face and hands. What makes the watch work are the hidden gears, which have been intricately designed to keep the hands revolving in time. Front and back of the watch are meaningless without each other. Similarly, all spaces in the restaurant should be considered not only on their own terms but also on how well they perform in relation to the whole. What this means is that front- and back-of-the-house design should be an integrated package, even if they are designed by different parties.

All too often, however, the two halves of the restaurant are designed by separate people looking at the space from different doors: the foodservice consultant from the back door and the interior designer from the front. Because their respective responsibilities ended at the swinging door between the two spaces, the resulting operation does not function smoothly.

The fact of the matter is that both sides of the door are influenced by the restaurant concept and by each other. If the front of the house is not designed to support the back of the house and/or the back of the house is not designed to carry out the concept manifested in the front of

the house, then the operation suffers. For instance, picture a classical kitchen with a full battery of ranges, ovens, steamers, and so on, all geared to produce a comprehensive menu for a gourmet restaurant. A typical fast food interior design scheme would be an obvious mismatch with this classical kitchen and would result in financial disaster for the restaurant. Another example would be the inclusion of a bank of deep-fat fryers in the kitchen of a 1980s style cafe serving Northern Italian cuisine. The deep-fat fryers are a costly and space-wasting mistake because fried foods are not commonly used for this type of menu.

Unfortunately, mismatches occur often because the restaurant concept and menu are not fully developed prior to the design programming. The secret to a good match is to conduct a careful market study and menu analysis prior to determining any specific design elements in the kitchen or dining areas.

Consideration of the following ten areas can help to achieve an integrative design process that results in a successful match of front and back of the house. They should be considered at the start of a project, before arriving at layouts and specifications.

The Type of Restaurant

One of the first decisions concerning all foodservice spaces has to do with the type of restaurant. There are many ways to classify the type of restaurant. Generally the owner decides which of the following categories apply:

Free-standing or within an existing
structure
Independent or chain
Take-out or eat-in
Theme or nontheme
Ethnic or nonethnic

The type of restaurant also encompasses market segment classifications such as fast food, coffee shop, hotel dining, family restaurant, gathering place, and corporate cafeteria (fig. 1-1).

The direct correlation between type of restaurant and choice of kitchen equipment is obvious: A Chinese restaurant calls for different equipment than a seafood family dinner house. Front of the house correlation with type of restaurant, however, may be more complex. In the case of the New York City restaurant Lox Around the Clock, for instance, the owners wanted a sit-down establishment where diners could get homestyle Jewish cooking twenty-four hours a day. From that directive, designer Sam Lopata created an interior scheme that supports a sit-down type of restaurant but bears no resemblance to the traditional Jewish deli. For the

1-1. *Type of restaurant can be expressed in many ways. At the Hilton Suites in Lexington, KY, for example, the dining area's location in an atrium lobby clearly defines it as a hotel restaurant. The design, by DiLeonardo International, expresses a subtle equine theme related to the local Kentucky Derby.*
(*Warren Jagger photo*)

Tex-Mex restaurant Home on the Range, on the other hand, the same designer effected a design scheme that bespeaks the rough-textured quality of a Wild West town. Here the reference to type of restaurant was more direct.

The Market

The importance of conducting a thorough market analysis before embarking on a restaurant design cannot be overemphasized. Even the most spectacular design, the most wonderful food, and the finest service can fail to save an establishment that doesn't meet the needs of the marketplace.

A good market analysis has four main components: potential customers, competition, location, and the economic environment. They are all interrelated, but each should be thoroughly analyzed.

POTENTIAL CUSTOMERS

Identifying the demographic and psychographic profiles of potential customers is crucial for restaurant design success (fig. 1-2). Lox Around the Clock works because it appeals to the twenty-four-hour eating sensibilities of youthful New Yorkers. Further, the menu offerings are suited to an ethnic city population that enjoys knishes and matzo ball soup. The unusual design scheme, which looks in part like a construction site and in part like a set from the old television show "The Addams Family," attracts chic, urban restaurant goers.

In some situations, the customers to be served at one meal period are totally different from those served at another period. In an Embassy suite hotel, breakfast is included in the price of the room and served almost exclusively to hotel guests, and lunch draws primarily a local business crowd. Many popular gathering

1-2. *At Rosalie's in San Francisco, the stylish lounge clearly attracts a sophisticated urban clientele.*
(Joseph Durocher photo)

places and cafes in urban areas serve lunch to a neighborhood clientele and dinner to a far-flung group of patrons who journey to the restaurant from different spots in the city.

In such instances, design needs to suit diverse groups of potential customers if the restaurant is to succeed. A room designed to act as an attractive backdrop rather than an imposing statement can appeal to different tastes. Changing certain elements for each meal period, such as tabletop appointments or lighting levels, can also alter the mood of a room. Similarly, different menu selections can be offered at lunch and dinner. Flexibility is a crucial design factor in both kitchen and dining areas for those establishments that serve a wide spectrum of customers.

THE COMPETITION

Sizing up the competition is critical to a good market analysis. It starts with identifying both the primary and secondary competition. Primary competitors are those restaurants located in close proximity that offer the same type of food and service as the proposed restaurant. Secondary competitors encompass the different types of restaurants located nearby. Even wildly divergent types—fast food from gourmet, coffee shop from singles gathering places—should be considered as potential competitors.

Next, the trick is to figure out how many restaurants the market can support and how well a particular type of restaurant can compete in the marketplace. Both data gathering and data analysis in this area can be very complex. Studies should indicate the financial health of competing restaurants and their volume of business. Every effort should be made to find out what future developments are planned for the neighborhood in question. When the owners of New York City's Zig Zag Bar & Grill (discussed in chapter 5) analyzed the restaurants on West 23d Street, they saw no direct competition for their proposed late-night gathering spot. Several months after Zig Zag opened, however, a hot new nightspot, Nells, invaded the scene and initially drew away business from nearby Zig Zag. As of this writing, it remains to be seen if, in the long term, competition hurts or helps Zig Zag's bottom line. If the addition of a competing nightspot helps to make 23d Street a popular destination neighborhood, then Zig Zag could ultimately profit from the competition.

LOCATION

"Location, location, location," the adage coined decades ago as the key to success, remains as true as ever. Restaurateur Joseph Baum says his acclaimed restaurant, Aurora (discussed in chapter 6), came into being in part because he was able to secure a location in Manhattan's midtown business district. Baum cites the ability to recognize a location that matches the type of restaurant as a crucial market factor. In the case of Aurora, a neighborhood business lunch crowd was enough to carry the restaurant while it developed a destination following for dinner.

Location also gives clues to customer psychographics. The high-tech, new cuisine restaurant that is a big hit in San Francisco would likely fail miserably if transplanted to a small Midwestern town because rural Midwesterners look for totally different dining and design experiences than trendy city folk.

The importance of location is exemplified by the story of New York–based restaurateur Michael Weinstein, who found that taking his wildly successful grand cafe concept out of Manhattan and into the New Jersey suburbs didn't work. Despite the fact that Jersey suburbanites throng to the Manhattan places, they did not respond favorably to the soaring, dramatic architectural milieu in their own backyard. Perhaps in the compressed urban environment, where most people live in small apartments, the huge restaurant space offers a welcome spatial experience, but in the suburbs, where most people live in houses, the same space might seem barnlike and intimidating.

Architecture is influenced by location as well (fig. 1-3). Free-standing restaurants in the middle of Manhattan or Chicago are rare, for instance. Moreover, different regions call for different architectural styles. The pitched roofs of New England are there to keep snow from collecting on the roof. Typical Southwestern architecture uses adobe—an indigenous material —to insulate the building from the hot summer sun. The exterior of a Chart House restaurant built several years ago in Rancho Mirage, Cali-

1-3. *The old factory that houses a Legal Sea Foods restaurant in Worcester, MA, designed by Morris Nathanson Design, is a building type typically found in restored inner city areas.*
(Warren Jagger photo)

fornia, looks rather like a prehistoric pterodactyl. It fits perfectly with the surrounding desert landscape but would have looked very strange in a Midwestern shopping mall. The point is to avoid grafting architectural style onto an unsympathetic environment. Successful restaurant architecture works in context with its location.

At times the owner's instinct plays a pivotal role in determining the relative strengths and weaknesses of the location. Michael Weinstein started out by opening restaurants in New York City's Upper West Side years before the neighborhood was gentrified. In this case, his timing was prescient.

The geographic location also affects kitchen design decisions. In most urban settings, for instance, food can be purchased on a daily basis. In more remote areas, however,

storage facilities are needed to hold food for a week or more, and extra storage space must be factored into the floor plan.

The importance of location may not be solely dependent on the geographic site. In the case of the Rattlesnake Club in Denver (discussed in chapter 6), an out-of-the-way location is less important than the architecture itself. The restaurant is located in the dramatic turn-of-the-century Tivoli Brewery. In this case, the location relates to the physical rather than geographic location.

ECONOMIC CONDITIONS

Finally, a market analysis should consider both regional and national economic conditions. The economic climate tends to influence restaurant longevity: In volatile times, planned obsolescence may be the key to a restaurant's success. In the late 1980s, the whims of fashion influenced the economic picture to such an extent that many restaurants were designed for a short but popular life-span. In these cases, front-of-the-house design elements were chosen primarily for their up-to-the-minute look, not for their enduring value. At any rate, a systematic analysis of current micro- and macroeconomic conditions as they relate to the restaurant business in the United States can help to assess the viability of any proposed restaurant.

Concept Development

Before designers involve themselves with concept development, a number of questions must be asked: What experience does ownership have in the restaurant business? Is this a renovation of an ongoing business, a new business, or a change of personality for an existing property? Is this a free-standing property or could special architectural considerations have an impact on the design? If ownership has not established a firm concept, then who will develop the concept—interior designer, architect, or foodservice consultant? Will it be a collaborative effort of many parties?

The concept is multifaceted and involves every aspect of the operation. It can revolve around a theme that has easily identified visual elements: a seafood theme with hanging lobster traps or a Mexican theme with cacti and over-sized sombreros, for instance. However, today's theme restaurants often reflect a more subtle approach—suggestions of a theme that give diners a feel for what they are about to get but leave a bit to their imagination. A display of fresh seafood coupled with architectural elements reminiscent of a cruise ship hints of a seafood restaurant. The adobe walls, pottery, tiles, and courtyard fountain of a Mexican villa prepare the diner for a south-of-the-border experience without screaming the message.

These subtle thematic references often engender a sense of realism. Fishermen eating fresh seafood do not eat under nets suspended from the ceiling, nor do Guadalajarans have brightly colored, oversized sombreros hanging on their walls.

In other instances, historic recreations evoke an authentic sense of place. Period design can range from a turn-of-the-century hotel dining room to an art deco cruise ship motif to a 1950s diner. In most cases, genuine restoration or renovation works better than attempts to create a period within a contemporary shell, but ingenious design can help a characterless modern building metamorphose into another time and place.

Concept can also revolve around a nontheme. A nontheme is an idea, an image, a shape, a pattern, an architectural style, or a central element that pulls the entire concept together. In Manhattan's classic Four Seasons, designed by Philip Johnson in 1959, the modern architectural backdrop of the Seagram building, designed by Mies van der Rohe, influenced every aspect of Johnson's cool, clean interior design scheme. The restaurant-nightclub Twenty:Twenty, designed by Haverson/Rockwell Architects in 1986 (discussed in chapter 5), provides a chic stage set for the hip, cosmopolitan crowd that frequents the establishment. Here esthetics define the concept.

In many popular restaurants, concept combines a food idea with a design idea. At New York City's America (discussed in chapter 6), the menu offers a range of food that is as broad as the country, from blue corn tortillas to meat loaf and mashed potatoes to Cajun chicken lips. The design by MGS Architects evokes America in a striking fashion, with such elements as a sweeping pastel mural and an abstract, neon American flag.

In other situations, the design concept bears no direct relationship to the food concept. Shezan, a Pakistani restaurant in New York designed by Gwathmey Siegel, reflects a clean architectural hand, with classic Breuer chairs and a silvery reflective ceiling that in no way relate to its Indian cuisine. Here, the concept of elegant dining rather than ethnic dining inspired the design.

Exterior architecture often becomes an integral component of the concept itself. Historically, elements such as Dairy Queen's gambrel roof, Howard Johnson's orange roof, and the ubiquitous golden arches of McDonald's all exemplify architecture as symbol of the restaurant. Vernacular roadside architecture like Tail

O' the Pup in Los Angeles literally portrays the concept in an architectural context. In San Diego's Horton Plaza, architect Tom Grondona has revived vernacular architecture in such operations as Boardwalk Fries, where the form of a French fry becomes a graphic architectural element. Here again, architecture helps to define concept (fig. 1-4).

At times the concept revolves around the cuisine. In restaurants such as New York's Rakel and Los Angeles's City, design functions as a backdrop for the chef's art. These establishments often utilize such devices as partially open kitchens to allow patrons a view of the cooking process. Dining rooms are often designed in neutral palettes, to permit the plate presentation to become the main attraction.

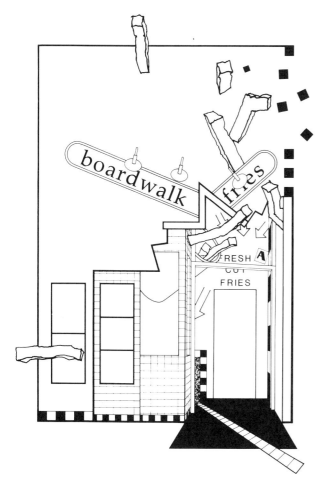

1-4. *Theme can become a strong graphic expression, as seen in this drawing of the facade of Boardwalk Fries in San Diego's Horton Plaza, designed by Tom Grondona Architect. (Tom Grondona drawing)*

The Menu

Menu planning plays an integral part in restaurant development. Depending on the type of restaurant, some chefs and owners say that the entire operation should revolve around the menu.

All too often, however, the menu is not planned in advance of the concept and the design. In fact, the chef is usually brought on board long after construction is underway. This is a practical decision that helps to limit pre-opening expenses but can cause greater expenditures in the long term because the chef's input can help with both front- and back-of-the-house design.

The design process is also helped if various members of the design team learn something about menu planning. The first fact to consider is that ultimately the diners mandate what stays on the menu, regardless of restaurant type. The owner, chef, or foodservice consultant may have a particular penchant for certain types of foods, but if they do not adapt these foods to what their ultimate consumers demand, then the restaurant is soon out of business. This is why operators often change at least 50 percent of the menu within the first six months of operation and why selecting equipment that affords flexibility in menu planning is very important.

Changing the menu, albeit costly, becomes necessary for many reasons. The menu may not conform to the production or service limitations of the facility. The restaurateur offering flambé service, for example, may find the ventilation system cannot handle the increased smoke created by tableside preparation. A health-conscious clientele might place an overwhelming demand on the one overworked steamer that steams seafood and vegetables. Regardless of the reason, a change of menu—and hence of kitchen and/or front-of-the-house design— should always be factored in as a possibility during the planning process.

Another important element to consider about the menu is that food may not be what brings people to a restaurant the first time, but it is traditionally what keeps people coming back. Anything that can improve the customer's perception of that food is important. Diners want hot food hot, and cold food cold. Although servers prancing through the crowd with uncovered plates piled with artfully arranged foods is a great merchandising technique, it leads to a negative experience if the food arrives at the table icy cold.

The Budget

The budget is nearly always a limiting factor in the design of a restaurant. A big design budget is only as big as the market will bear, and not even the best-financed project can afford wasted design dollars. However, adherence to a tight budget means little if the dining room looks ruined after two weeks of operation or if management can't afford proper maintenance procedures.

Budgetary planning has inherent contradictions. Every owner wants to stretch design dollars as far as possible and not go broke before opening day. A restaurant is, after all, a business. In contemporary times, however, with a grown-up, design-conscious baby boom generation and a younger mindset hungry for new visual sensations, design can be the ticket to success and is increasingly viewed as part of the value equation that helps the bottom line. Nevertheless, measuring its exact impact on profit is impossible.

The problem is that design is expensive. Furthermore, good architecture takes time, and time is money. Of course, design is a relatively unimportant backdrop for food and service in some very successful restaurants, and the charm of other totally undesigned bistros stems from their visual chaos. Such successes, however, are rare. Even simple interiors and rooms that appear to reflect timeworn patinas have often been designed—for a fee. Likewise, kitchen design is no free lunch, but back-of-the-house design dollars can buy increased productivity. An intelligent kitchen layout is crucial to both speed and efficiency.

The costs of design vary wildly, depending on the location, type of restaurant, intended life-span, and many other factors. Basically, the owner pays both for goods and for services. Goods translate into FF&E (furniture, fixtures, and equipment). Services include fees for the schematic design concept as presented in floor plans, elevations, renderings, and other architectural plans. Services also include FF&E specifications but not necessarily purchasing. Some design firms prefer to remain purely service oriented and leave the procurement and installation process to purchasing agents.

There is no uniform method of charging for design services. The design firm's fee may be based on square-foot costs, a percentage of total project costs, a consulting fee at hourly rates, or other methods. Many variables influence fee structures, but as a rule of thumb most firms charge a fixed fee based on the scope of the job and on the total project cost.

Some firms that provide purchasing charge a percentage markup based on FF&E prices. Owners should beware of design thrown in "free" by equipment or purchasing houses whose profit comes from markups.

Budget planning must begin in the very early stages of the design process. The owner should develop an initial budget as a guide, and a final budget should be agreed upon when the design contract is finalized. As the project progresses, the budget must be carefully monitored. Projects always have hidden costs, and renovation often presents more expensive surprises than new construction. In truth, any number of factors may drive up the costs of one or more elements of the construction budget, so buffer money ought to be built in somewhere.

A crucial aspect of budgetary control is how design dollars are allocated. Adding one dramatic design treatment in an otherwise simple room, for example, can elevate an ordinary interior into something special.

A good designer knows how to prioritize the FF&E budget and how to take from one area and give to another in order to adhere to the total budget. If unexpected surprises catapult costs so far that the budget needs to be adjusted, then the designer should inform the owner immediately. There's no excuse for running out of money midway through a project.

The Style of Service

How will the customers be served? Will guests serve themselves at buffet tables or queue up in a fast food line? Will a combination of service styles be offered so that guests help themselves to some items while servers deliver other items? Will full table service be offered? The answer dictates some specific spatial considerations on the design plan (fig. 1-5).

Any type of tableservice restaurant can have many styles of service: plate, platter, cart, or any combination of the three. Plate service, in which food is plated in the kitchen and then passed over to the wait person who serves finished plates to the guest, requires the least amount of dining room floor space. Platter service, in which food is assembled on platters and frenched (served onto a waiting dinner plate in front of the diner) requires larger tables and more floor space so that the server can manipulate the platter between the guests. Cart service requires the most space, as the gueridons (service carts) must be moved around the dining room and kept at a safe distance from tables when flambé cooking is employed.

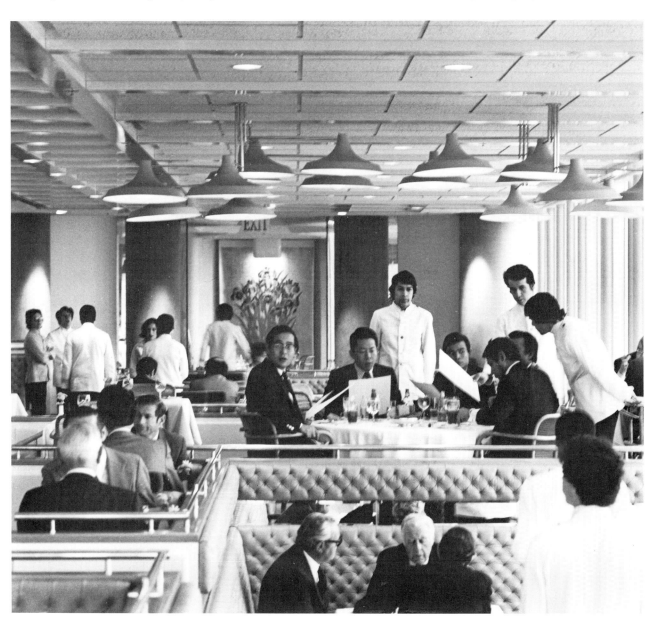

1-5. *The staff, decked out in their formal Mao jackets, conveys the formal style of service found at New York's Windows on the World, designed by Warren Platner Associates Architects.*
(Alexandre Georges photo)

The Speed of Service

Speed of service and turnover rate are closely allied with each other. Fast food operations, in which customers get their food within a few minutes, have the highest turnover rate, that is, guests occupy a seat for the shortest time. Tables typically turn over every fifteen to twenty minutes. In cafeteria operations, customers take more time to get their food and the turnover rate is a bit slower: fifteen to thirty minutes. The tableservice dining experience, especially the fine restaurant in which cuisine is cooked to order, is the most lengthy: Customers wait the longest for their food and spend the most time eating that food. In these operations turnover can range from an hour in a family-style facility to four hours in a gourmet establishment.

The amount of time a customer spends in an operation—both in getting food and in eating it—has many design implications for both front and back of the house. If customers are expected to dine on gourmet fare for an hour or more, then comfortable seating, such as upholstered armchairs, and an a la carte kitchen are in order. Conversely, if faster turnover is desired, then hard-surfaced chairs move guests out of the dining space as quickly as possible. Furthermore, the kitchen must be laid out and fitted with equipment that helps to speed the preparation and service of food to the guest.

Speed of service is too often overlooked in the planning process. In one case a group of owners, new to the restaurant business, approached the development of their pro forma statement without considering speed of service. They began with the following information:

> Menu: continental
> Style of Service: leisurely plate and cart
>   service
> Number of Seats: 235
> Lunch Turns: two per day
> Dinner Turns: five per day

Based on their projected fixed expenses, the owners determined that they would need $74,000 per day in revenues. To achieve this, they calculated their per check average by dividing the total daily sales by the total number of customers served.

$$\frac{\$74,000 \text{ required daily revenues}}{\# \text{ of lunch covers } + \# \text{ of dinner covers}}$$

The resulting $45.00 check average was considered appropriate for this type of operation and thus the project proceeded.

Neglecting to consider speed of service caused grave problems, however, because the restaurant could not meet the projected turnover rates and still provide the leisurely dining experience that is expected with a $45 check average. In other words, to meet the projected turnover rates, either the tables would have to be turned in less than an hour, or the serving time for lunches would have to stretch over four hours, and for dinners over ten hours! Management had failed to recognize the amount of dining time necessary in this type of establishment.

The Per Customer Check Average

Oftentimes not considered in design planning, the per customer check average nevertheless influences ultimate design success. Will a low check average dictate more turnover and thus a sturdy, low-maintenance design? If a low check average is expected, then the restaurant will generally attract a wide spectrum of customers. On the other hand, a high check average limits both turnover time and type of clientele.

The cost of the meal carries with it design expectations in the mind of the customer. People don't expect a $4.50 meal tab in a luxurious environment replete with rich materials, nor do they expect to pay dearly for fine cuisine in a room that looks like a fifties diner.

As can be seen in the section above, check average and speed of service must be carefully monitored and matched for successful results.

The General Ambiance

Before arriving at specific design solutions, define the type of atmosphere desired for a given restaurant. How should the customer *feel* in the space? Energized, ebullient, ready to eat and move on? Relaxed, at ease, comfortable enough to linger for hours? Stimulated? Cheerful? Nostalgic? Serene? Pampered? Protected? On display?

Obviously, different types of restaurants evoke different types of feelings. The feeling of dining in a homey neighborhood coffee shop differs from the feeling of dining in a highly contemporary corporate cafeteria, a gourmet establishment, or a see-and-be-seen grand cafe. These feelings are a function not only of food and service but also of interior design.

The Management Philosophy

Management philosophy helps to dictate design philosophy. In the case of the fast food chain restaurant, for instance, the philosophy of corporate-level management is to maximize profits for the shareholders who are looking forward to the next quarterly report. Here, design often represents a minimal investment. It tends to be pragmatic, derivative and safe. On the other hand, the entrepreneur looking to attract a young, sophisticated clientele may take a chance on innovative design and architecture. The restaurateur looking for the long-term growth of business may invest most of all, in the hopes of creating a classic design statement.

In summary, a successful design begins in the planning process and integrates front and back of the house. Careful consideration of restaurant type, the market, the budget, concept, menu, style of service, speed of service, per customer check average, general ambiance, and management philosophy can lead to the best design solutions.

THE DESIGN TEAM

The design of a successful restaurant does not come from the mind of one person. Rather, it reflects the efforts of a host of professionals, all of whom provide vital pieces of the picture, from kitchen equipment selection to architectural detailing to tabletop design to the integration of HVAC systems. Of course, ego is a factor to be reckoned with. Both owners and designers often view the restaurant interior as an extension of themselves. To the owner, it's the manifestation of his or her personality; to the designer, the manifestation of his or her talent. Quite often the chef (who may also be an owner) regards the kitchen as his or her private domain. Problems surface when individuals operate wearing their own personal blinders and so cannot make objective design decisions. Ideally, sensitive or damaged egos won't get in the way of professional collaboration.

Each professional also takes a different tack on where the design process begins. Some say that it starts with the menu, others with the market, and still others with the architecture.

Traditionally, however, the process of foodservice design begins with ownership. Ownership plants the initial ideas in the minds of the "design team." The design team, in turn, translates these ideas into a total concept and subsequently into a physical design.

The key team members should be involved from the very beginning. Depending on the size and scope of the project, key players typically include the owner, architect and/or interior designer, and foodservice consultant. As the project develops, the list of players may grow to include the chef, electrical engineers, lighting design consultants, graphic design consultants, and tabletop consultants. In the most inclusive scenario, involvement with restaurant planning extends to the employees themselves, as they (along with the customers) are the ultimate users of the space.

Problems arise when no clear leader emerges to guide the design process. A team leader, someone who has a balanced perspective of the many factors involved in the design of the restaurant, should be established by the owner early on. This individual coordinates the planning process, disseminates ideas, and has ultimate responsibility for the execution of those ideas. The team leader should be familiar with all aspects of the operation from menu items to the actual design and construction.

Often the owner takes on the role. After all, the owner has ultimate fiscal responsibility for the restaurant (to date, no restaurants have been built on spec). Yet in today's marketplace, many owners actually have little or no experience running a restaurant and thus farm out the individual responsibilities of the planning phase. Problems arise when they do so without understanding how each of the parts must be integrated into the whole.

In some projects, the foodservice consultant, interior designer, or architect becomes the team leader, which often causes difficulties as the design process develops and all of these professionals have their own priorities. The head of the design team—no matter what his or her orientation is—must maintain a neutral position and take into consideration all aspects of the operation.

The nature of the project, be it the renovation of a 60-seat independently owned bistro, the new design of a 250-seat chain restaurant, or the construction of a 400-seat corporate cafeteria, often dictates the choice of team leader. Many restaurant chains maintain their own in-house design specialist to oversee projects, for example, and the foodservice consultant is often the team leader for the remodeling of a kitchen. In new construction, the architect tends to become the team leader. Today increasing numbers of design firms specialize in restaurant design and provide a turnkey job by coordinating and handling every aspect of the design. In any case, without a strong team leader, the design process becomes an uncoordinated and frustrating procedure that yields disappointing results.

We have established that the team does not have a set number of players or a predetermined leader. This variety is due to the nature of restaurant design itself. Not all projects are the same, thus not all design teams are the same. A foodservice consultant might be the only necessary resource for one project, but another project might require a dozen team members.

The chef or the foodservice manager—those persons who will have ultimate responsibility for the smooth operation of the restaurant—ought to be involved, but they're frequently not brought on board until the restaurant is nearly completed. To better understand who should be involved on a given project, the following descriptions of each potential team member is offered as a guide.

Owner

The owner has ultimate financial responsibility for the project and frequently initiates the concept. He or she may or may not have experience in restaurant operations or possess a college degree in foodservice management. Restaurant owners tend to have aggressive, entrepreneurial

personalities and to be extremely dedicated to their work. Very often a restaurant is owned by two or more partners, each of whom has different areas of expertise.

Because owning a restaurant is thought to be a glamorous and profitable undertaking that does not require any specialized education, it tends to attract newcomers to the foodservice industry. These individuals may rely heavily on design consultants to determine the feasibility of the concept and interpret it accordingly. They often want design creativity and allow the design firm to develop original ideas.

At other times, owners possess skills that enable them to function in dual roles on the design team: chef-owners or architect-owners, for instance. These individuals tend to belong to the breed of owners who know exactly what they want and retain a design firm to execute their ideas.

Chef

The chef, and at times other members of the kitchen staff, should be considered an important member of the design team. The chef will be responsible for the efficient production of menu items. If the selection or layout of equipment does not match the menu or the style of preparation that is appropriate for the restaurant, this efficiency cannot be realized.

Chefs look at the layout of the kitchen from an operational perspective. They have the best understanding of what types of equipment will be required to produce the menu items. Today, there are an increased number of chef-owners, who often design minimal, very efficient kitchens with basic equipment. Because they are also responsible for the bottom line of the restaurant, they look for equipment that serves multiple functions, thus freeing up square footage for front-of-the-house seating. It is advisable to involve the chef early in the design process.

Manager

The manager of the restaurant can add important insight on operations to the design process. Managers are frequently on board during the construction process and may be called on to act as the owner's representative and to interface with the project team leader on an ongoing basis. It is important for them to have an understanding of the overall design scheme and to offer input into that scheme during the planning phase. Most managers carry with them a history of restaurant layout and design experiences that can provide invaluable information to the designers.

Foodservice Consultant

The foodservice consultant designs the back-of-the-house operation and provides space layouts, mechanical and electrical diagrams, and equipment specifications. Firms range from a single individual to large companies with offices across the country. The scope of services may include menu planning, equipment purchasing, engineering evaluations, and management advisory services such as feasibility studies. Larger firms, whose staffs include in-house architectural designers and who have a network of outside consultants to draw from, often become the team leaders. In this capacity, the foodservice consultant assists the owner in clarifying the concept for the restaurant, helps to determine the feasibility of that concept within a given marketplace, and may even be involved in site selection.

Methods of charging include a flat fee based on hourly rates or a percentage of the total project cost. Some equipment supply houses have kitchen design experts on staff who provide design services, but these foodservice consultants make their money primarily through selling equipment.

Interior Designer

The interior designer is responsible for the layout and décor of the restaurant's public spaces. Like the foodservice consultant, design firms vary in size and in scope of services. In general, designers develop floor plans, elevations, renderings, reflected ceiling plans, lighting plans, and furniture and accessory plans. They provide color schemes, material and decorative specifications, and all furnishing specifications. Some purchase as well as specify furnishings.

Today increasing numbers of designers have become restaurant design specialists and take on the role of team leader. They may supervise a total design package that includes everything from concept development to menu graphics to exterior signage to kitchen design. Other designers take on the role of team leader only for the front of the house.

Most interior designers have college degrees in interior design or architecture. Currently there are state and nationwide efforts to license the title of interior designer so that only those qualified by experience and education could use the name. Interior design fees are based either on a percentage of project cost, hourly consulting rates, or square-foot costs. If purchasing services are provided, then the design firm may charge a markup on items purchased.

Architect

Traditionally the role of the architect has been confined to the building structure and exterior design. Over the past few decades, however, most firms have expanded their practice to include interior design as well. Whenever a building permit for renovation or new construction is required, plans must be certified by a licensed architect. Restaurants designed from the ground up or facilities that require complex redesign of interior architecture, HVAC, and electrical systems may require the services of an architectural firm, and sometimes the team includes both an architect and an interior designer.

More frequently, however, the roles of architect and interior designer are interchangeable. In these cases, which represent the majority of projects today, one individual or one firm functions as restaurant designer. Architectural firms often keep interior designers on staff, and interior design firms often keep architects on staff.

The scope of services and methods of charging for an architectural firm whose practice includes restaurant design are basically the same as those of an interior design firm. The differences between the two often lie in design orientation and, at times, technical expertise in specific areas. Architects, for example, tend to deal with space, form, and volume rather than with surface decoration. Interior designers may be more knowledgeable about color and accessories.

General Contractor

General contractors are crucial members of the design team. All too often, however, they are not properly recognized for the important role they play. It is the GC who is ultimately charged with converting the architects' and designers' drawings into the reality of bricks and mortar.

If the GC is involved with the project during the design phase, difficult or impossible structural forms can be pointed out. In the long run, this knowledge improves the final execution of the project and may also lead to tighter controls over the construction budget.

The GC is frequently chosen by a bid process but should always be selected with the same care given to the selection of other design team members. Both the quality and the cost of their work greatly affect the success of the project. The general contractor heads up a team of subcontractors who together build the restaurant.

Engineers

Generally, three different types of engineers are involved in a restaurant design: structural, mechanical, and electrical. At times they may be on the staff of an architectural firm, but usually they are called in from private engineering firms as needed. Structural engineers are retained both for renovations and new construction to deal with problems involving the structural integrity of the building. Mechanical engineers handle mechanical systems such as heating, ventilation, and air conditioning (HVAC) and also work on pumping, plumbing, and elevator systems. Electrical engineers determine the amount of electricity needed for an operation and how best to distribute it. They are often called upon early on a job to determine the cost of new service or expanded service.

Lighting Designers

Lighting designers are often retained by the restaurant designer to highlight special features of the restaurant, deal with technical lighting problems, or program a computerized illumination system. Because lighting plays such an important role in creating restaurant atmosphere, the lighting designer is becoming an increasingly important team member, especially for complex projects that require intricate illumination schemes.

Other Specialty Designers

Like the lighting designer, other specialty designers are generally brought on board by the team leader for big-budget projects or those that require specialized problem solving. Graphic designers, for example, may be called in to design the restaurant's logo, interior and exterior signage, and menu graphics. Art consultants are often involved with foodservice facilities that are part of much larger organizations such as a hotel or a corporate headquarters. Tabletop designers become part of the team for gourmet restaurants or those establishments in which food presentation is key to the operational concept. Acoustic consultants are called upon when management wishes to control noise levels. Sound engineers are utilized to design music and video sound systems.

Financial Consultants

The real estate consultant becomes a team member when real estate is a critical factor in determining whether or not a project will fly. In such cases, the real estate interests in a restaurant are nearly as important as the operational interests.

The feasibility consultant conducts a marketplace study that identifies potential customers, the competition, and economic conditions of the locale in order to develop a pro forma statement.

In extremely large restaurant projects, each of these specialists and others may be involved with the design process. The complexity of the project has a great impact on the make-up of the design team.

As the design process develops, a clear understanding of responsibilities should be established. In certain instances, the team moves forward as a coordinated entity. In other situations, a maverick member of the group might attempt to divert efforts from the stated goals. In still another scenario, one member has to stand up as the leader and pull the rest of the team along. These interpersonal relations are, as restaurant designer Charles Morris Mount put it, "about 80% of the design process. The hard part."

THE SYSTEMS APPROACH

Market Segments versus Service Systems

Foodservice operations can be classified in many ways. Historically, classifications have been based on the check average, theme, ethnicity of the food, or market segment. Segmentation by market is the most frequently used means of classifying foodservice operations. Schools, employee feeding, hospitals, colleges and universities, military, and nursing homes are together considered institutional or non-commercial food service. Their primary mission is to feed in-house diners such as students or hospital staff.

However, this classification method does not really describe the type of food service that is being offered in a given operation. The elementary school operations, for example, could consist of the standard straight-line cafeteria, a scatter system of individual food stations where students help themselves, or a fast food system similar to commercial eateries such as McDonald's. Each type has different design implications.

Therefore, we present a nontraditional classification, one based on *service systems* (rather than market segments) and in keeping with a process-oriented approach to restaurant and kitchen design. An understanding of how the restaurant works can lead to a successful design.

Using the service system classification, the designer can accurately identify styles of service and types of food delivery systems. If, for example, the school board calls in a designer and says, "We want to put a foodservice operation in our new elementary school," then the designer has little insight into the characteristics of the design. If, however, the board says, "We want a fast food operation in our new elementary school," the designer has a well-established frame of reference to help determine which type of delivery system the board desires.

Market Segments
Full service restaurants
Fast food restaurants
Elementary and secondary schools
Employee feeding
Hospitals
Hotels and motels
Colleges and universities
Military
Recreation facilities
Convenience and grocery stores
Nursing homes
Transportation
Retail stores
All other food services

Service System
A la carte service
Tableside service
Fast food service
Banquet service
Family-style service
Buffet service
Take-out service
Delivery service
Cafeteria-style service
Tray service
Machine service
Satellite system
All other service systems

Service systems are loosely defined as the means by which the food is delivered to the customer. At times a foodservice operation has more than one service system. A hotel, for example, may have a la carte service in a gourmet restaurant, banquet service in a ballroom, and cafeteria service in an employee cafeteria. This is called a complex foodservice system.

Designers should familiarize themselves with the basics of each type of service system.

A LA CARTE

In a la carte service, a waitperson takes the orders from individual customers and then presents them to the chef for preparation. For the most part, the preparation is done to order, and in every case the food is plated specifically for a particular customer. A la carte service is frequently found in upscale restaurants, executive dining rooms, hotels, coffee shops, and other full-service operations. (It has been referred to as table service, which does not adequately convey information that can be used in developing an effective design scheme.)

TABLESIDE

The key element in tableside service is a service cart (gueridon). Food is brought from the kitchen and placed on the gueridon, where it is either finished, plated, and served or actually cooked at tableside. When foods are brought to the cart for cooking, a heating element (rechaud) must be added to the cart. Tableside service is most commonly used in gourmet establishments, although in recent years it has declined in popularity. Most often, tableside service combines with a la carte service in a given establishment, with one or two special tableside menu items, such as a Caesar salad or a flaming dessert.

FAST FOOD

Fast food is a style of service in which customers queue up in either a number of lines or one serpentine line to place their food orders. Typically the counter worker takes the order, assembles the food, and receives payment. This style of service is further characterized by speed and the use of disposables. Fast food service can be found in chain or independent operations, elementary and secondary schools, employee feeding, hospitals, colleges and universities, the military, and recreational facilities.

BANQUET

Banquet-style service involves a predetermined menu that is generally prepared and plated en masse. Payment for the meal is prearranged. Tangential activities such as speeches or entertainment often occur during the banquet service period, and these activities may necessitate modifying the service time of various courses.

In some instances, the starter course may be preset on the tables. Service of subsequent courses does not usually proceed until all customers have finished the previous course. Banquet service is offered through the catering departments of full-service restaurants, noncommercial feeders, and hotels, as well as in catering facilities.

FAMILY STYLE

Family-style service is characterized by one or more portions of selected foods brought to the diners on serving platters. The platters are often placed directly on the table for self-service. This style of service is used in full-service establishments; Chinese restaurants in particular favor family-style service.

BUFFET

In buffet service, customers can generally serve themselves unlimited portions of a number of items. In some cases, servers may assist in the portioning for control reasons. Buffets can be either in a straight line or in a scramble configuration. In the straight line, customers proceed in a logical flow from the beginning to the end of the line. In the scramble system, customers approach the buffet at random points. Buffet service is typically used for complete meal service in hotel restaurants, especially for Sunday brunch. It is often found in the form of a salad bar in full-service restaurants and noncommercial dining facilities.

CAFETERIA

Cafeteria service differs from buffet service in that customers select from preportioned food offerings (as compared to unlimited portions), hot food is portioned by a server, and diners assemble food and utensils on a tray. Cafeteria flow is based on cold items first, hot food items second, and beverages last. Whether the layout is a straight line or a scramble system, this type of service is the backbone of noncommercial foodservice and is often combined with a buffet-style salad bar.

TAKE-OUT

Take-out service relies on packaging, generally disposables. Food is either batch-prepared and then packaged or prepared to order and packaged as it "comes off the fire." In some instances the food is packaged in a partially cooked or raw stage for completion in the home oven. Seating is not required for take-out, but sufficient space is needed for customers to wait for their food. Take-out service is an integral part of many fast food restaurants and represents most of the food sales in the convenience and grocery store market segment. In addition, it is an increasingly popular and profitable foodservice system when combined with other styles of service in full-service restaurants.

DELIVERY

Delivery service relies heavily on telephone orders. Prepared food is delivered to customers via bicycles in urban areas and motor vehicles in suburban areas. The success of delivery systems depends on a sufficient population density to warrant the transportation costs. Delivery service systems are typically matched with take-out systems in a chairless storefront operation and combined with tray service in hospitals, hotels, and nursing homes.

TRAY

Tray service involves the delivery of preordered, fully assembled meals. Often temperature maintenance systems are incorporated within the tray or delivery cart in order to keep hot foods at proper serving temperatures from the time of assembly to the time of service. In other cases, hot foods are rethermalized just prior to service. This style of service is employed in hospitals, hotels, and nursing homes.

MACHINE

Machine service is coin-operated vending, in which a limited assortment of preportioned or electrically portioned food or beverages can be obtained at any time. Staffing is required only to fill and clean the machines, which can be found in all market segments.

SATELLITE

In satellite service, foods are generally prepared in bulk at one kitchen and then transported to other finishing kitchens and assembled for service at those sites. This style of service is most commonly found in schools and health care facilities. In addition, some full-service restaurants utilize satellite systems because of the economies and control available through a commissary kitchen. Satellite service systems are most frequently used in large foodservice operations with many points of sale.

Subsystems

The systems described above all involve a style of servicing guests or of delivering food, that is, the general means by which the food reaches the diner. Each of these service systems is supported by numerous subsystems, that is, the precise steps that must be taken in the back and front of the house to ensure that the food reaches the customer efficiently and properly. Another way of understanding the process is to think of the service system as the wheel and the subsystem as the spokes of the wheel (fig. 1-6). Every wheel (service system) encompasses some or all of the following spokes (subsystems): purchasing, receiving, storage, fabrication, prepreparation, preparation, holding, assembly, sanitation, accounting, and support stations. Each has design implications.

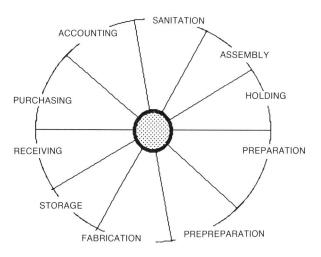

1-6. As with the spokes of a wheel, each of the subsystems of a restaurant depends on the other components for the success of the whole.

PURCHASING AND RECEIVING

The nature of purchasing and receiving food affects the layout of any foodservice establishment. Numerous factors must be considered before arriving at spatial allocations for loading docks and receiving offices. For example, will the food be purchased from many suppliers, all of whom require time at a loading dock? Will purchasing be done through a central, one-stop-shopping distributor, who delivers all items on a pallet? In some large-volume operations, the pallets move directly from the receiving docks to the production areas, with no intermediate stop in the storeroom. If the "purchased" foods come from a company commissary, then the purchasing function—and size of the purchasing offices—is minimal. In other instances, separating the receiving offices from the purchasing offices is a good idea in order to achieve tighter controls.

STORAGE

In order to design successful storage subsystems, the designer must understand the issuing policy of the house. Will cooks work from an open storeroom? Will they have a par stock of some ingredients issued to their work areas, with special items drawn as needed from the storage areas? Will a storeroom manager assemble all of the primary ingredients for the cooks, thus limiting the amount of space and time the cooks need to weigh and measure ingredients? Many questions must be carefully considered, and careful analysis of the menu, expected volume of business, frequency of delivery, and the storage characteristics of the foods to be ordered must be made before proper storage subsystems can be designed.

FABRICATION

Fabrication subsystems include those areas where food is first handled, or placed into process, prior to the preparation stage. In classical kitchens, before the advent of preportioned meats, fish, and poultry, fabrication areas were commonly used to break down primal cuts of meat; in effect the kitchen included a butcher shop area. Today, far fewer restaurants have these areas, but gourmet establishments often incorporate seafood or bake-shop fabrication subsystems. Fabrication areas have become particularly important in large operations located in high-rise buildings. Follow the delivery of lettuce as an example: Several cases of lettuce are delivered to a ground-floor loading dock. The lettuce is then moved to a ground-floor fabrication area where the heads are unpacked, washed, and stored in large containers for subsequent distribution to upper-level preparation areas. Without the fabrication subsystem, the cases of lettuce would have been delivered upstairs for handling, and then the empty cartons and wrapper leaves would have been sent back downstairs for disposal. The fabrication area helped to streamline the process and cut back on vertical transportation costs.

PREPREPARATION

In the preparation subsystem, foods are made ready to go to the final phase of preparation. For example, preparation may include breaking the lettuce into salad sized pieces and storing it in containers until ready for assembly in salad bowls. Preparation may be the "mis en place" work that is done for tableside flambé preparations. Preparation may also include mixing—and in some cases rolling out—pie crust that will be used to top made-to-order chicken potpies. A carefully planned preparation area can speed final preparation in an a la carte kitchen and improve overall productivity in any kitchen.

PREPARATION

The preparation subsystem involves the final cooking or assembly of food (fig. 1-7). Every kitchen has a cold food preparation area and a hot food preparation area. It may be where the preprepared salad ingredients are portioned onto the salad plates or the cooking station where the marinated ribs are broiled. This subsystem can also extend into the dining room when foods are cooked at tableside or on a buffet table. The characteristics of this subsystem need close attention when it is brought into the front of the house. For example, the food service manager who decides to offer made-to-

1-7. *The preparation subsystem includes a variety of equipment. At Scoozi restaurant in Chicago, designed by Aumiller Youngquist Architects, cooks poach, stew, sauté, broil, and fry items in the hot food preparation area. (Joseph Durocher photo)*

order omelets on the breakfast buffet table may encounter unsurmountable limitations due to an inadequate electrical supply, or the visual appeal of an open kitchen production area may be hampered by poor ventilation systems.

HOLDING

Once cooked, some foods may be held awaiting service. Consider a banquet situation in which twenty prime ribs are roasted. In this situation, a holding cart is essential while waiting for service. Along with the ribs, the holding box contains starch and vegetables: For example, baked potatoes that are ready for service along with steamed and seasoned green beans. A holding system is also helpful for sauces that are made in bulk to be drawn upon as needed during service. Holding subsystems are often necessary in order to keep hot food hot and cold food cold.

ASSEMBLY

Once cooked, the foods need to be plated or assembled for plating. In an a la carte operation, the assembly subsystem is adjacent to the preparation and holding areas. The steaks come off the broiler and go directly onto the plate and out to the customer (fig. 1-8). In a cafeteria or buffet service operation, many foods are prepared and delivered in bulk to the assembly area located behind the serving line, where they are then individually plated for the diner.

SANITATION

Dishwashing, pot and pan washing, and interim and after-hours cleaning are part of the sanitation subsystem. Sanitation is a frequently overlooked area in designing a restaurant. Hand sinks, soap, and adequate toweling must be eas-

1-8. *A well-designed assembly area provides adequate space for plating food and for service circulation.*
(Joseph Durocher photo)

ily accessible to all employees. Storage for mops, buckets, and cleaning supplies should be kept separate from food supply storage. A slop sink is essential, or floor mops will be cleaned out in the same sink used for washing greens. In addition, the decision to specify an expensive conveyor dishwasher or a more moderately priced rack machine should be based on careful analysis of type of operation and individual needs.

ACCOUNTING

Accounting subsystems, typically comprised of cash and credit control devices, must be carefully integrated into the design of the operation. Consideration should be given to the numbers and placement of credit card imprinters and other credit card paraphernalia, cash registers, and order-relay devices. These should be cho-

sen based on the needs of each given foodservice operation. Too often, sophisticated and expensive accounting subsystems are specified for small restaurants that would have done fine with a less elaborate scheme. Sometimes this equipment becomes an unsightly and noisy intrusion on the dining experience.

SUPPORT STATIONS

Support stations are too often neglected or underdesigned, especially in full-service restaurants. This is an extremely important subsystem for both front and back of the house. In the kitchen, support stations may consist of an area located near food pickup where the wait staff can get serving trays or soup spoons. If this is overlooked, waiters will run around the kitchen trying to find a tray—while the plated foods are getting cold—and then serve a teaspoon with

1-9. *Complete service stations incorporate accounting systems, backup condiments, space for dirty tableware, and all the materials needed to reset tables. Note how the exposed service station shown here, at New York's Home on the Range designed by Sam Lopata, Inc., melds with the wide-open design scheme.*
(Joseph Durocher photo)

the soup because they couldn't find a soup spoon. In the dining room, support stations are typically used to store extra silverware, glassware, and other tabletop accessories (fig. 1-9). Without them, waiters have to travel back and forth from the kitchen to set and reset the tables. In addition, if the guest drops a utensil or is served a dirty utensil, then the support station affords a quick replacement.

In fast food operations, the trash bins where customers deposit their waste are important support stations, as are the conveyor belts in cafeterias, where diners leave their trays.

The importance and complexity of each of these subsystems is a function of the service system and management philosophy. If, for example, management wishes to fabricate all steaks from wholesale cuts of meat, then the storage and fabricating subsystems are much more important to the operation than in a fast food op-

eration that depends on preportioned frozen foods. Therefore, designers must ask the right questions of each owner in order to figure out design criteria for any given restaurant. Without an understanding of these operational components, both kitchen and interior design will negatively impact restaurant functioning.

SPACE PLANNING: THE PROGRAM

The first concrete planning for a restaurant design should begin only after the players have thoroughly analyzed their market and have determined type of restaurant, style of service, the concept, the systems to be utilized, and the other factors we outlined. Then the data are organized into a design program, one which draws upon the following considerations.

Flow

An important goal of the design process is to optimize flow in terms of distance, volume, speed, and direction. Typically, flow patterns are charted for customers, employees, food, tableware, and service. A well-designed kitchen not only facilitates the transmission of food from the storage areas to the customer, but also the return flow of dirty dishes from dining room to kitchen.

DISTANCE

Distance from the back to the front of the house and vice versa is a crucial component of the floor plan. For example, a display kitchen can shorten the flow of food from the range to the guest, but if the service staff is forced to return to the back of the house to pick up salads, the efficiency of the open kitchen is lost. A more successful display kitchen was installed at Kuleto's in San Francisco (fig. 1-10). Here, all of the prepreparation for the hot foods is done in the

back of the house. The food is then brought to the display kitchen, where cooking is performed within view of the customers. Artfully arranged salads and desserts are also visible to patrons and located within easy reach of the service staff. Servers need not enter the back-of-the-house kitchen at all during service time. Interestingly, this setup is quite similar to the flow patterns in most fast food burger operations and diners with counter service, where these functions are performed as close to the customer as possible in order to speed the flow of food. In fancier restaurants with display kitchens, cooking is kept close to the customers so they can watch the drama of food preparation.

VOLUME OF BUSINESS

Initially, volume projections indicate the appropriate size of the space. Looking only at the overall volume of business over the course of a day can be misleading, however. A corporate cafeteria, for example, must be designed to handle a large volume of traffic during a short lunch

1-10. *Display cooking can add vitality to a restaurant and save steps for the service staff, yet it puts extra pressure on the chefs to keep the area clean. (Joseph Durocher photo)*

"hour," so seating and serving areas have to be larger than if the service were extended over a three-hour period. Another instance of misleading volume projections is a fast food operation on an interstate highway. Here, volume projections far exceed seating requirements because many customers take food back to their cars rather than use the seating area. Then again, larger bathrooms are needed as many travelers stop to use restrooms without buying food.

SPEED OF SERVICE

The faster the service, the more the restaurant depends on a well-designed flow pattern. Fast food operations and cafeterias, therefore, should be laid out so that each area of the restaurant, all food and supplies, and every piece of equipment help to maximize speed. These fast-paced operations should have clear, short lines of flow that do not cross. Conversely, the mannered service in a fine restaurant is an expected part of the leisurely dining experience, and placement of support equipment is not as important as in high-speed operations. Management might even decide to eliminate service stations from the dining room, thereby lengthening the distance traveled when servers reset tables. Such a decision could be acceptable in establishments where diners expect a lengthy, slow-paced meal.

DIRECTION

The ideal layout renders a straight-line flow that is unidirectional, with no crossing flow patterns. Such a design may prove impossible but should be aimed for in the planning process. In the back of the house, the flow should move—as much as possible—in a straight line all the way from the receiving dock to the server pickup station. The servers should then be able to take the food directly to the guests and finally bring dirty dishes and soiled table linen directly back to a cleanup area (fig. 1-11).

Moving through the Spaces

Space planning begins by looking at the parts that make up the whole of a restaurant. These parts are not the chairs or the artwork or any of

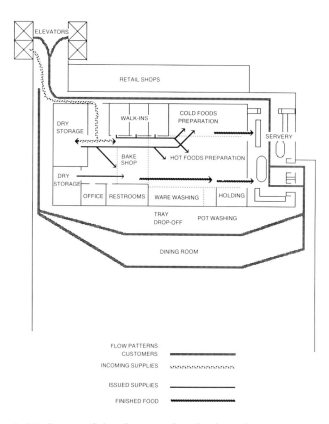

1-11. *Successful cafeterias, fast food, and tableservice restaurants depend on flow patterns that cross each other as little as possible. This cafeteria plan illustrates flow patterns for customers, incoming supplies, issued supplies, and finished food.*

the other décor items. Rather, they consist of the following spatial areas that together comprise the total front and back of the house.

EXTERIOR

The exterior includes every outside aspect: the parking lot, the building skin, exterior signage, landscaping, and exterior window and lighting treatments. The exterior of restaurants located in high-rise buildings consists of interior corridors. In shopping malls, public "outdoor" seating areas often comprise the exterior of a restaurant operation.

ENTRY AREA

The entry area begins when customers step inside the restaurant. Its form varies greatly, depending in part on whether the restaurant is free-standing or incorporated in a larger building. Climatic conditions also affect the appearance of the entryway. In general, it should look inviting and assist patrons to move in an orderly flow from exterior to dining. Doors usually separate the exterior from the entry, but in situations such as a shopping mall or employee cafeteria patrons may walk through open portals (which are typically secured at night). Where energy efficiency is paramount, double doors, revolving doors, or air screens are important considerations. The entry area itself includes such elements as the maitre d' station, coat-check area, waiting area with seating, public phones, space for guests to queue up for service, and frequently the cash-handling system.

DINING AREA

The dining area begins where the entry area stops, and it runs to the kitchen. It frequently interfaces with a beverage service area. Typical elements include seating and server stations, as well as all of the various decorative applications.

Quite often, architectural treatments such as raised or lowered floor and ceiling levels help to define dining rooms. Salad bars and buffet tables may be located here, and display kitchens are among the back-of-the-house areas often brought into dining rooms. Nonalcoholic beverage stations such as coffee or espresso stations may also be incorporated into this space. Because this is the restaurant's revenue-producing area, it takes up the largest amount of space.

BEVERAGE AREA

The beverage area is found in those operations serving alcoholic beverages outside of the dining area. It generally consists of a front bar and back bar, bar seating, and at times cocktail seating. The beverage area often incorporates music and video systems. The size of the beverage area depends on the importance of beverage sales to total revenue. In some restaurants, a single beverage area services dining room customers as well as bar customers, but other restaurants include separate service bars for the dining room.

RESTROOMS

Both front- and back-of-the-house restrooms are often included in a given restaurant. However, in some facilities a single bathroom located in the front of the house services both staff and guests. The size of the restroom(s) depends on the size of the restaurant. Larger establishments may include make-up areas for women and shoeshine stations for men.

KITCHEN

Nearly every restaurant kitchen can be divided into the following functional areas: hot food preparation, cooking, and plating; cold food preparation and plating; nonalcoholic beverage preparation and assembly; and warewashing and pot washing. In general, the kitchen is a third the size of the dining area, but this figure varies greatly according to restaurant type.

RESTAURANT SUPPORT AREAS

Restaurant support areas include receiving and storage areas (dry, refrigerated, and frozen), plus employee restrooms, locker rooms, dining rooms, and management offices. All of these areas are located in the back of the house.

Not every foodservice operation incorporates all these areas, and the significance of each functional area varies from restaurant to restaurant. In fact, every restaurant space has unique requirements and characteristics and should be analyzed individually in order to arrive at a successful program. The following breakdown by general type—fast food, table service, bar or gathering place, and cafeteria—is a good place to start.

FAST FOOD SPACES
Exterior

Exterior signage is of utmost importance to the fast food operation. Initial development of the design concept should include a signature ideograph or type face that establishes the logo. The logo helps to establish a clear identity that communicates instantly to people whizzing by in their cars. Operators tend to carry elements of the logo throughout the entire fast food environment by emblazoning appropriate surfaces with the name or ideograph as a constant reminder to their guests. Thus, signage and graphics are an important part of the total fast food marketing plan.

Signage often works hand-in-hand with architecture. The sight of an orange roof from the highway in the 1950s and 1960s heralded a Howard Johnson's. Today the golden arches indicate the location of a McDonald's. Primary colors and bright lighting are commonly used on fast food exteriors to further emphasize identity and create an upbeat, high-energy image.

Entry Area

In the fast food restaurant, the entry is the place where customers divide into queues (fig. 1-12). The two basic types of queues are: (1) several separate lines that lead to point-of-sale cash registers and (2) a single, usually serpentine line. Menu selections, ordering, delivery, and cash handling all take place in this one area. The amount of space needed is determined by expected volume; it is about the same no matter which queue system is used.

The obvious disadvantage to the single-line system is that the customer may be faced with being the thirtieth person in line when he or she enters the restaurant. The alternate method takes those same thirty customers and breaks them up into perhaps five lines with six persons in each line, so the customer's perception is of a much shorter line that will take less time. In

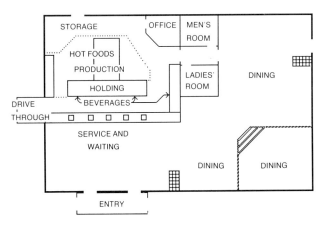

1-12. *The entry area in a fast food restaurant should be open to the serving and waiting area and the dining room, as seen in this floor plan.*

actuality, the throughput (the number of customers who are served in a given time) is about equal in both systems. What saves time in the single line is a division of responsibilities among the servers: One person takes orders and handles cash while others assemble the order. In multiple lines, just one person takes the order, assembles the order, and handles money transactions. An additional advantage of the single-line queue is that it limits the number of registers and amount of front counter space needed.

Dining Areas

Hard surfaces, bright lighting, and primary colors are the traditional design characteristics of fast food dining areas, because these elements facilitate easy maintenance, fast turnover, and upbeat energy (fig. 1-13). Recent years have witnessed a softening of the hard-edged atmosphere with applications such as greenery, artwork, soft accent lighting, and toned-down or muted color schemes. Glass-enclosed "greenhouse" seating areas and overhead skylights are increasingly utilized in fast food architecture to mellow the ambiance with natural light and plants. Spatially, the previously wide-open room is often divided into many small seating areas, and acoustic ceiling tiles or wall coverings are specified to mute noise levels. Fixed seating made of molded plastic has given way to smart-looking cafe chairs with padded seats and counter seating for single diners.

However, the design goals of easy maintenance, fast turnover, and upbeat energy remain. Today's fast food dining areas may look more up-to-date, with lighting levels soft enough that patrons don't need to wear sunglasses, but if the interiors are too comfortable, or can't withstand the spills and stains of constant turnover, then the design has failed.

Beverage Areas

Fast feeders don't serve alcoholic beverages, but some do install (nonalcoholic) beverage bars where customers fill their own cups with whatever cold or hot beverage they desire. Such beverage bars are a new addition to the standard fast food layout, and as of the late 1980s have not been widely utilized. They may catch on, however, because they help to improve speed of service: Unlike standard systems, the cashier

1-13. *The very successful stand-up "seating" at the Whopper Expresses in Manhattan helps to increase turnover and profits for the operators. (Joseph Durocher photo)*

does not have to assemble beverages along with the other food items.

Restrooms

In the fast food restaurant, restrooms must be planned for high-volume traffic in terms of both size and design elements. Fast feeders are typically used as roadside or walk-in rest stops, so the restroom volume can be greater than the diner volume. Spaces must be functional and easily cleaned with a minimum of periodic upkeep. The restrooms take such a heavy beating that all design applications should ensure durability and ease of maintenance.

Kitchen

Optimal efficiency is crucial in a fast food kitchen. Kitchen design for large chain operations has been researched, revised, researched again, and brought to a point where the placement of every element leads to the highest productivity output per employee hour. As with any kitchen, the key is to keep the flow of product in as straight a line as possible and not cross the flow of product with the flow of personnel.

A challenge to the design of fast food kitchens comes from expanded menus. The kitchen once designed to process only frozen fries and burgers now deals with fresh produce, soup, and even home-baked rolls. For new units the design is relatively simple—plan the kitchen to incorporate the expanded menu—but in an existing facility adding a convection oven or a vegetable prep area can make an already tight space into an impossible space.

Restaurant Support Areas

The storage areas of fast food restaurants are similar to other kitchens. Historically, limited menus placed limited strain on storage areas. As menus expanded, however, and more fresh ingredients were added, storage demands increased. For example, those fast food operators who are now making and baking their own biscuits must store large bags of flour instead of receiving ready-to-eat rolls.

The offices in fast food restaurants are usually quite small. Because of the very sophisticated point-of-sale (POS) systems in most fast feeders, much of the paperwork ordinarily completed in a standard restaurant office is done at the registers. Frequently this data is fed to a central data-collection office (not the on-site office), which sends reports back to the restaurant.

TABLESERVICE SPACES
Exterior

In chain-operated tableservice restaurants, the exterior image establishes theme and identity in much the same fashion as it does for the fast food restaurant. The logo or ideograph displayed on the building's exterior often carries through to the inside, and architectural form becomes a recognizable signal. Pizza Hut—which is really a tableservice restaurant—relies extensively on both its signage and its building shape for identity.

Other chain restaurants such as Rusty Scupper are recognizable not because every unit looks exactly alike but because each is designed in a dramatic fashion to complement a waterfront locale. Likewise, the Pennsylvania-based Seafood Shanty operations are a small regional chain of restaurants whose exteriors bear a common logo and similar but not identical architectural forms.

Retrofitting existing structures presents special problems, especially if the building in question happens to have been a known chain. In other words, to disguise a recognizable architectural form and create a new image requires extensive reconstruction. A bit of cosmetic overlay won't work.

Independent tableservice restaurants vary wildly in their architectural and graphic statements. Depending on the type of establishment and the marketing thrust, exteriors range from the undesigned and unembellished concrete or brick box to innovative architectural statements. Here, too, consumers recognize exterior symbols. The aluminum-sided diner, for instance, has become synonymous with a diverse, hearty, inexpensive Americana menu served twenty-four hours a day. Today, careful restorations or new knockoffs of this classical design have become late-night hangouts for everyone from the cross-country trucker to the urban clubgoer.

An investment in architecture and graphics is an investment in image that can pay off handsomely in the long run. The challenge is to create an individual identity that nevertheless remains in context with its environment, be it an urban streetscape or a rural country road (fig. 1-14).

1-14. B. Smith's stucco and glass exterior, designed by Anderson/Schwartz Architects, bespeaks its New York City location yet stands in stark contrast with the run-down Eighth Avenue surroundings. (Elliott Kaufman photo)

Entry Area

On the average, tableservice restaurants have small entry areas that function as pass-through spaces to the dining room (fig. 1-15). In some establishments, a coatroom is tucked into a corner of the entry area. In informal restaurants,

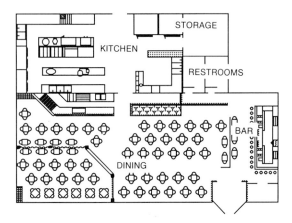

1-15. *In a typical tableservice floor plan, customers can easily access the bar and the dining room from the entry area. A dining platform and drink rail help to define different seating areas.*

the entry space often includes a dual-purpose host and cashier station. Fancier places have a maitre d' station where guests check in before being led to their table but the station does not include cash-handling functions.

The entry area in chains includes everything from the queue-up lines in steak houses to newspaper vending machines in coffee shops. It is usually an unembellished area where guests wait for a table.

In an upscale tableservice restaurant, however, the entry area can set the stage for the dining experience to come. Here, the entry is the transition zone between the outside world and the restaurant, and even in small spaces good design can help facilitate the transition with devices such as vestibules or angled entry doors. Lighting also plays a crucial role in creating a smooth transition between outside and inside.

Dining Areas

Due to the diverse nature of tableservice restaurants, dining areas reflect all manner of shapes, sizes, and décor. Large rooms are often broken up with levels or barriers to create dining nooks and the feeling of privacy. Small rooms are

often treated with mirrors and reflective surfaces to expand the sense of space. Comfort is paramount in any tableservice restaurant dining area, but in some contemporary places comfort is overshadowed by high style. The spatial plan should always take into account the traffic flow of the wait staff and the amount of space needed between tables.

Chain operations and independent family restaurants have traditionally relied upon theme treatments to carry forth the design idea in dining areas. Seafood houses were strewn with plastic lobsters. Pizza operations were decked out with red-and-white-checkered tablecloths, old Chianti bottles, and a little statue of a chubby chef handing out take-home menus. Coffee shops reflected bright colors, vinyl, and formica. Today many of these chains and independent restaurants have softened the spaces in much the same way as the fast feeders and capitalized on good design as a marketing tool.

In the tableservice restaurant, the dining area takes on critical importance as the patron's destination. Especially in fine dining establishments, where people sit for hours, the spatial plan and interior design must communicate appropriate messages.

Beverage Areas

Many tableservice restaurants incorporate a small beverage area or bar that is visually separated from the dining areas. The bar often serves multiple purposes: as a drinking spot, as a service bar for the dining room, and as a waiting area for diners. It is often accompanied by a cocktail lounge, especially when food is served. Today some restaurants serve complete meals at the bar, an effort aimed at the single diner.

Bar size ranges from tiny to gargantuan, depending on its role in the restaurant. The old-fashioned, dimly lit corner bar has given way to all manner of open, inviting bar areas. In New York City's Aurora, a centrally located bar is the first element customers view when they walk in the door, and it divides the dining room into two halves. Here, a singularly attractive bar has become an extremely popular lunch spot for single diners. Generally, however, bar design is not as important as dining room design in tableservice restaurants whose main mission is food service.

Restrooms

Restroom design in the tableservice establishment is too often neglected, although it plays an important role in the customer's overall perception of the restaurant. Materials and surfaces specified for the restrooms should be durable and easy to maintain in order to sustain cleanliness and efficiency. In addition, there are many ways to extend the dining room design into the restrooms and create something special. Flowers, wallcovering, piped-in music, and other design elements in the bathrooms go a long way toward engendering customer goodwill.

Kitchen

Both menus and kitchens are standardized in chain operations. The independent restaurant kitchen, however, does not follow a standard format. Frequently, batch-prepared foods are held in steam tables, where they are supplemented with foods prepared to order at a grill or fry station. In the a la carte kitchen, where all food is prepared to order and few foods are prepared in advance, fast-prep equipment capable of cooking food within minutes is most frequently included in the design. With few exceptions, kitchen space is always tight because the more space in the front of the house, the more revenue for the restaurant. Therefore, an efficient kitchen layout is absolutely vital: Every inch of space must be well utilized, equipment should do double duty when possible, and the spatial plan should save labor time.

With the exception of restaurants that have display kitchens in the front of the house, most of the food preparation and cooking in tableservice operations are performed in an enclosed kitchen. Pizza parlors, whether they are chain or independent, generally have open kitchens, as do some contemporary, high-design restaurants who showcase the chef's art as drama. In these cases, the back-of-the-house kitchen is even smaller.

Restaurant Support Areas

Because tableservice menus are generally more complex than fast food operations, they require more storage for the varied types of food items. Less space is needed for dry storage, however, because most tableservice restaurants do not use paper goods.

In the tableservice restaurant, the mix of dry to refrigerated to frozen changes as a function of management policy. In some independent operations, fresh foods are used wherever possible. Others, and many chain operations, depend heavily on frozen and canned goods. The type of storage facilities needed, therefore, depends on the particular operation.

GATHERING PLACE SPACES

The gathering place is a tableservice restaurant, usually with a bar scene, that relies heavily on "entertainment" as its raison d'être. In other words, patrons go to the restaurant not just for a meal but for an evening out. These places are the 1980s equivalent of the disco, and their primary market target is the young, upwardly mobile single. The gathering place provides a meeting place where the goal is to see and be seen, and it fills an important psychological niche in the lives of the customers.

Originally conceived as after-hour drinking places, the first gathering places, such as TGI Friday's, became synonymous with oversized bars, hanging plants, wood and brass furnishings and an endless list of drink specials. Today, the gathering place has evolved into a full-scale restaurant serving trendy cuisine. Northern Italian, Mexican, diner American, Cajun— whatever the hip menu of the moment, you'll find it at a gathering place. Finger (or grazing) foods such as tapas and pizza also figure prominently on the menus.

Exterior

Architectural design has played an important role in the gathering place. In general, suburban chain operations have been situated in free-standing buildings whose architecture is as recognizable as the chain fast food building. Independent urban gathering places usually sport distinctive, highly individual facades. Often they have huge windows open to the street, that allow passers-by to glimpse the electricity and excitement inside. This treatment is the reverse of the Parisian cafe, where people sit and watch the outside world go by. Other places use unusual, overscaled architectural elements to create identity. At any gathering place, the restaurant patrons are the show, and the architecture helps to promote the show.

Entry Areas

In most gathering places the entry area melds with the bar and dining area (fig. 1-16). Barriers are done away with in an effort to draw people into the space. This treatment creates a see-and-be-seen atmosphere that begins the minute people step inside. Patrons become instantly involved with the excitement of the space. Coatrooms are set aside and in some operations are placed in very remote locations.

Dining Areas

In the early days of the genre, dining areas surrounded the bar area. These dining areas were partially screened from the bar in an effort to provide a modicum of privacy and a quieter setting. With the advent of the see-and-be-seen ethic, however, this spatial relationship changed drastically. Barriers between the two spaces were lowered to create the feeling of one large space and to allow visibility between bar patrons and restaurant patrons.

In other words, everyone could look at everyone else. In the late 1980s barriers between dining and drinking areas began resurfacing but always with some visibility between the two. Many dining room elements differ from the stock tableservice restaurant. Because young professionals travel in groups, for instance, increased numbers of four-tops and larger tables replace deuces. Further, the noise levels often go off the scale and become a harbinger of success. Noise creates action, excitement, and energy and helps to develop the feeling of the place. Ear-splitting reverberation that makes conversation painful does not matter to youth accustomed to Walkmans blasting in their ears. Similarly, illumination levels are intense, with some places bright enough to assemble computer chips.

Beverage Areas

As mentioned above, beverage areas in gathering places are often integrated into the dining areas. Large bars—sometimes as large as the dining rooms—are designed to be conducive to conversation and people watching. Music, most often with a rock-and-roll beat, is de rigueur, and video systems have become commonplace as well.

The bar attracts its own crowd as well as diners who wait there for tables. This area is a critical revenue producer for the gathering place and merits special design consideration. It often takes up a sizeable chunk of space on the floor plan.

Restrooms

Restrooms take on a new meaning in gathering places. Frequenters of these facilities are very much concerned with personal appearance, and a trip to the restroom is often a lengthy visit. Make-up is checked and hair is adjusted. Women may visit in pairs and take the opportunity to chat in private. What this adds up to is

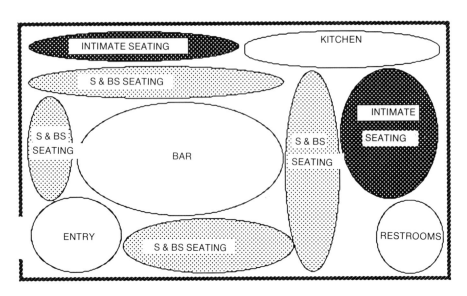

1-16. *This bubble diagram of a gathering place restaurant shows see-and-be-seen (S&BS) seating around the bar, and more intimate seating areas located further from the action.*

the need for extra space, particularly in women's rooms. Operators of the gathering place sometimes pipe music into the restroom in order to maintain the energetic pace.

Kitchens

As mentioned previously, the first gathering places did not emphasize food, yet they boasted a full menu and an attendant complement of equipment and support areas. In the beginning of the 1980s, a new awareness of and emphasis on food led to increasing numbers of display kitchen areas—from full open kitchens to large pickup windows—in the gathering place (fig. 1-17). Gathering place groupies had grown up with the open kitchens of McDonald's and enjoyed seeing every sort of food from pizza to linguini to broiled rack of lamb prepared in front of them.

With this emphasis comes the need to split the function of the kitchen into two spaces: the finishing kitchen in the front of the house and the storage and prepreparation areas in the back of the house. Consequently, the spatial plan allocates a display kitchen area adjacent to the back of the house for easy flow. This process shrinks the space in the back of the house and necessitates more esthetic treatments for the on-view finishing area.

Restaurant Support Areas

Storage areas for gathering places have followed a traditional format until recent years, when a greater emphasis on fresh foods has put pressure on the size of reach-in and walk-in refrigerators. The demand for fresh foods has necessitated more refrigerated storage along with additional space for the prepreparation of fresh foods.

NONCOMMERCIAL CAFETERIA SPACES
Exterior

In general, the exterior of a cafeteria operation consists of the exterior building shell that houses not only the cafeteria but also many other facilities (offices or hospital beds, for example). Therefore, the exterior of the cafeteria has not traditionally been integrated into its overall design program. In some operations, however, the exterior approach to the cafeteria

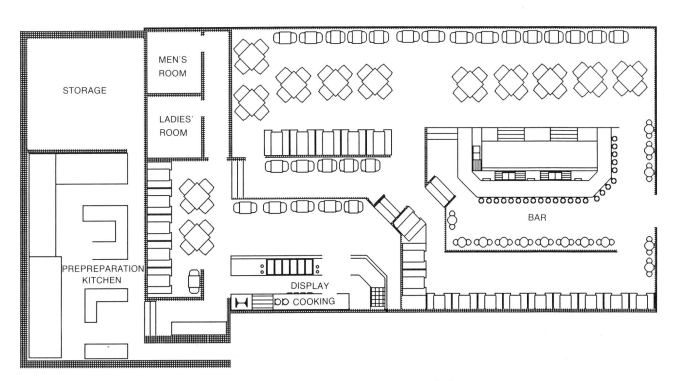

1-17. Some gathering place restaurants have two focal points: the bar and the display cooking area, as is illustrated here. Note the prepreparation kitchen in the back of the house.

—actually located inside the building—has been designed to attract patrons into the space. Floor treatments, artwork, and windows into the serving area can capture the attention of people as they walk by the cafeteria. Large operations dedicate an entire floor to the cafeteria, which has its own elevator or elevator access. Thoughtful design treatments such as menu displays in the elevator or hanging banners over the escalator can arouse interest in the cafeteria and lead people into the space.

Entry Areas

The cafeteria entry area is minimal in size and limited to the space where customers pick up a tray and gain their first introduction to menu offerings. Entry areas in the traditional straight-line cafeteria needed to be larger and longer, because they served as holding areas where guests queued up. Today's scramble designs, where patrons do not enter a line but travel to individual food stations, eliminate the need for an entry queue.

Servery

The servery, where patrons pick up and pay for food, is the design feature that distinguishes cafeterias from other types of food service. In general, it needs to be large enough to allow a smooth and continual flow of traffic during the peak lunch hour, when cafeteria customer counts swell considerably and patrons' time is limited (fig. 1-18). The scramble-system servery was conceived to cut down queueing and to speed customers to the food items they wish to

purchase, for instance, to hot foods, grilled items, sandwiches, and beverages. The marketing advantage of the traditional straight-line design was that customers were paraded past all food offerings and conceivably would make impulse purchases. With the scramble system, customers can be more selective in the choices they make and the queues they enter, so attractively designed food stations are critical. In addition, exhibition cooking and preparation, such as made-to-order grilling, stir fry, and roast carving, have proven to be enormously popular draws.

Care must be taken to position food stations so as to maximize flow with minimal cross-traffic. Another goal—reached through careful placement of service stations and cashiers—is to ensure that once seated, customers' hot food is hot and cold food is cold.

Efforts have been made to de-institutionalize serveries, with less emphasis on stainless steel surfaces and more attention to lighting, color, finishes, and textures that improve the look of the food and add warmth to the feeling of the space. Scramble systems depend on well-placed and descriptive signage to educate and direct customers.

Dining Areas

Gone are the days when noncommercial cafeteria design was typified by institutional green masonry block walls. In fact, today's cafeteria dining room design is often indistinguishable from that of a full-service restaurant. Elements such as greenery, carpeting, and artwork help

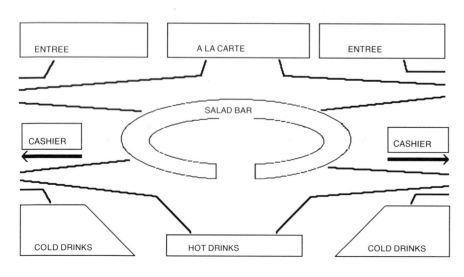

1-18. *The complex circulation patterns of scramble-system serveries can initially cause confusion, although they keep queues shorter than in straight-line systems.*

to stylize the setting. At Emory University's R. Howard Dobbs Student Center in Atlanta, for instance, architects John Portman & Associates sculpted interior space into a spectacular environment with a domed central rotunda and curving dining terraces. Here, students enjoy a theatrical eating experience comparable to the see-and-be-seen grand cafes. At Philadelphia's award-winning La Salle University student center entertainment and dining room renovation, architects Bartley-Bronstein-Long-Mirenda created a multifaceted facility with exposed brick walls and soft, incandescent lighting that bears no resemblance to its "institutional" predecessor (fig. 1-19).

In these and other noncommercial facilities, the dining experience serves as a respite from daily business activities, and design should be engineered to provide a restful, comfortable escape from workday tasks. Acoustic control is a particularly important design consideration. Maintenance and durability of furnishings and materials is also critical.

Spatially, cafeteria dining rooms should be divided by barriers, levels or other devices to allow customers the choice of more intimate dining. These semiprivate areas also enable informal meetings to be conducted over a meal or a break period. Depending on the needs of the institution, private dining rooms are sometimes included for more formal gatherings. Cafeteria dining areas are often utilized for special evening functions, so design flexibility should also be incorporated into the spatial plan.

Beverage Areas

Alcoholic beverage service is not offered in most cafeterias. Several nonalcoholic beverage stations are frequently situated in the servery area. In some newly designed cafeterias, beverage stations have been placed in the dining areas, as in newer fast food designs.

Restrooms

Generally, restrooms are incorporated into an overall building design that includes the cafe-

1-19. *Architects Bartley, Bronstein, Long, and Mirenda transformed a typical student center cafeteria into Intermissions, a stylish cafe at La Salle University, Philadelphia.*
(©Tom Bernard)

teria. Thus, their design is not an integral component of the cafeteria interior. Like all foodservice restrooms, however, they should be functional and easy to maintain.

Kitchen

Cafeteria kitchens were traditionally designed with banks of steam-jacketed kettles, pressure steamers, and deck ovens, all aimed at bulk preparation of large batches of food. Recent changes in menus and servery design have changed the fare and the face of cafeteria kitchens. In many instances, as with grill stations, foods are cooked at the point of service. Another example that moved back-of-the-house space to front-of-the-house serveries is a la carte preparation of such items as fresh vegetables, steamed off as the need arises by the counter staff in high-pressure steamers located right on the serving line.

This shift of production out of the kitchen not only changes spatial allocation—requiring more servery space and less back-of-house space —but also creates different demands for cooking and refrigeration equipment in the back of the house. The introduction of the tilting fry kettle, convection oven, and the combination oven—multipurpose units that speed cooking time—has decreased the reliance on traditional pieces of equipment. When vegetables are cooked in the kitchen, the low-pressure steamer is being replaced with the faster and smaller high-pressure steamer.

The floor plan of the noncommercial cafeteria kitchen depends in large measure on the type of institution. Hospitals, for example, require separate patient food assembly areas. The larger and more complex the institution, the larger and more complex the kitchen. A smooth, straightforward flow from receiving to preparation to servery pass-through is always the spatial goal. Multipurpose equipment and labor-saving layouts also help achieve an efficient, successful design.

Restaurant Support Areas

Storage and receiving areas for cafeteria operations are frequently separated from the production areas because most cafeterias are located within a multistory building shell. In many instances, one receiving dock serves the entire building, and the storage of foodservice goods may be overseen by the storeroom manager for all departments within the building.

Offices and employee spaces are similar in size and nature to a commercial restaurant, but additional office space is required in complex foodservice operations such as hospitals, where multiple styles of service are supported by a single kitchen and support facilities.

SUMMARY

Space planning for any type of foodservice enterprise incorporates some common design principles. A well-designed restaurant, however, is one where the design team has carefully attended to the particular character of the operation and designed spaces so that they work most effectively for the customers, the staff, and management. Time must be spent developing the floor plan and considering, rejecting, and refining spatial options until arriving at the best possible solutions.

2

THE PSYCHOLOGY OF DESIGN

"We shape our buildings and our buildings shape us." Winston Churchill expressed this thought to the House of Commons just after World War II. He was concerned about a proposed plan to change the shape of the legislators' meeting room, concerned that a change of physical environment would in turn effect change in the legislative process.

Churchill's point—that environment affects behavior—is a well-documented fact, but only recently has the knowledge of social scientists—the environmental and behavioral psychologists—been deliberately applied to architecture and interior design. This knowledge is just beginning to be applied to the field of restaurant design.

ENVIRONMENT AND BEHAVIOR

Despite the lack of applied research, we know that customers' attitudes and behavior are influenced by their interaction with environmental elements. For an example, consider the chair you are now sitting in. You might be able to read this text for hours because of the design of the chair and the texture of the seat covers. Conversely, you might already feel uncomfortable and want to move on. This psychological reaction is important to the selection of seating in a restaurant, because it can influence guests either to eat quickly and move on or to linger over a meal and choose to stay for an after-dinner cordial.

Seating selection is but one of many decisions made by the design team that should re-

flect a working knowledge of design psychology. The combination of all environmental elements affects how people feel and consequently how people act in a given space: how long they stay, how comfortable they feel while they are there, what they remember, and perhaps if they want to come back again.

HOW SPACE IS PERCEIVED

In order to analyze the psychological impact of design elements, one must understand the many ways in which people perceive their surroundings. According to the anthropologist Edward T. Hall in his book *The Hidden Dimension* (Anchor Books, 1969), sensory apparatus falls into two general categories: distance receptors and immediate receptors. The distance receptors—the eyes, the ears, and the nose—are used to examine faraway objects and sensations. The immediate receptors—the skin, the membranes, and the muscles—examine the world up close. The world of touch incorporates such diverse sensations as temperature, texture, hardness, and shapes.

Hall also defines different distance zones because distance from any given object influences the perception of that object. A classic example is the impressionist painting, which looks like blobs of color on close inspection, but from a distance reveals itself to be a Parisian landscape. So too in a restaurant must the design consider the sensory impact of objects that are close to the guest along with objects that are across the dining room. Hall's distance zones, which are excellent guidelines for environmental design planning, are as follows:

1. Public distance—12 feet and beyond. The feeling of distance one gets when entering a high-ceilinged gathering place or a large, open lobby. Public distance encompasses the view when walking into the dining area itself or when entering a spacious pickup area in a kitchen.
2. Social distance—4 feet to 12 feet. The feeling of distance guests perceive when they are at a cocktail party or in a restaurant and have a sense of the people milling about them. Social distance is people watching the television screen above the bar, entertainers in a nightclub, chefs working in a display kitchen, or the service staff bustling about the restaurant. Similarly, the kitchen staff experience social distance while working in a display kitchen where guests walk by or in a bakery station where workers at other stations can be seen.
3. Personal distance—18 inches to 4 feet. The feeling of distance experienced in conversing with a single person or several people at a cocktail party or in speaking across the table to dining companions. This is also the feeling of distance a worker in the kitchen gets when two people are working in a double-sided work station or when one station, such as the broiler station, is positioned next to another station, such as a fry station.
4. Intimate distance—physical contact to 18 inches. The feeling of being close enough to touch a dining companion, as when seated side by side in a banquette. It is the sometimes crowded feeling when a diner's chair is bumped by passing service staff or a cook brushes past a co-worker in a cramped kitchen environment.

Another important influence on the way people perceive space is their ethnic background and country of origin. In Paris, for example, people are comfortable in crowded dining conditions, hence the popularity of the cozy European-inspired cafes where tables and people press together in a way that other cul-

2-1. *The tight seating scheme creates the atmosphere of a European cafe in New York's Ciao Bella. (Joseph Coscia, Jr., photo)*

tures might find stifling (fig. 2-1). In contrast, the hushed atmosphere of the Japanese teahouse—be it in downtown Tokyo or in a rural town—with its sense of serenity and spaciousness, reflects a totally different cultural orientation. Yet another cultural orientation can be found in the wide open space of the New York City grand cafe gathering place, which offers urbanites a spacious escape from their cramped working and living settings.

If management can identify the cultural characteristics of their target market, then design can be geared to suit that market. For example, the vaulted ceiling and unbroken floor space of the gathering place in New York City provides a welcome spatial experience for a New York City clientele but may fail in the suburbs where people take spaciousness for granted.

DISTANCE RECEPTORS

Visual Space

Visual perspective is affected by the structure of the eye and the angle at which objects are viewed. The retina—the light-sensitive part of the eye—is composed of three different areas, each of which performs a different function. One of the most important of these areas is peripheral vision, the field of vision outside the line of direct sight.

Edward T. Hall cites the following example of peripheral vision:

> A man with normal vision, sitting in a restaurant twelve to fifteen feet from a table where other people are seated, can see the following out of the corner of his eye. He can tell that the table is occupied and possibly count the people present, particularly if there is some movement. At an angle of 45 degrees he can tell the color of a woman's hair as well as the color of her clothing, though he cannot identify the material. He can tell whether the woman is looking at and talking to her partner but not whether she has a ring on her finger. He can pick up the gross movements of her escort, but he can't see the watch on his wrist. He can tell the sex of a person, his body build, and his age in very general terms but not whether

he knows him or not. (*The Hidden Dimension*, p. 72).

Only when someone is directly in front of the retina can all specific details about the individual be perceived.

The more designers understand how vision zones work, the better they can effectively manipulate visual space. For example, the field of vision is broader when sitting on a banquette than when sitting in a booth. Consequently, guests are more affected by surrounding elements in a banquette and more private in a booth, where the field of vision is narrower. This implies that banquette seating—which provides more visual stimulation—could encourage faster turnover and is especially appropriate for a see-and-be-seen environment, whereas booth seating limits visual stimulation and distractions, provides a feeling of intimacy, and leads to slower turnover of tables.

In a room with free-standing tables, a sense of intimacy can be created by changing the angle of tables and chairs in relation to each other. The purpose of angling the tables is to

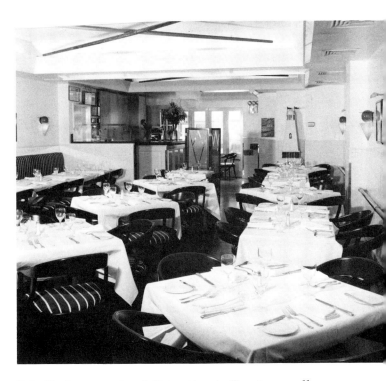

2-2. *To decrease visual distraction in Remi, a small New York restaurant, designer Adam Tihany angled the tables to redirect sightlines.*
(Joseph Coscia, Jr., photo)

cut visual distraction (fig. 2-2). Visual distraction can also be lessened by increasing the space between tables, although this is a costly technique. Lighting levels can be modified, thus limiting the scope of vision, and light or cool colors can help to create an overall sense of spaciousness.

Designers often manipulate visual space with mirrors and reflective surfaces. Mirrors expand the sense of space as well as the field of vision. Used incorrectly or to excess, they can cause visual confusion and disorientation. However, mirrored columns or mirrored horizontal or vertical planes can open up an otherwise claustrophobic room, while at the same time adding sparkle and visual excitement. In the Gwathmey Siegel–designed Shezan restaurant, a reflective ceiling creates a subtle, shimmering effect as candlelight bounces off it in this underground space. The mirrored strips at eye level for patrons facing banquettes in figure 2-3 permit a selective (and secretive) view of the bustling waiters, sparkling tabletops, and other diners behind them.

Another effective means of modifying visual space is to minimize sight lines. A frosted glass or glass brick wall, for instance, limits visual perception. Light and motion can be perceived through the glass, yet the diner maintains a feeling of intimacy. In some cases, one-way or reflective glass is used on exterior window walls. Diners can thus look out, but passers-by can't look in. From a practical sense, however, these reflective windows can—from the outside—give the impression that the restaurant is closed.

2-3. *Mirrored strips at eye level above banquettes allowed diners a selective view into New York's Fino restaurant, designed by Stephen Leigh.*
(Norman McGrath photo)

Auditory Space

Auditory space involves how the ear works and what exactly we hear. The ear actually picks up sound from two main zones. Primary audio space, that space where one hears and is heard clearly, is up to 20 feet away. Background audio space is from 20 to 100 feet away. In many dining areas, part of the primary audio space must be modified and turned into background noise so that diners can hear table companions and speak to them without strain but be conscious of a friendly background buzz. This state is what architect Warren Platner (who designed Windows on the World) calls convivial intimacy. It means that guests feel secure in their privacy, yet part of a larger whole.

Control of primary and background auditory space is also important in the kitchen. Kitchens are innately noisy spaces made louder by communications between kitchen workers and the service staff. Although background noise can add vitality and energy to the kitchen, the sound must be controlled to minimize carry-over into the dining area. This carry-over sound is of particular concern in display kitchens because of their proximity to dining areas.

Controlling sound at the interface point between service and production is also important. In some cases the communications between the front of the house and the back of the house flow through an expeditor, and in others servers call out their own orders to the line personnel. Whatever the system, it must be quiet enough for personnel to hear clearly. Sound control in this area of the kitchen can be controlled by placing processing equipment far from the plating and serving area.

Because the restaurant by definition is a noisy environment (fig. 2-4), acoustical control often involves the skillful application of sound-absorbing materials with the goal of achieving

2-4. *In the cavernous interior of Sports restaurant and bar, New York, architect Patricia Sapinsley used acoustical panels on the wall behind the bar so that noise would not reach deafening levels.*
(Joseph Coscia, Jr., photo)

background buzz. Soft materials like carpet, upholstery, wallcoverings, and curtains, as well as acoustical ceilings, panels, or banners, help deaden noise levels.

When such materials are properly selected and applied, the correct audio level for any type of restaurant can be artfully created. Designers can effectively combine acoustical materials with decorative treatment. A treatment composed of fabric-covered baffles that temper noise levels may serve as a unifying design statement that pulls together the entire room. Baffles, which are generally made of glass or mineral fiber batts encased in perforated metal or fabric, are especially effective in high-ceilinged spaces.

For retrofit, the acoustical panel is an efficient and cost-effective choice because installation does not involve structural work. Faced with woven fabric or perforated vinyl, the panels come in a variety of shapes and sizes and are easily attached to walls or ceilings. They can even be formed into the restaurant's logo or another graphic symbol.

Another technique that can be particularly effective in helping to soften loud conversation is the use of background music. Here the principle at work involves masking undesirable types of noise—people's voices at other tables, the clatter of dishes, and other operational sounds —with the desirable sounds of music suited to the taste of the restaurant's clientele.

The obvious solution of cutting up the size of the dining spaces to quiet primary audio space is not always effective, however, because sound waves travel through floors, walls, and ceilings. Just because adjacent dining rooms are visually separate doesn't mean that they are acoustically separate. In operations that require one single dining area, careful attention to sound-catching corners, shapes, and spaces can significantly limit reverberative sound.

In some types of operations, such as the fast food restaurant or the bar-dominated gathering place, little attention is given to controlling primary audio space because high noise levels create movement, excitement, and action, which are highly desirable in these types of places. In fact, the most popular new see-and-be-seen places all share remarkably high noise levels, in part created by the use of hard surfaces: steel, glass, wood, concrete, marble.

In some cases, domed ceilings also reflect or focus sound, thus generating "hot spots" of high noise levels. In addition, all of these sound-reflecting surfaces and materials can generate reverberation and cause an echo effect.

Olfactory Space

Olfactory space involves the sense of smell, one of the most significant yet frequently overlooked areas of restaurant design. Smell evokes the deepest memories of any of the senses, but how often does the design allow pleasant aromas to waft through the restaurant   aromas that customers will remember the next time they think about where to eat? Given current interest in fresh, real ingredients, perhaps their accompanying smells should be allowed to enter the front of the house. Because the lack of smell obscures memories, the indiscriminate elimination of all odors can have a negative psychological effect. Evidence of the importance of smell can be seen at Claudia's, a San Diego cinnamon bun bakery at Horton Plaza (discussed in chapter 5). Here the delicious aroma of baking cinnamon buns seems to correlate with the number of customers lined up to buy them.

The technique of bringing desirable cooking aromas to the guest is not limited to bakeries. The effectiveness of tableside cooking relies heavily on the sense of smell. In many recipes a dash of Worchestershire sauce is added to the heated pan. The aroma of the vaporizing sauce fills the area—along with the sizzle—thus tantalizing palates and promoting further tableside preparations.

Of course, off-smells can create negative feelings. The stale smell of beer or slightly soured mixers at a bar tells the customer that the bar lacks a good sanitation program. The smell of cigarettes where customers are trying to savor a vintage Bordeaux indicates an ineffective ventilation system. The smell of garbage in the parking lot sours the stomach.

IMMEDIATE RECEPTORS

Tactile Space

Tactile space includes both what is actually perceptible by touch and what relates visually to touch. A wineglass, for example, is an item that a guest touches in a restaurant, and a nubby wallcovering is a surface whose texture engages the visual perception. Tactile space is extremely important because it can psychologically warm up a room, which makes people feel comfortable.

Likewise, tactile elements involve people with their surroundings, which is particularly important in modern interiors and in very large, high-ceilinged spaces, because both tend to make people feel separate from the environment. Diners often like to feel impressed by the design of a restaurant, but they don't like to feel overwhelmed. Textural architectural and decorative surfaces like fabric, brick, upholstery, and artwork can keep the environment from feeling distant or intimidating (fig. 2-5).

The touchable items in a restaurant—seat and tabletop elements—have a lot to do with people's enjoyment of the dining experience. The degree of seating comfort, for instance, has a great deal of influence on the length of the meal and should be chosen to suit the type of facility. Natural materials, upholstered seats, and padded armrests maintain high comfort levels and are recommended for high-ticket establishments. Comfortable seating also helps to keep customers content as they sit through the multiple courses that play a pivotal role between profit and loss in many fine restaurants.

Tactile sensations can also be negative. No one likes the sticky sensation of plastic upholstery in warm temperatures, as in figure 2-6, the

2-6. *Surface textures with which guests come in direct contact should never cause embarrassment or discomfort (Brad Elias, Hochheiser/Elias Design Group drawing).*

2-5. *Anderson/Schwartz Architects utilized a variety of surface textures to create interest in the banquette seating areas at Cinco de Mayo, New York. (Elliott Kaufman photo)*

feeling of pitching too far forward in a hard seat, or leaning against a seat back that is uncomfortable to the human back. Yet some degree of uncomfortable tactile experiences—often caused by smooth, hard surfaces—can be appropriate for a restaurant that depends on fast turnover, like a fast food eatery. Here the seating can be pleasing to the eye but not comfortable to sit in for very long. This reflects an increasingly common design technique in the fast food environment: furniture that is good-looking but becomes uncomfortable to sit in after about 15 minutes.

Turnover in thirty minutes or less is not only essential to the success of fast feeders but also plays a pivotal role in customer satisfaction and the ultimate profitability of cafeteria operations. Frequently cafeterias serve large numbers of diners in a very limited time period. Comfortable seats can slow table turns and lead to dissatisfied customers who wander around the dining room with trays full of food in much the same way they hunt for parking spaces for their cars.

In any type of facility, the tabletop elements—table surfaces, flatware, glassware, dishware, table accoutrements—play a major role in customer satisfaction. The feel of a perfectly balanced fork, the coolness of a chilled beer mug, and the pleasant touch of a linen napkin add to the dining experience. Even in an inexpensive eatery, the choice of tabletop items is critical to diners' enjoyment of a meal because of the direct contact with these items. Tabletop elements—both paper plates and crystal goblets—should always be carefully chosen.

Tactile sensing devices are finely tuned. The fingers detect smoothness and temperature, but the muscles in the fingers, hand, and arm weigh tabletop items, calculate how well built they are, and determine any imperfections in balance or form. The oenophile sipping a 1961 Chateau Lafite-Rothschild from an improperly balanced wine glass does not fully enjoy the experience. A five-degree rise in temperature as growing numbers of diners overload the cooling system can make guests irritable and hasten their departure.

On the tabletop, as in the restaurant interior itself, avoiding a homogeneous textural weight is advisable (fig. 2-7). The tabletop could offer a pleasing tactile experience through the contrast of a smooth marble table surface, nubby linen-blend napkins, and cut crystal glassware. Likewise, a more casual restaurant might feature smooth, polyurethane wood tabletops with woven placemats and heavy stoneware. Tactile space is also an important concern with take-out foods. A thin napkin for fried chicken tells guests they will have trouble wiping their fingers when they are through. Flimsy forks and knives tell the guest to take two of each and prepare for all of them to break, hardly the message that should be sent to paying customers. Such attention to tabletop detail also helps to create a strong impression of value in the minds of clients. It shows concern for the things people touch, and implies a high regard for the food as well.

Tactile sensations are also important in the kitchen. Well-balanced knives, solid work tables, and a substantial cutting board give kitchen workers a sense of security and comfort that is extremely important. Nonslip flooring is another crucial design element in the kitchen. The tactile sensation of secure footing is essential.

Another part of the restaurant where tactile attention is important is the bathroom. We all tend to equate a dirty bathroom with a dirty kitchen. Like attention to tabletop detail, attention to bathroom detail causes customers to feel that management cares about the quality of their experience. Skillful use of tactile space, for example, might mix Corian surfaces to give the feel of marble, terra cotta flooring, attractive dried flower arrangements, and tile walls. Such textural diversity creates a very pleasant effect yet provides surfaces that can be cleaned and easily maintained.

Food, of course, is the most tactile element of all. Food presentation works on many levels to impress—or distress—the diner. In addition to the visual appearance, mouthfeel—the texture of food in the mouth and the complete organoleptic experience that includes taste, texture and temperature—is an element that leads to customer satisfaction.

If presented in a nondescript way, even well-prepared dishes can look unappetizing. Conversely, a carrot curl on a sandwich plate or a sprig of dill on a poached filet of black cod go a long way toward creating the impression of good food. A delightful textural balance of foods is literally mouthwatering and carries with it the same excitement when eaten.

Even in the fast food environment, tactile cues can create the impression of food value. Packaging design often plays an important part: If the standard ketchup container that spells out the word ketchup on one side and names the manufacturer on the other also shows an image of red, ripe tomatoes, the customer is more likely to perceive the value of its contents. Another example is the average fast food package, whose nondescript surfaces give little insight into the contents of the package and in no way helps to sell the product or provide the diner with any visual cues as to the tactile characteristics of the contents of the package. McDonald's has taken two important steps toward realizing the importance of the textural experience to consumers' happiness. First, they intro-

2-7. *A rich assortment of tabletop ware provides textural interest in the dining areas at Porter Wright Morris & Arthur Headquarters in Columbus, OH, designed by Warren Platner Associates Architects.*
(Jaime Ardiles-Arce photo)

duced their McD.L.T., in which "The hot stays hot and the cool stays cool." Here the hot parts of the meal are contained in one side of the package and the cold parts in the other, all in an effort to limit the possibility of tepid tomatoes and limp lettuce. In the second case, they introduced see-through containers for their packaged salads. Customers can visually inspect the textural variety of the salad components.

Thermal Space

Thermal space relates to temperature. In the restaurant, the most important psychological effect of thermal space is its influence on one's sense of crowding: Hot rooms feel more crowded than cool rooms. Consequently, a full restaurant should be kept comfortably cool so that diners do not experience the discomfort of feeling hemmed in. Half-empty restaurants might benefit from warmer temperatures because the warmth helps to create a feeling of more people in the room.

Overheated kitchens result in overheated tempers and ultimately have an adverse effect on productivity. "If you can't stand the heat, get out of the kitchen" does not carry the weight in a labor-short marketplace that it once did.

Temperature control is a particular problem in the design of ballrooms or restaurants with window walls. In both of these cases the heat loads—from the occupants of the room or the rays of the sun—can periodically overload cooling systems and render the rooms uncomfortable.

Kinesthetic Space

Kinesthetic space is the psychological (not physiological) perception of space. Kinesthetic perception can be caused by the physical conditions. A room that can be crossed in one or two steps creates a different sensation from a room that takes fifteen steps to traverse. A room with a seven-foot ceiling feels a lot smaller than a room with an eleven-foot ceiling.

Designers can manipulate kinesthetic space in the restaurant by a variety of techniques—mirrors, barriers, furniture arrangements—that help to achieve a desired psychological effect. A lowered ceiling over perimeter seating, for in-

stance, affords a more intimate dining experience than a high-ceilinged central area in the same restaurant. The bright, reflective surfaces of the walls in the limited-menu Burger King operations called Whopper Express make these narrow spaces feel a great deal larger than they really are.

Another aspect of kinesthetic space is that the fewer restrictions to movement, the larger the space feels. When comparing two identical rooms with different furniture arrangements, the one that permits the greater variety of free movement is perceived as larger. This principle can be effectively applied in compact urban storefronts, where a wall-hugging seating arrangement keeps the space from feeling cramped.

The vocabulary of the social scientist can now be applied to the process of restaurant design. We will examine next the psychological effects of three crucial design applications: spatial arrangements, lighting, and color.

SPATIAL ARRANGEMENTS

Spatial arrangements should always be orderly, guiding people in a logical progression from space to space: from exterior to entry zone to dining room to kitchen. The restaurant exterior, including signage, parking lot, and landscaping (when applicable), is very important because it creates the first impression and gives visual cues about the type of facility. Different feelings are created by a colorful logo versus a completely understated logo whose only identification is a discreet street address. Such restraint carries a great deal of snob appeal, implying that only those people "in the know" frequent the establishment.

Architecture—both exterior and interior—also conveys psychological messages. Building design can act as an enticement from the highway or from the street (fig. 2-8). Special architecture implies a special experience—and special food—inside.

As for the interior, social scientists divide space into two main areas: barriers and fields. Barriers include walls, screens, symbols, and objects. Fields include shapes, size, orientation, and environmental conditions. In the restau-

2-8. *No one could mistake the 1950s message of Ed Debevic's exterior architecture and signage.*
(Joseph Durocher photo)

rant, both serve functional and psychological purposes.

Barriers often act as space dividers to create feelings of privacy. In some cases, a dividing wall can separate the functions of entry and dining, and potted palms can help delineate small, intimate dining areas in a large room.

Fields can be thought of as the complete architectural plan: the overall layout of space with its accompanying environmental conditions of climate and lighting. These elements substantially influence how people feel in a space. A small room helps to create a cozy feeling for a gourmet restaurant, and a large room helps to establish a theatrical feeling for a see-and-be-seen grand cafe. The mixed sensation of barrier and field of the open kitchen impacts on both the kitchen and the diners.

Shape also has psychological impact (fig. 2-9). Because people tend to be attracted to curved forms, architects often build large, curved walls. The upward sweep of these curved lines can be very uplifting. However, as the New

York–based designer Lewis Dolin cautions, "Curved walls, as well as any other space dividers, should be well thought out in smaller spaces so as to create a sense of larger space."

Lastly, the interaction between spaces—between the outside and the inside, between the front of the house and the back of the house—can help to communicate information about the quality of the dining experience and about the food itself. An exhibition kitchen or more subtle kitchen references, like woodburning pizza ovens or pickup windows, not only signal messages about the food itself, but also allow diners a privileged glimpse of the back of the house. Psychologists maintain that people like seeing what goes on behind the scenes and that those "staged regions" that form a bridge between the front and back of the house can generate a lot of customer interest. In this context, service staff uniforms also link kitchen and dining room and send messages about both the food and the type of establishment. A black jeans and T-shirt uniform, for example, carries

2-9. *Sweeping curvaceous forms soften the impact of the hard-edged architecture at Toscana, New York, designed by Piero Sartogo and Nathalie Grenon. (Joseph Durocher photo)*

a completely different set of associations from the full-skirted, blue-and-white-checked gingham uniform, the former belonging to a hip, expensive inner city bistro and the latter to a popular, moderately priced pancake house.

Within the dining area, designers can manipulate spatial arrangements for a variety of psychological effects. A really "bad" table is never necessary. Terraced floor levels rising back from windows, for example, can provide each table with a view. In a large room, terracing from side to side defines spatial areas and creates islands of intimacy. Other techniques that facilitate comfortable dining and camouflage room size include lowering parts of the ceiling (mentioned previously in kinesthetic space) or closing up an area with architectural or decorative dividers. The larger the room, the greater the need for such enclosures.

Furniture arrangements can also facilitate or retard interaction between people and should be chosen to suit the type of facility. For example, a restaurant that functions as a gathering and meeting place, such as a Bennigan's or TGI Friday's, wants to encourage interaction between guests. In the ever-popular gathering places, face-to-face seating and an asymmetrical bar shape can help to draw people together. Other facilitators include uncluttered lounge seating and casual-looking furniture. Conversely, when privacy is desired, widely spaced tables can be arranged at angles to each other to restrict views of other diners. Chairs in a row, barriers between chairs, and circular or linear bars act to retard conversation between people.

In the back of the house, equipment arrangements can serve to retard or improve interaction between employees. The equipment itself or divider walls serve as barriers. However, half-high divider walls can help interaction between workers. In these cases employees can talk from both areas, thus eliminating barriers to communication. Limiting barriers can also improve supervision. Management that can easily see every corner of the front and back of the house can more easily supervise employees.

Rooms with a regular layout of tables all neatly lined up in rows seem formal. Tables that are randomly spaced throughout the room with different sizes of tables mixed together and rooms divided with barriers lead to a feeling of informality. The divided room can also lead to a feeling of intimacy.

LIGHTING

Lighting is arguably the single most important element in restaurant design because incorrect lighting can obviate the effectiveness of all the other elements. Lighting is a critical psychological component as well: More than any other design application, illumination creates the mood of a space. Lighting can make a room feel intimate or expansive, subdued or exciting, friendly or hostile, quiet or full of electrifying energy. Not only is the intensity of the lighting important, but also the light source, the quality of the lighting, and the contrast of different light levels in different areas are all crucial design considerations. In the kitchen, lighting intensities must be maintained at levels that do not lead to eyestrain.

Ideally, a lighting design consultant is retained to handle the complexities of designing an effective illumination scheme. If the budget prohibits the hiring of a lighting designer, then the architect or interior designer must be well versed in lighting psychology and sensitive to the specific demands of the facility. A bustling cafeteria calls for a bright ambient light level and brightly lit architectural surfaces to help move people through the space. An elegant French restaurant should have a more subdued illumination scheme to encourage leisurely dining. A source of illumination between diners, like candles or reflected light bounced off the tabletop, draws diners together while providing a complementary glow that helps to overcome the negative aspects of typical downlighting in many restaurants.

Although the lighting scheme should always respond to the type of facility, the following guidelines for psychologically effective illumination apply to any restaurant. Remember that restaurant lighting is similar to theatrical lighting. Both set the stage for a dramatic production that relies heavily on the setting and atmosphere to effectively carry it off.

Important to any effective lighting scheme is a dimming control system that can modify illumination levels for optimum psychological effectiveness. The system needs to be changed to react to the time of day and to create different moods for different occasions. The same room can feel bright and cheerful for breakfast, restful for lunch, animated for cocktails, and romantic for dinner—all due to carefully planned light programming. If the budget permits, an automated system can be programmed and preset to react to external light conditions and deliver the desired light levels for any time of day or type of function. Dimming systems should never be adjusted during dining hours, as that can be very distracting to clientele. Further, control systems should be clearly marked to facilitate manual lighting level changes, should the need arise.

Light transition zones are important so that customers don't feel blinded when they enter from bright sunlight or disoriented when they leave at night. When people step into a dimly lit restaurant from the sunlit outdoors, for example, their eyes need time to adjust before they can see clearly. Light transition zones help eyes adjust before people move on to the dining area and give a logical psychological procession from outdoors to indoors.

Sparkle is said to enhance and encourage conversation. Sparkle comes from light fixtures such as chandeliers and multiple, small pin lights. It is also produced from certain reflected light, such as light bounced off glassware, mirrored surfaces, or shiny tableware. Especially appropriate for leisurely dining, sparkle seems to create an almost magical effect that makes people feel animated but not restless.

For environmental comfort, and to avoid a homogeneous, boring effect, direct lighting (light cast directly onto an object, without reflections from other surfaces such as walls or ceilings) should be counteracted with indirect lighting. The juxtaposition of direct and indirect lighting can create an interesting yet comfortable effect. Indirect lighting can create small shadow patterns that feel friendly; however, large, dark shadows may appear hostile and should be avoided.

One of the most important aspects of psychologically effective restaurant lighting—and the most often overlooked—involves making people look good. When people feel attractive, they not only enjoy the environment more but

also tend to return for repeat visits. If fleshtones look good, food also tends to look good. Both look best under incandescent lamps, but a careful mix of warm (or tinted) fluorescent and incandescent lighting can also provide a rosy, flattering glow. Strong downlighting, however, is extremely unbecoming to people because it highlights every imperfection, and light sources improperly angled can throw unflattering shadows over people's faces. Guests also tend to feel uncomfortable when their table is lit more brightly than the environment around them; the effect is something like looking into a black hole. Therefore, people should not be spotlighted as if they were on stage but rather surrounded with soft light. Although strong downlighting centered on the tabletop can be used effectively, designers must install easy-to-aim lamps that can be adjusted when tables are moved.

Perhaps the most crucial element of psychologically effective restaurant lighting is balance. If a room is too bright, too dim, too deeply shadowed, or too homogeneously lit, it won't feel comfortable. Achieving the right balance involves not only the correct selection of light sources, but light programming that is sensitive to overall brightness, daylight, and the color spectrum.

COLOR

Color should always be chosen in concert with lighting because the two are so closely associated. Together they communicate a variety of psychological messages on both obvious and subliminal levels. Their interrelationship stems from the fact that color perception is a function of the type of light source and the reflective surface itself. In other words, the same color takes on different hues or appears to be a different color when seen under different light sources (fluorescent or incandescent, for example) or when viewed in direct or indirect light. Light is also color, whether the source is a tinted bulb, a neon tube, sunlight, or a candle.

Another consideration is that the source of light will affect the perception of color. Some of the light is absorbed, but the light that is reflected is highly charged with the color of the surface material, or in other words, its hue. In addition to hue, brilliance and saturation further affect the perception of color. Combined, as seen in figure 2-10, the Munsell color system gives a graphic depiction of how these three elements interact. The higher the value of the color, the greater its reflectance. The saturation of each value level can be thought of as the purity of each of the colors. Pure yellow has a higher saturation level than a shade of yellow produced by mixing yellow with black or some other less reflective color.

Light and cool colors recede. This principle can be used in restaurant design to expand a sense of space. Conversely, dark and warm colors advance and can be used in large rooms to keep the space from feeling vast and impersonal and instill a sense of intimacy. Warm colors become excellent highlights as points of color on a tabletop and add to a feeling of elegance.

Bold, primary colors and bright lighting encourage turnover and are appropriate for fast food or casual restaurants that depend on fast turnover. Extremely high illumination, however, washes out the effects of colors (as well as the effects of texture), leads to eyestrain, and lessens the impact of detailing in design.

Muted, subtle colors create a restful, leisurely effect. Pastel color schemes, in addition to making a small room appear larger, evoke a calm atmosphere.

Light colors can also make a room look brighter because the brightness of a color is a function of its hue. Light colors such as yellow appear brighter than dark colors such as navy blue, even when measured brightness is the same. Measured brightness is expressed in lumens that are "absorbed" into dark-hued surfaces and reflected from bright surfaces. As mentioned earlier, brightness is also affected by the light source.

Because all colors carry with them various associations, color can evoke a theme, a style, a culture, or a country. Purple, for example, is the color of royalty; green is the color of nature; muted pastel hues reflect the palette of postmodern architects; and red and gold color schemes are common in Chinese restaurants.

Color schemes should relate to climatic conditions. Simply put, warm colors feel right in colder climates and cool colors feel right in warmer climates. On their own, however, cool colors are generally unappetizing (maybe this is partly why food is never blue). Therefore, even in a tropical climate, cool color schemes should also employ warm accents.

Stylish color schemes reflect general trends in the consumer marketplace. In the early 1980s, restaurant color palettes began to coincide with the shift toward cool hues like seafoam green, deep blue, and aqua; often combined with burgundy, peach, or rosy terra cotta. In the late 1980s, bright, clear colors became the leading fashion statement and found their way into the color palettes of the restaurant designer. Color cycles literally move around the color wheel, gradually shifting from the cool colors to the warm colors with all of these trends each having a life cycle of about eight years.

An analysis of the colors themselves must

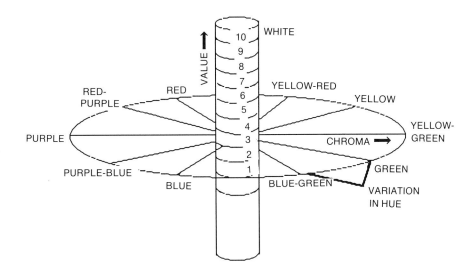

2-10. *The Munsell color system offers a way to conceptualize the relationships of colors, within the context of value, chroma, and hue (Adapted from W.J. McGuiness and B. Stein.* Mechanical and Electrical Equipment for Buildings, *5th ed. New York: Wiley, 1971.)*

be tempered by at least three facts. First, the effect of any color depends on its hue and intensity. Sky blue, aqua, and navy are all blue, but each carries a different association. Second, the perception of color changes with distance from the color. When choosing colors, designers must compensate for the public distance from which customers view a restaurant when they enter. Third, ongoing research by various experts and associations has yet to quantify scientifically the effects of colors. On the contrary, there is much disagreement regarding color psychology. Given these limitations, individual colors can be evaluated in part by their psychological effects.

RED

Historically, reds suggest aggression, hostility, and passion. There are a limited number of colors that harmonize with red because it is so intense, but the edge can be tempered with gold, wood, brass, crystal, or mirrors. Red and black is a classic combination, with an upscale, stylish association. Some say that red enhances the appetite.

GREEN

Green is associated with nature and general well-being. Because of its link to the outdoors and therefore to good health, it has become a trademark of "natural" and salad bar restaurants. Green is also linked with light and good foods. Live plants, light, and white woods can all complement green. Although it can be refreshing in moderate doses, green should not be overused because its reflective nature negatively affects the appearance of skin tones and some foods.

YELLOW

Yellow suggests radiant sunlight, expansiveness, and high spirits. In small doses, it can evoke cheerful, exuberant feelings and is particularly appropriate in breakfast areas. Yellow commands attention and can be used effectively as a color accent or an architectural symbol, as in the McDonald's arch. Green-cast yellows, however, have a disturbing effect.

GOLD

Like yellow, gold has a warming influence, and it can help offset cold materials—like stone—or brighten dark materials like dark wood. Gold is associated with wealth and power, and it tends to invoke a timeless feeling because of its historical overtones.

BLUE

Blue is stark, cool, and refreshing. It can visually expand a room, but it does not complement most foods and so should be avoided on the tabletop. Blue goes particularly well with warm colors and materials. It is said to have a calming effect.

NEUTRALS

Darker browns suggest masculinity, and lighter terra cottas suggest warmth and femininity. A rosy hue complements food and people. Neutrals are excellent for the tabletop because they tend to enhance the colors of food. Another advantage of neutrals is that they provide an excellent backdrop and an effective canvas for a variety of color effects. A neutral backdrop also allows for flexibility, because the mood of a room can be changed just by changing the color accents.

PEACH

Peach, which has passed a recent peak in popularity, is a spinoff of the terra cotta family. Peach is associated with feminine, intimate feelings. It can be effectively highlighted with deep blue, black, or white, all of which downplay its feminine overtones.

WHITE

White is extremely effective when it is harmonized with other colors. It works well as a background or as a statement in its own right, but it is not ideal for walls because its brightness produces glare that can lead to eyestrain. However, in a fast food environment, where contact time is minimal, white walls can encourage turnover and are in keeping with the bright, clean atmosphere of these types of restaurants. Although white is traditionally associated with tabletops, it is not always the best choice because white tends to neutralize the color of the food and the tabletop pieces. White tabletops can also contribute to glare in sun-filled restaurants.

BLACK

Black has negative sociological connotations. It is associated with depression and mourning, but it can be very stylish and it works well as an accent with all other colors. Black goes especially well with white—its opposite—creating a classic statement (fig. 2-11). It does not usually work well as a background color, with the exception of nightclub environments or in conjunction with colored lighting.

SUMMARY

All design applications in the restaurant engage the senses and manipulate them for various ef-

fects. Today design elements are being looked at separately and analyzed for their psychological contribution to the whole. Whether or not intentional, almost every design element and environmental condition in the restaurant works as a psychological tool. From lighting to color to texture to temperature, the nuances that influence people's feelings and behavior number in the hundreds. Design choices, therefore, should reflect careful consideration of their psychological impact. Customers can be encouraged to leave or linger, feel exuberant or mellow, feel like part of the action or secure in an intimate enclave—all as a result of design applications. Such attention to the psychological impact of design can have a marked effect on the diner and hence on the operation's profitability.

2-11. *Stanley Jay Friedman Associates juxtaposed black and white in a classic checkerboard pattern in the Cafe at Shun Lee West, New York. (Elliott Kaufman photo)*

3

DESIGN IMPLEMENTATION: FRONT TO BACK THROUGH THE CUSTOMER'S EYES

The creation of a successful restaurant design is based, in part, on its operational effectiveness. To an even greater extent, its success depends on the customer's perception of the restaurant. That perception develops from many pieces of information. A potential customer may hear about the restaurant from a friend, read an advertisement, see a newspaper article, or watch the construction of the building that will house the restaurant. All of this information comes together as a go or no-go decision to visit the restaurant the first time. Over the course of that first meal, many customers decide whether or not they wish to return.

This chapter addresses the ways in which front-of-the-house design impacts the customer, from his or her first glimpse of the facade to the end of the meal. It follows the progression of spaces as the patron perceives them, starting with the exterior and moving on to the entryway area, the dining room, the bar and lounge and the restroom. It also covers the basic principles of design decision making for such areas as signage, seating, tabletop elements, lighting, color, and floor, wall, window, and ceiling treatments.

The act of dining out, regardless of restaurant type, involves the sequence of destination, progression, and arrival discussed here. In an effective design, this sequence is a harmonious flow, a spatial organization that helps to orchestrate a memorable restaurant experience. Once the customer enters the doors of the restaurant, the design should continue as an integrated sensual and operational experience that reinforces the decision to visit and compels the decision to return.

EXTERIOR IMAGE

The exterior image of a restaurant influences the customer in many ways. Obviously, location plays an important role in determining an appropriate architectural style. Ventana, a free-standing wooden building nestled in the redwoods of Big Sur, California, creates different expectations than Rocky Aoki's Big Splash, located on the loading dock side of a suburban shopping mall in Florida. In these cases, the customer is preconditioned by the restaurant's surroundings to expect a certain type of establishment.

Similarly, the architecture built along the "miracle mile" situated on the outskirts of many cities and towns portends a certain type of restaurant. People have been conditioned to expect greasy spoon diners and fast food restaurants on these stretches of highway, and other types of restaurants seem incongruous.

Preconditioned expectations can sometimes be overcome by the exterior design. For example, the image of noncommercial cafeterias suffers from perceptions of sterile, uncomfortable, noisy environments. Today, many institutions have upgraded their exterior, signage, and entry areas to beckon patrons inside the cafeteria, where people find that their recollections of the boring, straight-line cafeterias of yesteryear do not match the restaurant-style atmosphere.

Facade

To succeed in a cluttered visual environment, a restaurant's facade must stand out from the rest of the pack. This is particularly important for restaurants on roadways but should be considered even when the restaurant has little

competition. The same problem has faced advertisers in magazines who have opted for color ads in an effort to stand out from the crowd. Today, with so many color ads, some marketers have moved back to black-and-white images. The key is to be distinctive. In terms of restaurant design, the facade of the building itself can help to differentiate it from the competition and create memorable images in the minds of the customers. Scoozi in Chicago, for instance, has a giant red tomato hanging outside over the entryway. The tomato became a symbol for this popular gathering place (discussed in chapter 5), with people arranging to meet "under the red tomato" before entering. Another equally effective but totally different type of treatment is the facade of the tiny Aussie Eats fast food store at San Diego's Horton Plaza. Here a dramatic architectural element shaped like a stylized Sydney Opera House, crowns the neon logo and helps to distinguish the eatery from its fast food neighbors (fig. 3-1).

In chain design, recognizable architectural elements, such as the red roof of a Pizza Hut or the golden arches of a McDonald's, communicate instantly to the customer. However, reliance on architectural imagery can restrict the flexibility of the building for future occupants. It can also, if not properly protected, be easily copied. The gambrel roof developed as a Dairy Queen symbol has been used by many copycat chains, for example.

Historically, fast food exteriors relied on vernacular imagery to impart the idea of the restaurant. The Tail O' the Pup in Los Angeles (protected from demolition by landmark status) was a hot dog stand built to look exactly like a hot dog. Would-be customers had no questions regarding what type of food would be served here. Although most fast food chains have moved to more generic building types, individual places, such as Boardwalk Fries in San Diego's Horton Plaza (discussed in chapter 5), have resurrected vernacular architecture with great success. Here, a giant container of styrofoam

3-1. *The unusual architectural facade of Aussie Eats —drawn from the Sydney Opera House—helps to distinguish it from its fast food neighbors at Horton Plaza, San Diego.*
(Joseph Durocher photo)

french fries "explodes" from the store interior right through to the restaurant's facade. Not only does the exterior stand out from the competition but also it tells passers-by in a whimsical, dramatic way what they can expect to purchase inside. In a subtler interpretation of vernacular architecture for Seafood Shanty, a Pennsylvania-based seafood dinner house chain (discussed in chapter 5), DiLeonardo International fashioned a facade suggestive of a seafaring vessel.

Other building types can communicate to the potential customer what type of experience he or she can expect inside the doors. The exterior of Le Cygne in New York City looks rather like an elegant, postmodern townhouse. It implies an elegant dining experience as well. The discrete, screened window facade of New York City's Aurora, which prohibits pedestrians from looking inside the restaurant, promises exclusivity. Palio, located inside a Manhattan office tower, takes the theme of exclusivity even further. Here, patrons reach the restaurant by entering an elevator located on the ground floor bar. Only the privileged reservation holders whose tables are ready can enter the elevator and be whisked upstairs to the chic dining room.

Restaurants with big storefront windows that allow views inside signal a more informal, convivial type of restaurant. The facades of bistros and large gathering places, for instance, often have windowed walls totally open to the street. Restaurateur Michael Weinstein pioneered the wide-open gathering place in New York City with places like The Saloon, Ernie's, and America, all of which allow pedestrians unobstructed views of the lively scenes inside, and vice versa. At Los Angeles's City restaurant (discussed in chapter 6), architects Schweitzer and Kellen designed a new glass front that opened up a view to the interior of this hugely successful restaurant. They intentionally kept the gritty industrial look and art deco lines of the old carpet warehouse that houses the restaurant, however. The effect clearly says "urban chic."

Often customers browse for a restaurant in much the same way they look for a book. If they like the cover, chances are good that they will look inside.

Signage

Signage is such an important component of exterior building design that it merits its own discussion. Often it is the most recognizable element of the facade, the one that arrests people's attention and remains in their minds as a symbol of the restaurant. Especially in a shopping mall or on a highway, signage can be an extremely effective attention grabber. When the average time a motorist traveling 55 miles per hour has to read a sign is six seconds, then an easy-to-read, eye-catching sign is essential. A classic example is the Hilltop Steak House in Saugus, Massachusetts, whose 68-foot-high cactus emblazoned with the restaurant's name in red neon can be seen from both sides of the highway—a mile away (fig. 3-2). Just one quick glimpse, and the motorist knows for sure that Texas-style steaks are being cooked up inside the barnlike structure.

Today, graphic designers create effective signage—with type, color, form, and light—that carries strong, clear visual messages. The style of the typeface should echo the style of the restaurant, thus giving people cues about what they're going to encounter inside. No matter what type of establishment, readable typeface is essential. At times, the signage becomes an integral component of the architectural design; in other instances, it is a separate element. Even when it is free-standing, however, sign design should mesh with architectural design.

Whether mounted on sign posts high above the highway or integrated into facades, a well-conceived, well-designed sign can become a recognizable ideograph that symbolizes the restaurant. Used as a logo throughout the space, it often creates a lasting impression. At the Wildflower Inn in Vail, Colorado, architect Warren Platner developed an entry sign whose typeface and floral form is echoed throughout the interior (fig. 3-3) and effectively symbolizes the design theme of the restaurant (discussed in chapter 6). Such ideographs can also be integrated into advertising programs that play an important part in developing the first impression of a restaurant. Although advertising is not an integral part of the design program, it should work in conjunction with the design to invoke a coordinated message.

3-2. *Sign as symbol is nowhere more dramatic than at the Hilltop Steak House, Saugus, MA.*
(Joseph Durocher photo)

3-3. *At the Warren Platner–designed Wildflower Inn, Vail, CO, the restaurant's ideograph is established with the entry sign (Warren Platner Associates Architects drawing).*

Landscaping

Patrons driving or walking past a free-standing restaurant notice not only the building itself but also the natural surroundings. In fact, landscaping helps to form people's first impression of the restaurant. Like the facade and the signage, it gives cues about what type of dining experience awaits them inside. Formal landscaping—such as an eight-foot-high, manicured hedge flanking an iron gate driveway entrance—prepares the customer for a formal dining experience in which multiple courses are served by multiple service persons. Informal landscaping, such as nonordered gardens or free-flowing bushes and trees, prepares the customer for a more casual experience. This type of landscaping is appropriate for moderately priced family restaurants with friendly interior settings that don't impose a "suit and tie only" feeling.

Sometimes landscape design works in concert with architectural design to create a dramatic first impression. Chart House restaurants, for example, were routinely situated at spectacular settings and then each individual unit was built—and landscaped—to fit its natural terrain. The exterior package was so special that it set people up for a dining experience that was out of the ordinary. The steak dinner may not have tasted any different, but its value was enhanced by architecture and landscaping.

Landscaping is also a critical concern when parking areas are situated on the restaurant property. A sea of asphalt can be hidden from the view of diners with a few artfully placed trees or shrubs. Landscaping can also conceal unsightly neighboring buildings or dumpsters.

ENTRY

As noted above, the exterior image creates first impressions and heightens people's expectations about what they will find inside the restaurant. The next move is arrival, stepping through the front door and into the entry area. It's important that this experience of arrival flows smoothly from an operational point of view and also creates appropriate esthetic impact. Spatial progression comes into play here as well, especially in upscale restaurants where the design team wants to provide people time to shift gears from the outside world. In these situations, small vestibules between door and reception give patrons a brief pause before they enter the fray.

The ways in which the outside is separated from the inside must be matched to both the type of restaurant and its location. In Hawaii the problem is easily resolved: The weather allows restaurant entrances to do without physical doors. In most places, however, a door is necessary, and the form of that door affects the customer's perception of the restaurant. A glass door allows customers to see into the restaurant, but a solid wood door creates a feeling of anticipation. In some instances, the anticipation may be deliberate and desired, but in others it may be intimidating enough to turn a guest away. Note the effective combination of wood and glass used by Morris Nathanson Design for the Legal Sea Foods restaurant located in a Burlington, Massachusetts, shopping mall (fig. 3-4).

3-4. *The entry door can create anticipation, as it does in Legal Sea Foods, Burlington, MA, designed by Morris Nathanson Design, Inc.*
(Warren Jagger photo)

The design of the door, with its dramatic, wood-framed crown arch, creates expectations of an exciting experience; as patrons get close, they can see the welcoming entryway right inside the glass.

As a general guideline, the portal to a restaurant should be as unencumbered as possible. In addition to invoking a feeling of the theme of the restaurant, it should be easy to use. A heavy oak door with a cast iron ring handle may give the feeling of entering a castle, but if not carefully balanced, it may be too hard for people to open. Glass doors or doors with windows in them invite guests to preview the interior and in some cases allow diners to look out on the show outside. Particularly in cold climates, double sets of doors minimize the blast of cold air that enters when single doors are used. In some settings, energy-efficient revolving doors may be appropriate.

Reception

The reception area or landing area serves as a conduit from the exterior to one of the destination spaces. In a fast food operation, the landing area should lead directly to the order counter. If the fast food pickup counter is not immediately visible, the customer can become disoriented because they expect to find the pickup counter as soon as they enter the restaurant. A similar phenomenon exists in tableservice restaurants. Designer Sam Lopata originally placed the maitre d' stand in Batons—an upscale tableservice restaurant (discussed in chapter 5)—some 40 feet from the landing area past the open kitchen and the bar. His motivation came from French restaurants where diners are drawn well into the restaurant before they are guided by the maitre d' to their destination. In New York City, however, customers expect to be greeted and guided as soon as they step through the door of the restaurant, and the management at Batons was forced to move the maitre d' stand to meet this expectation.

The reception area of a cafeteria plays a very important role. Here customers stop and begin to think about their options. In newer operations trays are dispensed in the reception area, and menu specials are highlighted. Cus-tomers gain an overview of the servery food stations and begin to develop a sense of where to go and what to buy. The design of this space is particularly important in a cafeteria because, unlike the tableservice restaurant with a maitre d' or the fast food operation with its pickup counter, customers must make decisions about which areas of the servery they should approach and in which order.

If the customers can clearly see each of the stations in the servery—even as they stop to pick up their trays—then they can calculate whether or not they want to wait in line for hot entrees, grilled burgers, individually prepared sandwiches, or perhaps to make their own salad at the salad bar. Further, they must figure how many stations they will approach. Customers must move quickly through this reception area. Any delay may make them decide to skip lunch, jump in a car for a trip to the local fast food eatery, or bring a brown-bag meal in the future.

Coat Room

The coat room should be included in the entry area for guests to store items they do not wish to carry to the table. Typically coat rooms are found in tableservice restaurants; they may have an attendant or may be self-service. If they are not controlled by a member of the staff, then they should be designed so that several guests can use the space at one time. The maitre d' should be able to watch the space to limit the potential for theft of guest property. In very upscale restaurants, care must be taken when guests arrive in furs and other expensive coats. A separate storage space for this outerwear should be considered.

Although coat rooms are common to tableservice restaurants, they are frequently overlooked in other types of establishments. In a university cafeteria, a coat room or lockers at the entryway would be a welcome design addition for storing books and coats. Students may make additional purchases because their trays are not crowded with books—purchases that might otherwise not be made. In malls, shoppers are frequently burdened with packages when they drop into the food court and may limit their food purchases because their arms are full. Again, a coat room or a set of keyed, self-service lockers could alleviate their burdens and increase sales.

Without coat and package storage space, problems can arise in any type of dining area. In casual restaurants that do not have coat rooms, hat and coat racks should be provided in the dining area, although this does not solve the confusion of people setting their belongings on empty chairs at neighboring tables. People drape their coats over the backs of chairs or over the drink rails in bars if the restaurant has no provision for garments, and thus destroy the look of even the most carefully developed design.

Waiting Area

Often people enter a restaurant only to be told that they have to wait before being seated. After this communication takes place, patrons sit down in a waiting area, if one is provided. Too often, waiting areas are eliminated from the design because they are not revenue-producing

space. However, a thoughtful design can provide needed waiting space plus potential for sales. An example is Wildflower, designed by Warren Platner, where patrons walk past an entrance gallery lined with wine cabinets and then wait in a banquette surrounded by wine cabinets and displays (fig. 3-5). This treatment suggests that management is serious about the selection and handling of wines and conditions guests to think about the purchase of wine as they wait for a table.

In some types of restaurants, waiting areas have the potential of becoming incremental sales areas. For example, on Sunday mornings in most chain coffee shops, the inadequate waiting area forces guests to stand in a cramped entryway. With just a little additional space, a self-service coffee bar and take-out station could be added to the waiting area to provide a carry-out continental breakfast for those diners who would rather not wait and a welcome cup of coffee for guests who did choose to wait. The additional business generated through coffee and take-out sales, as well as customer goodwill,

3-5. *The wine cellar in the waiting area at Wildflower Inn, designed by Warren Platner Associates Architects, helps to merchandise the establishment's wine selection.*
(Jaime Ardiles-Arce photo)

would justify the bit of extra footage and expense.

In tableservice restaurants, the waiting area can incorporate design elements that serve as merchandising devices. Posting a menu or menu board with the specials of the evening markets the meal before the guest arrives at the table. Previewing the menu during the waiting period may ultimately speed up the ordering process and lead to faster turnover at the tables. Food displays in the waiting area also prepare diners for the experience to come. In many of the Legal Sea Foods restaurants, Morris Nathanson Design located fresh fish display cases for retail sales adjacent to the entryway, so that diners could preview the wares (fig. 3-6). Similarly, at Big Splash, located in a South Florida shopping mall, diners view a lavish display of fresh seafood as they wait to be seated. The idea of a fresh fish dinner becomes increasingly attractive as people contemplate the display.

Another menu merchandising technique that depends on design is the addition of a dessert cart or espresso station adjacent to the waiting area. Both of these elements precondition guests to make purchases after the meal. Although a dessert cart or wine rack can be added

to the waiting area as afterthoughts, they are most effective when incorporated into the original design.

The vision of an open kitchen is another excellent means of merchandising food to waiting guests. The open kitchen may be positioned so that it is at the back of the dining room, yet visible to guests in the waiting area. This placement works best in small square or rectangular rooms. In more complex layouts, the open kitchen can be placed adjacent to the waiting area so that customers can have a close-up preview of things to come, plus an entertaining view of chefs at work. Dunkin Donuts uses this approach in many of their waiting areas. Customers watch their doughnuts being mixed, rolled, cut, and fried through a large picture window as they wait to make their purchases.

A successful waiting area previews the design as well as the menu. Connie's restaurant in Chicago, for instance, features a waiting area strewn with chair cushions made of flour and onion sacks and old barrels that serve as tables. As people wait, they are immersed in the old warehouse atmosphere that designer Robert Donahue created throughout the restaurant (fig. 3-7).

Two environmental conditions make an enormous difference to customer comfort in the waiting area: light and temperature. Lighting levels must be controlled to provide a painless transition from outside space to interior space. Entering the waiting area of a restaurant with an entrance facing west can be an ocular assault, for example, because going from bright daylight into a dim room is temporarily blinding until the eyes can adjust. In all circumstances, both entry and waiting area lighting should be dimmer-controlled to relate and react to the exterior lighting levels.

Temperature control in entry and waiting areas is also very important. In free-standing units located in northern climates, customers feel very chilly on cold days unless the building has been properly insulated. As mentioned earlier, double sets of entry doors can help. In southern locations, an air screen can be used to limit the mixing of outside and inside air. In general, the design team must always be aware of the infiltration of outside air and program the space for maximum temperature comfort.

3-6. *The view of fresh fish entices diners at Legal Sea Foods, Cambridge, MA, designed by Morris Nathanson Design, Inc.*
(*Peter Vanderwarker photo*)

3-7. *Generic warehouse elements in the waiting area preview the theme of Connie's restaurant, Chicago, designed by Donahue Designs. (Steinkamp/Ballogg photo)*

Both the exterior image and all of the entry areas should work together to preview the restaurant. Together, they help create an image of things to come. If carefully designed, they support the functions of the destination spaces.

DESTINATION DINING

Seating

When patrons progress to their dining destination, the first element they come into direct body contact with is the chair. Seating affects how people perceive a space and how long they stay in the space. The surface and shape of the seat, its height, its position at the table, its spatial relationship to other seats, and its visual relationship to other parts of the room design all affect the customer's perception. Obviously, different types of chairs make different types of impressions. The ubiquitous bentwood cafe chair signals informal dining, and an upholstered armchair tells patrons that the meal will be long and formal.

At New York City's Aurora, for instance, the chairs send out multiple signals, all tied in to the type of restaurant. First of all, they are

office chairs, an image ideally suited to the concept of holding business discussions over a meal. Second, they swivel and have arms, and they are very comfortable over a multicourse repast. Third, their soft leather upholstery gives a sensuous tactile sensation. An equally distinctive but less comfortable chair design is used at New York City's Toscana restaurant. Here, architects Piero Sartogo and Nathalie Grenon fashioned a highly unusual chair design whose curvilinear profile becomes a visual focal point in the room. With its dissymmetrically curved, burled wood back and squared-off black leather seat, the Toscana chair epitomizes the high-style Italian design theme of the restaurant. For the dining rooms at Porter Wright Morris & Arthur headquarters in Columbus, Ohio, Warren Platner Associates gave a new twist to the famous, Platner-designed wire chair (fig. 3-8) by upholstering the seats with floral tapestry. Here attorneys can wine and dine their clients in an evocative combination of modern and residential styling.

In addition to the covering of the seat, its size and the pitch of the back and bottom affect the guest's comfort levels. For optimal comfort levels, seats must be matched to their intended

3-8. *Special chairs can help to create a singular identity for dining rooms, as the Warren Platner–designed wire chair does here at Porter Wright Morris & Arthur Headquarters, Columbus, OH. (Jaime Ardiles-Arce photo)*

use. In cocktail lounges, seating can be lower and deeper than at dining tables. Dining chairs, on the other hand, must be matched closely to the height of the dining table. Although tables and chairs come in standard sizes (tables from 26 to 30 inches high and chairs from 16 to 18 inches high), the designer should always double check that the table and seat height are matched for comfort. All too often, chairs are too low (or tables are too high), causing the discomfort illustrated in figure 3-9. This problem seems especially prevalent with custom-designed banquettes, whose seats sometimes sink so low that eating is difficult and getting in and out of the seat requires a dancer's flexibility.

The structural integrity of the chair is also a crucial consideration. A good chair should be able to withstand the weight of even the most portly individual. In the restaurant, wear and tear take their toll so quickly that seating made for residential use generally won't hold up for more than a few months. On the other hand, commercial seating is built with extra structural reinforcements in order to withstand more abuse. The commercial bentwood cafe chair in figure 3-10 shows the structural support features critical to restaurant chairs. A retail version would look exactly the same to the customer, but not for long, because it would soon begin falling apart at the stress points.

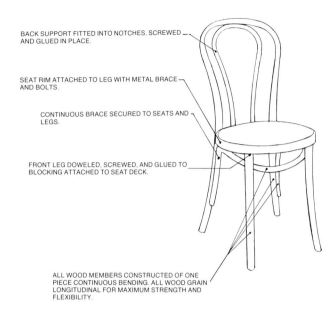

BACK SUPPORT FITTED INTO NOTCHES, SCREWED AND GLUED IN PLACE.

SEAT RIM ATTACHED TO LEG WITH METAL BRACE AND BOLTS.

CONTINUOUS BRACE SECURED TO SEATS AND LEGS.

FRONT LEG DOWELED, SCREWED, AND GLUED TO BLOCKING ATTACHED TO SEAT DECK.

ALL WOOD MEMBERS CONSTRUCTED OF ONE PIECE CONTINUOUS BENDING. ALL WOOD GRAIN LONGITUDINAL FOR MAXIMUM STRENGTH AND FLEXIBILITY.

3-10. *The abusive foodservice environment requires seating with structural reinforcement (Brad Elias, Hochheiser/Elias Design Group drawing).*

The materials of choice for seating depend on the type of restaurant. Natural fabrics always impart an upscale ambiance, and in casual or fast food restaurants, vinylized upholstery fabrics can achieve a residential look that is also easy to maintain. Vinyl, the time-honored choice for diner seating, lasts forever and today can be specified in a full spectrum of popular colors and a leatherlike texture. Nylon also holds up extremely well and can be blended with wool or wool and silk for a more luxurious look. Even in high-ticket establishments, maintenance is a key consideration when choosing upholstery because the finest silk won't impress a customer if it is stained or worn. In general, delicate materials should be used on seat backs rather than on seat bottoms.

In fast feeders, cafeterias, and other restaurants that depend on high turnover, the seat itself can play an integral part in moving people through the space. For the past twenty-five years, molded-plastic fixed seating was the standard in high-turnover restaurants. Recently, however, in an effort to expand market share and make the space more conducive to dining, the variety of seating has greatly expanded to include wooden benches or cafe chairs, fashionably styled metal chairs in a spectrum of colors, and even upholstered chairs. Such seating

3-9. *Poorly matched chair and table heights create awkward dining conditions (Brad Elias, Hochheiser/ Elias Design Group drawing).*

choices really do create a totally different impression from the old institutional-looking furniture, but consideration must always be given to the desired turnover time. When a restaurant depends on thirty-minute turnover, chair design should not encourage patrons to linger for two hours.

Seating can create a feeling of intimacy. Booth seating, curved banquette seating, and high-backed chairs engender a private feeling, for example, because in each of these seating arrangements sight lines have been restricted and the seating wraps around the guests. The atmosphere is also affected by the relative position of seats to each other. The crowded feeling of a French bistro depends on tightly packed seating at small tables, but in a fine dining operation generous spacing between tables can give a feeling of elegance. In the front of the house, the amount of square footage allocated per seat can range from 8 square feet in a cocktail lounge or tightly packed bistro, to as much as 18 square feet in a gourmet establishment with tableside cooking. Similarly, table size varies according to the type of restaurant and the style of service, as discussed later in this chapter.

The shapes of tables and the number of seats at tables are other important considerations, again depending upon the type of restaurant as well as the dining habits of typical customers. The gathering place type of restaurant, for example, has more large tables than small tableservice restaurants where the emphasis is on food. In gathering places groups of individuals or couples meet to drink, eat, and watch people, but single couples tend to frequent traditional restaurants whose emphasis is on the meal.

Although part of the goal of good design is to carefully match the mix of deuces, four-tops, and larger tables with the size of parties that frequent the restaurant, a mix of table sizes and seating configurations creates more visual interest than a single type of table. Seating variety also offers patrons the choice of more intimate or more open seating, depending on their mood. In the Hobey Baker restaurant remodel in Santa Barbara, California, architect Barry A. Berkus specified a mix of square tables, round tables, and redwood booths capped with vaulted canvas (fig. 3-11). The variety of forms enlivens the space, and the mix of seating appeals to different types of clientele.

3-11. *A variety of square and round tables and redwood-lined booths gives diners a choice of seating options at Hobey Baker, Santa Barbara, CA, designed by Barry A. Berkus.*
(Del Hayden photo, courtesy of the California Redwood Association)

Every guest wants the best seat in the house. Ideally every table should be perceived as the best table. Every seat, of course, isn't a window seat, and there is only one natural prime spot such as the center of the bow window at Tavern on the Green—a table that is the visual focal point of the restaurant, one from which the entire dining room can be viewed. However, designers can employ a variety of techniques to ensure that every table is indeed desirable. Terracing backwards and upwards from a window view, for example, as Warren Platner did at Windows on the World (fig. 3-12), allows patrons in the back of the room a spectacular vista of both the outside and inside panoramas spread out below them. Note on this same cross-section drawing how carefully the architect considered sight lines from one area to another: One person's unrestricted view did not interfere with another person's privacy.

Sight lines and flow patterns of both guests and employees are crucial considerations in laying out the tables in a restaurant. Customers disdain a view of the bathroom, the smell of the garbage room, and the clanging of the pot sink. Until recently, they shunned a view of the kitchen and still do if it is not brought to them deliberately. However, well-designed display kitchens can turn the table closest to the kitchen into a prime table. Deuces elevated on a side wall, as in New York City's America,

highlight those seats and put the diners on display. The secret is to take what could be a bad situation and make it something special. A nook adjacent to the wine cellar can become a special party space because it overlooks the wine display. A large antique table positioned in the center of the dining room can become a captain's table for single diners.

Tabletop

The tabletop provides the guest's most immediate and personal experience in the restaurant because diners come in direct contact with their plates, food, glasses, and flatware. The texture, temperature, color, and balance of each element separately and in concert should all be taken into consideration during the design process. An entire book could be written on the selection of tabletop elements, but some basic principles can guide the development of an effective tabletop design.

THE TABLE

The tabletop material is most important when it is visible to the guest. Hard surfaces such as granite or marble give a different feeling from the warmth of wood tabletops or the fine-dining image of linen-covered tabletops. In any case, the choice should be visually compatible with the overall design. Resin-coated fabric table-

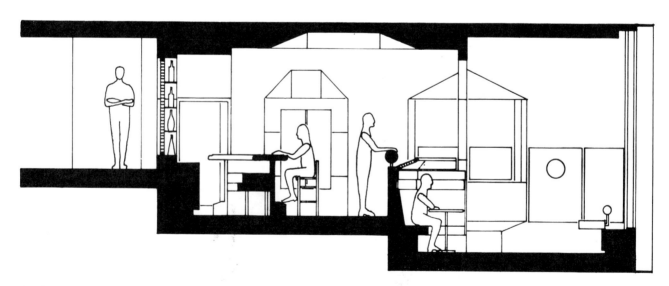

3-12. *Sight lines must always be taken into consideration in the design, especially in complex spaces like Windows on the World, designed by Warren Platner Associates Architects. (Warren Platner Associates Architects drawing).*

tops, hard materials such as marblelike compressed stone, and in pricey establishments granite or marble are often specified for bare tabletops. These materials are easy to maintain and also mesh with modern design sensibilities.

With cloth-covered tables, the tabletop itself is invisible to the guest ninety percent of the time, but it flashes into view when the linen is changed between guests. In some operations an inexpensive plywood top may still be acceptable, but high-ticket establishments should carry through the high-end esthetic, even though guests may view the tabletop for only a few seconds. The solution doesn't have to cost a fortune. At Shun Lee West in New York City (discussed in chapter 5), the dining room is basic black with pale pink accents. Tables are fitted with an ink black covering and set with pink linen. When the wait staff changes the linen, the flash of black tabletop is almost indistinguishable from the black background (fig. 3-13).

Table bases should always be substantial enough to support the table's size and weight and convey a secure and stable feeling to the customer. Table bases should also be adjustable so that wobbling can be eliminated. Levelers or floor glides can help keep tables steady on rough or uneven floors and prevent floor damage.

The actual size of the tabletop depends on the restaurant's style of service. An average place setting is 24 inches wide, but more room is needed to serve a formal meal, and conversely space can be tightened for banquet-style service. In cafeterias, the size and shape of the trays must be considered when specifying table size. All too often, the table becomes too crowded with oversized plates, a deuce is too long for comfortable conversation, or five people have to cram around a table meant for four. One versatile choice to help accommodate large parties is the drop-leaf table, whose squares can be easily opened up to form a round top with greater seating capacity.

3-13. *The tabletops at Shun Lee West in New York, designed by Stanley Jay Friedman Associates, are fitted with a black covering that matches the restaurant's black background. Because of this, even when waiters change linens, the room has a finished appearance.*
(Elliott Kaufman photo)

NAPERY

The color and design of tablecloths and napkins should be integrated with the overall design scheme. At Pizza Piazza restaurant in New York City, for instance, tabletop consultant Barbara Kafka specified grid-patterned tablecloths to coordinate with the restaurant's grid-patterned graphic wall designs. Napery design forms such a strong image in the restaurant that at times a change of tablecloths and napkins can create a fresh new look for the interior.

When specifying linen, attention should also be given to flame retardancy, stainability, and texture. The feeling of a linen napkin is quite different from that of a polyester, cotton, or cotton-polyester-blend napkin, and all of these napkins react differently to stain-removal efforts. The material also determines whether or not the napkins can be used for fancy folds or if they can be folded only flat. In some cases one type of material for the tablecloth and another material for the napkin may be advisable. In any event, guests always touch table linens and their feel leaves a lasting impression.

The colorfastness of the linens is very important. A well-set dining room generally includes napkins folded in some appropriate shape. If, after several washings, some napkins are light blue and some are dark blue, the impression of the overall design can be adversely affected.

FLATWARE

Flatware is handled by guests more than any other item on the tabletop: its pattern, heft, cleanliness, and material affect guests' perception of the meal.

Stainless steel is the most common material for restaurant flatware, but the various grades give varying appearances after even limited use. Some inexpensive flatware shows scratches and a dull finish after only a month of use. Better (more expensive) grades take on a shine that lights up the tabletop. Experts say that a stainless steel mix with eighteen percent chrome and eight percent nickel yields the best results in terms of both corrosion resistance and luster.

The selection of silver-plated flatware is appropriate for high-ticket establishments but places additional responsibility on the operator. The several grades reflect the quality of the silver, the number of platings, the weight of the blanks that form the individual pieces, and the flatware's durability. Some manufacturers plate more silver on the backs of the pieces because then the touch points, that is, those areas that come in contact with the table or dishware, are better protected. One popular choice is silver plate flatware made from stainless steel, which experts say is both durable and relatively inexpensive. However, any silver coating tarnishes quickly and needs to be burnished or polished periodically. This can be done with a machine, in soaking bins, or by hand, but the process must be incorporated into the overall design of the warewashing area. Sterling silver is rarely used in restaurants, not only because of its expense but because it requires even more care than silver plate.

When considering shape, heft, and balance, beware of forks that are very thin where the base of the handle attaches to the top of the tines. When too thin, the fork rolls in the hand and is all but impossible to use for cutting. Knives pose a special problem because the blade, if not made of high-quality stainless steel, shows scratches and mars the appearance of even the most beautiful tabletop. For those operations specializing in steaks and chops, serrated knives should be a part of the tabletop hardware. When seafood is served, fish knives should be included as an added tabletop feature. For any item, the construction of the flatware should be considered. Adequate metal at stress and touch points and proper grading or thickness yield a sturdy and well-balanced piece of flatware.

The selection of holloware—those extra tabletop elements such as salt and pepper shakers, candlesticks, and sugar and creamer sets—must be coordinated with the flatware and the overall design of the restaurant. In simple terms, an insulated plastic coffee pot should not be used when fine linen and silver plate flatware cover the table. In addition, the designer must consider all flatware and holloware items necessary for each menu item to ensure that the look is integrated. Manufacturers don't always offer a total set of holloware in the same design pattern as flatware.

CHINA

Along with the flatware and holloware, the serving plate plays an important role in the customer's perception of the food, and it also anchors the esthetics of the tabletop design. The plate's size and heft should reflect the foods being served on it. Heavy plates give the customer a feeling that they are getting a lot of food. (Bar operators use this technique when they serve beer in sham pilsners or heavy bottomed beer mugs.) Oversized plates imply that the restaurant takes its food seriously. Fine china portends a gourmet meal.

In any type of foodservice operation, no matter how casual, the plates that foods are served on should be considered a canvas. The chef carefully places food on this canvas, and the servers should present the plates to maximize the visual appearance. Heavily patterned plates that make strong design statements can serve as excellent base plates, that is, those plates that are already set on the table when the guests arrive, but they should never be chosen for serving food. Not only aren't the patterns complimentary to many items, but also they can actually detract from the appearance of foods. Other types of base plate designs, such as one with a 1½- to 2-inch band of color around the rim of the dish, can make a striking statement in the dining room and also be suitable for serving food. All too often, however, the colored rims are marred with the fingerprints of careless service personnel. The selection of any plate must always be an informed one that recognizes the visual limitations and operational considerations involved with the choice (fig. 3-14).

Equal care should be taken with the selection of other china items. Consider the handle design of cups, for instance. Some handles withstand the wear and tear of brutish people,

3-14. *Even the smallest variation in the construction detail of a plate affects its durability.*

and others break with a simple tap. The feel of the handle is also important. The heavy, large handle of a commercial coffee mug, although not suited to a fine dining operation, is easy to grasp. In contrast, the dainty handle of a bone china teacup is fine for sipping afternoon tea in a leisurely fashion but impossible for all but the most slender individuals to slide a finger through.

The selection of coffee cups and other tabletop items often reflects painstaking design considerations. At Manhattan's Aurora, for instance, restaurateur Joseph Baum knew that he wanted a round cup, not a can-shaped one. After looking at hundreds of designs, he found an unused mold that perfectly fit his concept and had the china manufacturer put it into production for Aurora.

Replacement schedules and costs are also important considerations when selecting china. Shape, material, and design all affect life-span. Thin china is perceived as fine china, but it may not hold up to the rigors of a restaurant. Conversely, heavy china is not necessarily strong china. Types of china commonly utilized in restaurants include stoneware, glassware, porcelain, bone china, and restaurant dinnerware, which is a cross between bone china and porcelain. The strength tests manufacturers usually provide for their china can be a useful reference. In general, commercial china, because it is produced especially for the hospitality market, has been designed for strength and resistance to breaking and chipping. In addition, commercial china manufacturers tend to recognize the importance of a design suitable for storage and restaurant warewashing. Residential china, like residential furniture, won't last long in the restaurant environment. Another advantage of commercially made designs is that stock patterns are maintained for quick delivery from the manufacturer. For a little extra investment, customized plates can be created to coordinate with the restaurant's graphics program.

Another design consideration is the glazing process, the number of glazes and the temperature at which they are fired. Gold-rimmed plates look good but are prone to premature wear. They are fired at relatively low temperatures that leave a less resilient finish than high-temperature firing.

In recent years, increasing attention has been paid to the esthetics of the tabletop. In New York City's Aurora, Milton Glaser's bubble design motif is used on the china as well as on the carpeting. In Denver's Rattlesnake Club, a Charles Gwathmey–designed plate, with its elegant black and white tuxedo design, works beautifully to showcase the restaurant's innovative cuisine. At City in Los Angeles, plates in a variety of solid colors from creme yellow to pale blue, were each chosen for use with particular dishes. The rainbow of plates, along with the different-colored little side dishes that hold condiments, help to anchor each tabletop as a visual highlight in the monochromatic interior—a treatment appropriate to a restaurant whose raison d'être was a wide variety of original dishes.

In the case of tableservice restaurants, the design team should remember that there are numerous courses to each meal and many variables to each course. Traditionally a meal includes an appetizer, main course, dessert, and beverages, but the appetizer selection alone might include the choice of a dozen or more items, each of which comes with its own garnish, serving plate, underliner, eating utensils, and condiments. The same is true for all of the other courses.

According to experts, the average piece of dinnerware is used about seven thousand times and lasts approximately three years of typical restaurant use if handled properly. Some china manufacturers estimate that 25 percent of a restaurant's china is broken each year. Needless to say, replacement costs can become astronomical. The design team must not only specify well-constructed items but also make sure that all of the back- and front-of-the-house support stations are adequately designed for storage. The greater the variety of tabletop elements, the greater the need for storage in the kitchen dishroom and at the front-of-the-house server stations.

GLASSWARE

A fine Bordeaux is best appreciated in a high-quality, thin-walled, clear, stemmed wineglass. Sherry should be served in a stem sherry glass and champagne should be served in a champagne flute. However, if a different glass is selected for each type of drink, the bartender may have to stock twenty-five different types of glasses. The use of a single glass goblet for all beverages—wine, beer, soda, champagne, and mixed drinks—may not always be the most esthetic means of serving these drinks, but from an operational perspective it is certainly the easiest.

Although the variety of glasses used for beverage service is usually determined by management, the designers—both back and front of the house—must be cognizant of this decision as they design storage spaces. With more types of glassware, additional storage space is needed in the clean dish storage areas as well as at the bar itself. In some cases, a variety of glassware may also affect the requirements for storage at the server stations.

The two basic kinds of glass are lime, or plain glass, and lead, or crystal glass. Some high-quality plain glass is indistinguishable from crystal except for a slightly thickened, rounded rim. As with all tabletop items, many grades of glassware are available, and longevity should always be factored into the initial price.

Lighting

As noted in chapter 2, lighting influences diners in subtle and direct ways, from the rosy glow it can impart to people's complexions to the mysterious patterns it can throw on wall surfaces. Lighting that is too bright or too dim may lead to serious eyestrain. Lighting that is too uniform makes the atmosphere seem dull, and lighting that is too harsh can cause food to look very unappetizing. Moreover, light can totally change the perception of colored surfaces.

Lighting the variety of spaces in a restaurant is an art in itself, and in complex or big-budget projects a lighting designer is often enlisted to help develop an illumination scheme. In other instances, well-informed architects or interior designers implement the lighting program. No matter which is the case, the operator should be educated about the basic ideas of the plan so that he or she can properly regulate light levels on the dimming system if it is not automatically programmed and communicate the right information to maintenance people about relamping and focus adjustment. One of the reasons that restaurant lighting is so complicated is that it involves not only the selection of light sources but also the programming of many light levels, levels that respond to both various time periods and various types of places in the room. To be effective, light levels, light sources, and quality of light must all react and interact consistently with other design elements in the restaurant.

When establishing lighting plans for interiors, the design team should be concerned with the following lighting classifications:

1. Mood, décor, and art lighting
2. People and food lighting
3. Motivational and task lighting
4. Safety and security lighting

Mood, décor, and art lighting is often the most dramatic illumination in a restaurant. It really begins outside the restaurant with signage and architectural lighting and carries forward to the interior of the restaurant, where objects or surfaces are spotlighted with overlays of direct or indirect lighting. Artwork is usually lit with carefully focused track lights manipulated to avoid glare yet allow the images to be clearly viewed. Plantings and wall surfaces are often uplit so that they glow. Generally, objects are spotlit with direct light for the most powerful effect, but some lighting designers caution against juxtaposing brightly spotlit objects with a dark backdrop because the contrast can cause discomfort.

Effective people and food lighting involves delicate manipulation of light sources and light levels. Obviously the goal is for both to look as attractive as possible, and different designers have different theories about the best ways to achieve this goal. Certainly people and food look best under incandescent light. Designer Brad Elias recommends dimming an incandescent bulb in order to achieve a natural glow rather than tinting it pink. Some experts say that the room should be lighted in such a way that the tables and diners become the focus of the room. "You don't want lighting to become entirely focused on the design features of the room, no matter how good they are," believes architect Warren Platner, who also cautions against using a single source like wall sconces to wash the room in light and leave diners sitting in relative darkness. Jimmy Schmidt, chef-owner of the Rattlesnake Club in Denver, maintains that incandescent ceiling spots, perfectly aimed at white tablecloths so that indirect light bounces up to softly illuminate people's faces, are ideal. However, this indirect lighting depends on precise aim and light levels. Nothing is more distressing to diners than a bright, glaring light shining up into their faces (fig. 3-15).

Motivational and task lighting is most important for the employees of a restaurant. Bright but not blinding light levels help them perform their assigned tasks and in some instances drastically affect productivity. Task lighting is all too often overlooked in the front of the house. The bartender needs good task lighting when mixing drinks, the service staff when filling out guest checks, and the flambé chef while preparing duck a l'orange.

Safety and security lighting are essential for the well-being of guests, employees, and management. Exit signs inside the restaurant, emergency lights, parking lot and other exterior lighting, plus task lighting so that employees can work safely are all important. With strategic planning, none of these light sources need be offensive to look at. Emergency lights, for example, can be totally recessed into the ceiling.

3-15. *If direct light is not carefully controlled, it can cause glare (Brad Elias, Hochheiser/Elias Design Group drawing).*

NATURAL VERSUS ARTIFICIAL LIGHT

When a restaurant is entirely interior with no outside source of light, controlling lighting levels throughout the day is relatively easy. However, when sunlight (natural) or other external lighting sources (hallways or parking lots) enter the restaurant, establishing a lighting scheme becomes more difficult. The location of windows relative to the sun can limit the impact of sunlight, because indirect sunlight entering a restaurant is quite different from the glaring direct rays of the sun. In new construction, the architect can plan northerly facing windows or windows that do not face the sun during service hours, roof overhangs, or tinted glass to help alleviate the problems associated with glaring sunlight. In existing buildings, exterior plantings and window-shading elements, such as curtains, drapes, and blinds, can minimize the impact of the sun on interior lighting levels.

The main dining room of New York City's Tavern on the Green exemplifies good control of natural light. The room has a long wall of windows that during the summer is partially shaded by trees, with just enough light filtering into the room to create a bright and cheery atmosphere. In the winter, the leafless trees allow the sun, low on the horizon, to pour all of its warming rays into the room. During evenings throughout the year, thousands of miniature lights festooned on tree branches outside the windows allow guests to dine by sparkling urban starlight.

The rapidly expanding use of greenhouse units in fast food and family-dining restaurants also calls for a careful balance of natural and artificial light. During the day, sunlight is a welcome light source in these spaces, although as always glare should be tempered with shading devices. At night, lighting from mercury or sodium vapor parking lot fixtures make complexions and food look pasty and unappealing if allowed to pour in through uncovered greenhouse windows.

LIGHTING LEVELS

Lighting levels should be carefully monitored throughout the restaurant for tasks such as reading the menu and for atmosphere. As mentioned in chapter 2, a light transition zone at the entry area is essential. In the dining area, light levels help set the mood yet must not interfere with the diners' enjoyment of the restaurant. A dim dining alcove may create an intimate milieu, but low lighting levels can prevent guests from reading the menu and identifying the food. Even the most artful plate presentation cannot be appreciated in the dark. A single light level in the restaurant can cause the environment to feel monotonous.

A multiple-dimming system, either preset by the lighting designer or carefully controlled by the operator, is essential to achieve proper light levels in all of the areas of the restaurant and at all the different times of day. At the Wildflower restaurant in Vail, for instance, a typical programmed dimmer system has preset lighting levels for different times of day keyed to the various rooms. The restaurant manager simply pushes a number that relates to an outside brightness condition ranging from intense sunlight to total darkness, and the light level dims or brightens accordingly. Albeit more expensive than a manual system, such "automatic" dimming control is the superior choice because once worked out and set into the circuit, the levels remain in the unit's memory forever. Management doesn't have to fool around trying to find the right light levels, and patrons don't have to experience the discomfort of a room going from bright to dim to dark to bright, as operators fiddle around for the right level.

DIRECT VERSUS INDIRECT LIGHTING

As discussed briefly in chapter 2, an artful mix of direct and indirect lighting in the dining room can create an intriguing combination of shadow and sparkle that enlivens the environment. Indirect lighting—lighting where the lamps (bulbs) cannot be seen—minimizes shadows that make people look unattractive and gives an overall glow to the space. These concealed sources can create what is called the ambient light level, filling in all the nooks and crannies with even, diffuse illumination. They can also help to achieve different light levels and, as is often the case with wall sconces, cast soft patterns of light on the walls. Some designers like to use indirect lighting almost exclusively in a restaurant, but to add the sparkle that enlivens a space, direct lighting should be applied in a controlled manner. Direct lighting usually involves some sort of visible bulb, such as exposed bare-filament lamps or chandeliers. The direction of the light path, the spread to the beam emitted from the lamp or luminaire, and the glare from the lamp must always be considered. Another direct lighting application frequently utilized in restaurants involves high-intensity lamps that provide a pinpoint of light on tabletops. These lights highlight the tabletop and the food placed on it, but the effect can backfire if the light is too bright or is improperly angled. In any scenario, direct and indirect lighting must work in concert to create a lighting mix that matches the overall design image of the restaurant.

SPECIAL EFFECTS

Special-effects lighting is used not so much to illuminate the room as to dramatize it. Neon, in many colors and configurations, has assumed quite an important role in many restaurants. Most effective when used in moderation, it is often used for signage: as restaurant logo outside and inside, or to identify a space in the restaurant such as a raw bar or salad bar, for instance. Neon can also become an effective directional signal. In Chicago's Mama Mia! Pasta (discussed in chapter 5), a single red neon tube on the ceiling soffit follows the undulating flow of the ceiling design that anchors the restaurant's main seating section (fig. 3-16). On a more elaborate scale, the red, white, and blue neon tubes that form a stylized flag on the ceiling of New York City's America, help to guide guests down a central runway that leads to tables on either side of a monumental bar in the back.

Often, theatrical fixtures are used in much the same fashion as they are on stage to highlight interesting details in the restaurant. Theatrical framing projectors might cast varied patterns, called light paintings, on floors, walls, or ceiling. These framing projectors are devices

3-16. *Architects Banks/Eakin used a single band of undulating neon to mark the boundary of the dining room in Mama Mia! Pasta, Chicago. (Orlando Cabanban photo)*

that, just by the change of a template, can cause a variety of effects. A good alternative to the more expensive fixtures made for theaters are scaled-down versions offered by commercial lighting manufacturers, which are better suited to the restaurant environment. In either case, light can transform a monochromatic backdrop into a fascinating design of color and pattern, depending on the template design. Theatrical light projections can communicate virtually any image. In the cafeteria of Miami's Southeast Financial Center, for example, entryway walls were illuminated with the company's abstract sunburst logo.

A new and increasingly popular direct light source is the low-voltage halogen miniature reflector lamp that is frequently used to highlight tabletops, displays of art, or in some instances to wash a wall. These very efficient lamps, which require a transformer, work best in balance with other light sources, unless they're used to provide task lighting to a very limited area.

Special-effects lighting often incorporates clever or unique decorative applications. At New York City's Extra! Extra! (discussed in chapter 5) bare bulbs with exposed filaments were housed inside a metal grid—resembling a mechanic's trouble light—and wrapped around the suspended ceiling grate with a sturdy fabric that looks like old fashioned iron cords. The total effect is lighthearted and whimsical, perfectly matched to the restaurant's playful design scheme.

The direct light of chandeliers, especially sparkling off glass and crystal, has been a staple of banquet lighting. Typically used in large, open spaces, they also find their way—in highly stylized formats—into restaurants. In such cases, these ceiling luminaires can provide both direct and indirect lighting to a restaurant interior. At New York City's Cinco de Mayo (discussed in chapter 5), large commercial restaurant colanders that were painted gold, turned upside down, and hung from the ceiling look like big, sparkling lampshades and throw pretty spirals of light onto the ceiling of an atrium seating area (fig. 3-17). This clever application provides a neat special effect for a very low cost.

3-17. *Inexpensive restaurant colanders were turned into sparkling chandeliers by Anderson/Schwartz Architects for a dining alcove in Cinco de Mayo, New York.*
(Elliott Kaufman photo)

OPERATIONAL CONCERNS

From an operational perspective, the design team should be aware of several lighting concerns. To begin with, the accessibility and easy changeability of the lamps is important. In some high-ceilinged restaurants, the only way to change ceiling lamps is to hire lift scaffolding. The lamps in the lounge atop the John Hancock Building in Boston, for example, are so difficult to reach that they have not been used as intended since they burned out in the early 1980s.

Easy relamping should be a goal of every restaurant lighting scheme, but it becomes difficult when many different lamp types are used. One trick that can make the operator's life easier is to specify much higher wattage lamps than the space requires, and then keep them dimmed down. A 150-watt lamp run at full capacity burns out quickly but lasts almost indefinitely if it is never turned up to more than 50 percent of capacity.

Another concern is the need for auxiliary lighting to be used during cleaning periods. If the restaurant does not have a dimming system, then an entirely separate lighting system with different light sources might be required. A dimming system not only allows light levels to be turned up enough for the cleaning crew but on slow nights in large restaurants it also enables management to leave unused sections darkened. Also, task lighting for the various service functions performed in the front of the house should always be considered as part of the illumination plan.

ENERGY EFFICIENCY

Energy-efficient lighting is important in any type of restaurant operation. Fast food operations use a little more than a quarter of their total energy consumption and tableservice restaurants use less than a tenth of their total for lighting, but in both types of operations energy conservation plays an important role. Energy conservation pertains to the amount of energy used by the lamps themselves for illumination and the energy that is converted to heat by the lamps. Certain lighting plans may actually necessitate increased ventilation capacity to prevent the dining areas from overheating.

For any given lighting situation, lighting energy management options (LEMOs) should be considered. Every area of the restaurant has several potential LEMOs. One option might show a low initial installation cost for the luminaire, moderate energy consumption, and high replacement frequency. Another option might entail high initial installation costs, low energy consumption, and very low frequency of replacement. The second option seems to be the obvious choice, yet with a lighting package costing an average of $6 to $7 per square foot a restaurateur may be strapped for cash and choose the first option, hoping to retrofit the lighting scheme after the restaurant becomes profitable.

THE LIGHTING PLAN

All of the information noted here and much more goes into a good restaurant lighting plan. Most experts recommend that a variety of concealed and decorative fixtures are desirable in order to achieve successful results. To recap, the following factors must be considered before final decisions are made.

Location—Precisely which space will be lit affects all other factors.

Types of lighting—Will a single type of lamp (bulb) be used or a mix of lamps? Will a single luminaire (fixture) or a mix of luminaires be used?

Light quality—What are the spectral characteristics of the light and how will they affect the people using the space and the appearance of colors in the space? If more than one light source is used, how will the quality of light be affected by the mix, both overall and in specific areas?

Quantity of light—How much light is needed? Must some points be lighted more than other points?

Energy utilization—Total energy consumption, total energy cost, and the coefficient of utilization (CU; how well a fixture converts electrical energy and delivers it as light energy) of the luminaires must be considered.

Maintenance—How often must the bulbs

be replaced? Can the luminaires be cleaned, and how?

These and other factors must be considered in planning an illumination scheme. In the end, everything comes together as something subliminal for the patrons. The better the lighting plan, the less aware the customer is of such a plan. Instead, diners bask in an atmosphere both comfortable and exciting, bathed in flattering light.

Color

Color is linked closely with light because without light there is no perception of color. With certain types of light, colors appear more vibrant, but with other types of light the same colors look dull and gray. This basic principle of light reflection is essential to the selection of colors and lighting in restaurants.

When white light—light that is composed of equal color components (violet, indigo, blue, green, yellow, orange, and red)—strikes a surface that is painted red, more red is reflected from the surface than any other component of the light, and the surface appears red. The same is true when light passes through red glass or gel: the red component of the light is transmitted while the other components are filtered out of the resulting beam.

There are many classifications of color. The Munsell system as a point of reference, as illustrated in chapter 2, includes three important means of classifying a given color: hue (shade of a given color), value (brilliance of the color), and chroma (the saturation of or purity of the color). Colors appearing on opposing sides of the color wheel are complementary colors. If a wall painted red is illuminated with a blue-green light source, then the wall appears gray. In effect, the light reduces the apparent chroma level of the wall. Chroma levels are also affected by intensity of lighting. A peach tabletop that looks good under indirect sunlight may look washed out when sunlight falls directly on it. Heavily saturated paints with high chroma levels should be used in interiors where high light levels are expected. Pastels (colors that are mixed with white) appear faded in brightly lit rooms.

Floors

Restaurant flooring means more to patrons than just a surface to walk on. Flooring can act as a directional signal, yield a soft, cushy feeling of elegance, and either absorb or reflect sound in the restaurant. Selecting a floor material seems easy: It should last forever, be easy to clean, be available in colors that complement other colors in the space, deaden or heighten noise as needed, and cost only a dollar per square foot installed. However, such flooring does not exist. As with lighting systems, therefore, a careful analysis of the advantages and disadvantages of any floor covering plan is important.

By most standards vinyl composition is the least expensive floor covering to purchase and install, and terrazzo and marble are among the most expensive. In fact, the installed cost of the terrazzo is approximately six times greater than the vinyl. Again, the owner short on cash may opt for the inexpensive floor solution, but added to the installation cost should be the cost of maintaining the floor, the usable life of the floor, and its replacement cost. These factors give a total cost per square foot of flooring over time.

Vinyl composition flooring, for example, must be replaced after a number of years, whereas the terrazzo has a much longer usable life-span (over a forty-year life-span, the total cost per square foot of terrazzo is only twelve percent higher than vinyl). Unglazed ceramic tiles, if properly maintained by mopping and occasional sealing, hold up almost indefinitely, but the finish on glazed ceramic tile wears out very quickly. Marble can take a great deal of abuse, but alcohol spills soak in and leave stains. Granite, a less porous material than marble, withstands abuse even better than marble. Composite stone flooring, made of small, compressed bits, has become a popular, easy-maintenance flooring option. Wood floors, often chosen for their warmth and eye appeal, have to be refinished approximately every nine months. Carpeting is the floor covering of choice for acoustic control. The thicker the carpet and padding, the more noise it absorbs. Nylon or a nylon-wool blend is a practical choice because of its flame retardancy and stain resistance. A solid-color carpet always shows dirt, stains, and spills far more than a patterned carpet.

Building codes and safety issues must always be considered in choosing floor materials for the restaurant. In some locations, certain types of flooring may be excluded because of building or health codes. Especially in the grease- and water-laden kitchen, some applications are safer, prevent the buildup of dirt, and minimize chances of fire.

In the front of the house, specifying flooring for its esthetic appeal is more appropriate. In New York City's Toscana, three different floor surfaces were artfully applied in the dining area: marble, wood, and carpeting. The result gives the visual and aural sensations of being in an open garden courtyard or in a secluded villa interior. However, three different cleaning techniques are required to properly maintain these surfaces, which involve different cleaning chemicals (and polishes where necessary), plus special equipment and training. In this extremely elegant, high-ticket establishment, management feels that the expense was well worth the visual effects.

In other restaurants, different flooring materials perform various functional roles. At B. Smith's in New York City (discussed in chapter 5), for example, the bar floor is covered with gray-colored ground concrete that is well suited to the beating taken from spilled drinks, snuffed-out cigarettes, and dripping umbrellas. In the dining room, a center island of sound-absorbing carpet is surrounded by a boardwalk of warm wood flooring. These three surfaces are not intermixed as closely as in Toscana and have functional as well as esthetic purposes.

In the fast food environment, just one practical flooring material can take on new meaning if cleverly applied. Such is the case in the Vineland, New Jersey, McDonald's (discussed in chapter 5) designed by Brad Elias (fig. 3-18). Here, Elias specified unglazed ceramic tile in a custom-designed pattern resembling a needlepoint rug. The floor has an esthetic in keeping with the restaurant's postmodern-Victorian motif but remains eminently practical.

Entry areas, because of the high wear and tear brought on by street dirt, should be covered in highly resilient materials. The designer

3-18. *Unglazed ceramic tile was transformed into a needlepoint rug by Brad Elias of the Hochheiser/Elias Design Group for this McDonald's in Vineland, NJ. (David Schindler photo)*

should also be aware that polished stone flooring becomes very slippery when wet. If specified in entry areas where rain and snow could be tracked in, polished stone flooring should be covered with runners. Relaxed dining settings benefit from carpeting that deadens noise and gives a warm feeling to the space. However, restaurant dining areas that depend upon high noise levels to generate excitement often rely on hard flooring surfaces that reflect noise, can take abuse, and are easy to clean.

For any floor material subject to the rigors of restaurant traffic, the following points should be considered in concert with the esthetics of the materials:

Flammability—Particularly important in display kitchens and dining rooms where tableside cooking is offered.

Colorfastness and Lightfastness—An especially important consideration with carpeting, fading can also be a problem with wood flooring.

Flooring Adhesive—For wooden flooring, nails may be sufficient, but in some cases box-coated nails reduce squeaking. Box-coated nails plus glue ensure a squeak-free wooden floor. For carpeting, proper adhesion prevents carpet slippage and premature wear and wrinkling. For vinyl, rubber sheeting or tiles, the choice of adhesive material—along with the subfloor—plays an important role in the life-span of the surface. Although the best adhesives are significantly more expensive, they are generally worth the investment in extended, trouble-free usage.

Subflooring—The wearability of the finished floor depends a great deal upon the subfloor. If the subfloor cracks and splits or does not take well to an adhesive, then the finished floor won't last long under normal restaurant conditions.

Walls

Walls enclose patrons, provide surfaces for points of interest such as artwork and lighting sconces, and open up vistas to the outside world. Windows are important parts of walls in many restaurants, especially free-standing restaurants and large urban gathering places, and should be selected with energy conservation and lighting concerns in mind, as noted previously. The glazing itself has great impact on energy conservation. Single-pane windows are the least efficient insulators, and thermopane units are the most efficient insulators. As with daylight control, window coverings such as shades, blinds, screens, and exterior awnings impact energy conservation.

Walls and their coverings play an important role in the overall design of a restaurant. The shapes of walls, the materials they are made of, and the finishes placed on them can range from simple sheetrock covered with paint to elaborately curved walls trimmed with rare wood and marble. Wall treatments perform a number of esthetic and practical roles. At Chicago's Art Institute dining room, Norman DeHaan Associates specified stepped tiers of upholstered wall panels that align with various beams, soffits, and ceiling planes in the room to help unify and enhance the physical characteristics of the space (fig. 3-19). In addition, the fabric walls help to mute sound in this calm, upscale establishment (discussed in chapter 5).

The intricacy of the design and the quality of the wall coverings drastically affect the cost of the wall and in many cases its durability as well. Like floors, walls take a beating in the restaurant environment. Long-lasting, wear-resistant materials such as vinyl wallcovering in high-impact areas can keep maintenance costs low and wall surfaces looking new. Scuff marks from the backs of chairs can be eliminated by specifying chair rails or, as used to be the norm in fast food operations, bolting chairs to the floor. In most restaurants, however, chair rails are the preferred option.

Much artistry can be used in the selection and application of wall finishes. In Lox Around the Clock, designer Sam Lopata exposed the history of the space by breaking through walls to reveal old studs, BX wire, lath, horsehair plaster, and sheetrock patches—a solution that works well for the irreverent design of this all-night restaurant. Similarly, the rough brick, plaster, and concrete of the patched-up walls at Chicago's Scoozi and Denver's Rattlesnake Club, create a fascinating textural milieu. In

3-19. *Fabric-covered wall panels further the architectural characteristics and absorb sound in the dining room of the Chicago Art Institute designed by Norman DeHaan Associates.*
(Van Inwegen photo)

New York City's fashionable yet formal Aurora, cherry-paneled walls reminiscent of high-powered boardrooms add to the clubby atmosphere of the space.

In some designs—most notably fast food environments—wall elements are fashioned from plastic materials and slapped on as an overlay. These don't trick the customer for very long. Walls offer one of the most accepting palettes for interior design and art elements, but these should always be thoughtfully applied. Just because a wall is there doesn't mean it should be covered with "decor."

From an operational perspective, walls and their coverings should be easily cleaned and resistant to wear and tear. In high-impact areas, special attention should be given to wall finishes. Although some finishes may detract from the otherwise seamless design, a scuff mark or hole punched through a wall can be even more distracting to the customer.

Ceilings

Too often neglected in the restaurant design scheme, the ceiling is always noticed by the clientele. The designer Sarah Tomerlin Lee once said that in an otherwise simple room a special ceiling treatment could work like a woman's hat: The ceiling could dress up a plain room in the same way that the hat could transform a simple sheath into a fashionable outfit.

Technically the ceiling is frequently comprised of several elements: the basic ceiling structure, luminaires, acoustical treatments, and ventilation grillwork. The basic ceiling structure may be the framework to which the other elements are attached, or the framework and its covering. Painted sheetrock is often the material of choice on fixed ceilings, but in some designs structural elements are deliberately left exposed, along with the lighting, plumbing, and HVAC mechanicals, or suspended ceilings are installed.

Today, few restaurants have the 2-foot-by-4-foot fluorescent luminaires commonly used in office buildings, with the exception of some corporate and other noncommercial cafeterias. Instead, many restaurant designers specify recessed lighting, track lighting, or indirect lighting coves as part of the ceiling design. These treatments increase the complexity of the ceiling structure but also serve to improve the quality of lighting in the space. In some cases skylights—either real or simulated—become a light source and a ceiling element. When cove lighting is used, the ceiling serves to reflect light into the dining space and to conceal the luminaires. In still other applications, the ceilings merely hide the can of recessed luminaires or provide a solid base from which to suspend light tracks.

Acoustic elements integrated into the ceiling are often used to control unwanted noise in the restaurant. Acoustic ceiling tiles, insulation, and other sound-absorbing materials applied to ceilings minimize reverberation and absorb sound. Ceiling alcoves—such as lighting alcoves or simply dead air space above a perforated ceiling—also serve to trap and thus limit reverberation. Fiberglass panels wrapped with fabric, banners, and color-coordinated, vinyl-coated, acoustical drywall panels are also popular choices for ceiling treatments.

Many good designs combine a number of the above-mentioned treatments. At Caffe Luna in Newton, Massachusetts, for instance, Morris Nathanson Design created a ceiling treatment that worked with other design elements to transform a small, ordinary, shopping mall storefront into a snappy bistro setting (fig. 3-20). Here, a ceiling soffit edged with hidden cove lighting runs down the length of the room. The soffit creates a raised, central ceiling section, which the designers covered with a cloud-dappled "sky" that evokes lazy summer afternoons. This prominent design feature crowns the room and also defines the circulation path. It is edged with a ceiling of acoustic tiles that hangs over the seating areas and helps to soften sound in the hard-edged space. A track of low-voltage, high-intensity luminaires attached to the acoustic ceiling adds dramatic lighting to the environment.

The distribution of fresh and at times the elimination of unwanted air is usually integrated into the ceiling treatment. Care must be taken to ensure that adequate air is supplied to all areas of the dining room without creating a draft in any one spot. This air supply is best accomplished by installing oversized ventilation grilles, but unless they are designed to tie in

3-20. *An effective combination of floor, wall, and ceiling treatments created a fashionable cafe environment in Caffe Luna, a shopping mall restaurant in Newton, MA, designed by Morris Nathanson Design, Inc. (Warren Jagger photo)*

with the ceiling design, the appearance of the grilles can detract from the appearance of the ceiling. In some cases, make-up air can be piped into the dining room via coffered ceiling spaces, thus providing indirect ventilation that limits the chances of drafts. In any case, exhaust air must be carefully balanced with the kitchen exhaust system; a positive pressure must be maintained in the dining room to ensure that smoke and airborne grease do not enter from the kitchen. What this often translates into is a system in which all air sweeps across the dining room, through the kitchen doors, and out the exhaust hood in the kitchen. If smoking is allowed in the restaurant, however, then this air-handling technique becomes less effective because cigarette smoke can drift past many tables before leaving the room. Judicious placement of smoking sections or the installation of "smoke-eater" machines on the ceiling can help.

DESTINATION DRINKING

Customers progress to the bar for many different reasons, depending on their needs and on the type of restaurant. Sometimes, the bar is the patron's sole destination, a place for socializing. Other times, it acts as the waiting area of the restaurant, and customers sip drinks there while waiting for their tables. In still other situations, people drift over to the bar after their meal for an after-dinner drink. When food service is offered at the bar, single diners in particular may prefer to eat there rather than at a table.

In gathering place restaurants, the bar is usually a very important operational component that serves large numbers of people and makes a lot of money. In serious gourmet restaurants, where food is the raison d'être, the bar may consist of no more than a few token stools. Bars are most often located at the front of restaurants so that customers don't have to wend their way past diners to get there. A view of the bar, with its throngs of patrons and bustling conviviality, can help to merchandise the restaurant to passers-by. This technique works especially well on urban streets and inside hotels, where too often bars are located separately from restaurants. In some restaurants unusual bar

placement—at the back of the room or up a flight of stairs—works to the operation's advantage. The decision depends on many factors, but circulation paths should always be considered.

Designing a bar operation is every bit as complex as designing a restaurant. The ten factors outlined in chapter 1 should be considered. When a bar is affiliated with a restaurant, it must meld with the concept of the restaurant to make both bar and restaurant supportive of each other. The selection of any equipment or décor items should begin only after the nature of the bar and a managerial philosophy are established.

In a time when numerous groups are taking positive steps to curtail excessive consumption of alcoholic beverages, beverage service operations must be sensitive to alcohol-related issues. Many operators used to aim at a sales mix that was composed of 60 percent food sales and 40 percent liquor sales. The high profitability of liquor led to many promotions—for example, happy hours and two-for-one specials—that increased beverage traffic.

Today, however, even gathering place operations with deliberately big bar scenes have worked to shift the sales mix. New York City's America, for example, reduced an initial sales mix of 40 percent beverage sales to only 30 percent because management did not want to promote the establishment as a drinking place. America maintained its profitability and its reputation as a restaurant while decreasing many of the headaches that excessive drinking can cause.

A well-designed bar can help to control beverage consumption yet increase the overall bottom line of beverage sales. The design of the backside of the bar and the service side of the bar can add profit to the bottom line through increased customer counts and decreased operating costs. Because these functional aspects of bar design are usually far less successfully realized than the esthetic aspects, a detailed discussion follows.

Drinking spaces can be divided into three distinct, related areas:

1. Beverage production and storage areas, including the inside service side of the bar

2. The outside service area located in front of the bar
3. Cocktail seating

Beverage Production and Storage

The type of equipment installed at a bar is a function of the type of operation. The low-volume neighborhood tavern may elect to serve bottled beer because the volume does not warrant installing a draft system. A large-volume gathering place, where the potential for selling draft beer is apparent, may also opt for bottled beer, with numerous special offerings, rather than draft as a marketing angle. In still other beverage operations, where a very large volume of beer sales is expected, dozens of beers can be served from a draft system. The same is true of other pieces of equipment. Draft wine systems, frozen marguerita dispensers, glass chillers, liquor-dispensing systems, and a host of other specialty equipment must be specified and installed only after a careful analysis of the market has been conducted.

On the other hand, certain pieces of equipment are essential in any work station if the bartender is to work at peak performance. A typical, double-sided bar work station is shown in figure 3-21. At the center of any work station is the ice bin, and every other piece of equipment should be placed around this central focal point. Following the assumption that most bartenders are right-handed, the undercounter glass storage, plus the bottled and gun-dispenser mixes, should be placed to the right of the ice bin.

In a bar layout with more than one station and more than one bartender at the bar, the layout becomes more complex. The glass washer is often placed between the two stations. For the bartender located to the left of the glass washer (on the right-hand side of the drawing), this placement is most convenient because he or she can easily take clean glasses from the washer and set them on the drainboard to await service. The other bartender has a harder time because the glasses must be carried several steps to be set on a drainboard. A manual washing system with separate sinks in each station could be installed. This two-sink system costs less than a glass-washing machine, but in the long run it takes bartenders away from their primary business of selling drinks.

Sales-control systems must also be integrated into every beverage station. In some cases these systems are merely cash drawers, but increasingly they are sophisticated electronic cash registers that are integrated with beverage-dispensing equipment. In one of the most elaborate systems, the bartender need only enter onto a cash register keypad the desired mixed drink and place the appropriately iced glass under the beverage head, and in seconds the glass is filled with the requested beverage. Such a system requires only three running feet of bar space, and contains the cash register plus a beverage-service head that can dispense seventy-one different products.

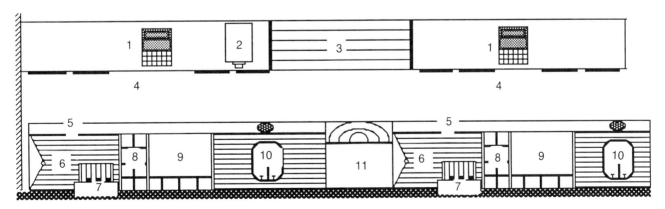

3-21. A *typical double bar incorporates: (1) cash registers; (2) frozen drink machine; (3) liquor display; (4) undercounter refrigeration; (5) speed rail; (6) glass drainage and storage; (7) beer- and soda-dispensing heads; (8) mixer storage; (9) ice bin; (10) sink and dump station; and (11) glasswasher.*

Fully integrated cash- and beverage-dispensing systems generally are installed in large-volume operations or operations in which management is not constantly available to supervise the bartenders. The liquor and mixes are frequently stored in a central location and piped to the work stations.

One storage area can be used to supply several work stations at a single bar or at multiple bars. An advantage of this centralization is that pilferage can be minimized because no bottles are issued to the bartenders and the only drinks that are served come out of the beverage-dispensing head. No drinks can be ordered unless they are rung into the cash-control device. Further savings occur because liquors can be purchased in half-gallon containers rather than liter bottles. Draft beer, when drawn from a central location, stays fresher, and labor costs are limited because bottles and kegs do not have to be carried to and from the bar area.

In general, one of the greatest advantages of centralized storage and control systems is that the amount of space required in the backside of the bar can be significantly limited. A viable alternative, especially for modest bar operations that realize a moderate volume of draft beer sales, is to install a keg storage and serving unit in the bar itself. Such systems transport the beer direct from a walk-in to the bar and do not require complex refrigerated tubing.

Storage procedures of alcoholic beverages must be even more stringent than with food products (fig. 3-22). Alcoholic beverages are

3-22. *At Cafe Majestic in San Francisco, wines are stored under the circular bar top and issued to the wait staff by the bartender.*
(Joseph Durocher photo)

3-23. *Well brands—the brands of liquor used in most mixed drinks—are kept in a speed rail along the front of the sink, and call brands—those liquors asked for by name—are displayed on the back bar.*
(Joseph Durocher photo)

prone to theft and therefore must be secured both before and after issuing to limit stealing and unauthorized consumption. In storerooms, security is accomplished by locked spaces kept separate from food storage areas. At the bar itself, a means of securing the liquor and dispensing equipment is imperative.

At the bar, storage of well brands, that is, those liquors that are used for most mixed drinks, is done in speed rails, which should run along the face of the underbar (fig. 3-23). For call brands, those brands that are specifically requested when ordered, storage is generally on top of the back bar, with backup storage in cabinets. In some restaurants, call brands are stored in plexiglass cabinetry above the front bar, which effectively merchandises these higher-priced spirits.

Bottles of beer can be stored in back bar refrigeration or in undercounter bottle coolers, which are more convenient for high-volume operations because they give more storage capacity than back bar refrigeration in the same amount of floor space.

Glass frosters and chillers, which lower the temperature of glasses before drinks are poured into them, are also included in the bar work stations. At draft beer stations, glass chillers bring the temperature of mugs and pilsners down to as low as 0° F, helping to maintain the

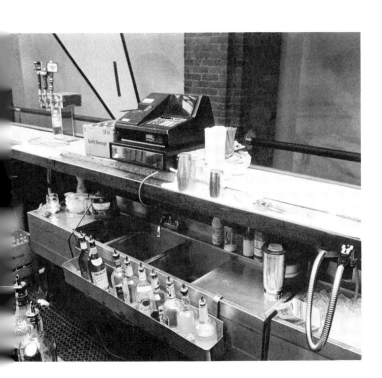

drawn beer at the icy drinking temperatures preferred by most Americans. In other countries, beer is consumed at higher temperatures, which should be considered if the bar is to appeal to an international crowd. Glass frosters can chill a glass down to −20° F, which is perfect for frozen or slush drinks. However, the two units are not interchangeable. A beer mug chilled to −20° negatively affects the flavor of the beer.

Workboards are important elements of any bartender's work station. The workboard should provide a counter with a sink and a waste disposal area. The sink is used for cleaning hands, drawing water, and draining glassware. A dump station for straws, napkins, and waste fruit is also needed to keep the workstation clean.

Operational Layout Concerns

Straight-line bars are the most common and most economical to build and service. In many new installations, however, free-form bars have become very popular. Although equipment manufacturers will gladly construct high-priced customized bar pieces, modular units can generally be installed at a much lower price and still function well.

One of the most important visual concerns in laying out a bar is the appearance of the underbar area. When a straight line bar is installed, the clean lines of the back bar liquor and refrigeration systems are esthetically acceptable. However, when L-shaped or curved bars are installed, customers can view the underside of the front bar, an area that is often a jumble of ingredients, glassware, and cleaning materials. A glasswasher is well suited for such installations, as glasses are taken from the bar top, dumped, and placed directly in the glasswasher, where they are out of sight of the guests. As glasses emerge from the clean side of the machine they can be loaded into a glass froster or chiller where again they are out of sight. Pipes, wires, and tubing must be carefully concealed where the underbar is exposed so that their appearance does not detract from the esthetic of the bar.

Additional pieces of equipment are needed in most bars. Blenders, frozen-drink dispensers, bottled wine, and bulk wine dispensers must each be added to the bartender's arsenal, based

on the expected clientele and drinks to be offered. In the layout of any beverage production
and storage area, the bartender's primary job of
mixing and serving drinks must be kept in mind.

The pickup area (service bar) used by the
dining room wait staff should be carefully designed. All too often, this area interferes with
patrons who are standing at the bar. Ideally, this
pickup area is at one end of the bar. A good
example of an efficient layout was designed by
the Hochheiser-Elias Design Group for Banditto Ditto, as seen in figure 3-24. In cases such
as this, the service staff ice and garnish their
own glassware, thus saving the bartender's valuable time.

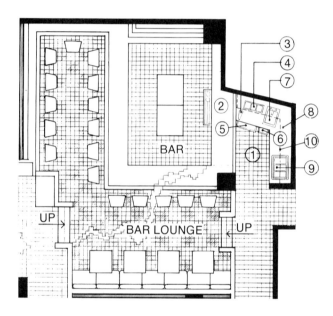

1 BAR SERVICE AREA
2 BARTENDER STATION
3 SODA GUN
4 GARNISHES
5 ICE BELOW
6 TRASH
7 SINK
8 WORK SURFACE W/ DISHWASHER
   RACKS BELOW
9 BAR SNACKS
10 GLASS SHELVES ABOVE

3-24. *In a well-designed service bar area, like this
one at Banditto Ditto, New York, designed by Brad
Elias of the Hochheiser/Elias Design Group, the
wait staff sets up and garnishes the glasses for
service (Brad Elias, Hochheiser/Elias Design Group
drawing).*

Bar Service Area

The bar service area includes the bar stools and
the standing area immediately behind the
stools. Typically, for each 18 inches of bar
length, one stool can be added. In a 20-foot-
long bar, eleven guests can be comfortably
seated at stools. Of course, seating is important
at a bar, but the real profits come from the
guests who are standing behind the bar stools.
Typically, the standing area holds enough
guests to triple the total clientele at the bar.
When a large number of standees is expected,
additional work stations may be needed. The
profitability of the bar is adversely affected if the
standees—or for that matter any bar customer
—must wait while bartenders mix drinks for
other guests.

If standees are expected at a bar, drink rails
should be installed to separate standees from
guests seated at cocktail tables or dinner tables.
Without this separation, dinner guests end up
being bumped against while dining.

Hard, smooth-surfaced floors should be installed under bar stools and in standing areas.
The smooth surfaces make entering and exiting
from bar stools easier. They are not easily damaged, even when smokers snuff out their cigarettes on the floor. Ventilation is very important
in bar areas (fig. 3-25), as people light up cigarettes more frequently here than in the dining
room. Illumination sets the mood of the space
just as it does in the dining areas, and in recent
years the typical bar atmosphere has gone from
dim to bright. Bar lighting has played an important role in transforming the dark hideaway into
the animated meeting place. Similarly, hard
materials such as wood, brass, and tile are typically specified in bar areas. These materials are
generally easy to maintain, and their sound-reflecting qualities are an asset if operators want
to create a high-energy bar area.

Music and video systems have become
increasingly important components of bars
because they contribute to the kind of entertainment milieu that today's patrons look for
when they go out to socialize. Like other design
elements, these systems should be integrated
into the bar design from the start of the project,
taking into account such issues as speaker quality and placement and choice and placement of

3-25. *DiLeonardo International created an animated, yet comfortable bar and cocktail lounge for Hilton Suites at Lexington Green, Lexington, KY. (Warren Jagger photo)*

video projection screens or TV monitors. At Sports in New York City, architect Patricia Sapinsley designed a high-impact, high-energy bar on a very limited budget for this gigantic gathering place restaurant. She cleverly placed video projection screens so clientele could watch sports events from every seat in the house.

Cocktail Lounge

Table seating in lounge areas plays an important role in many operations, especially when it serves as a waiting area for diners. Table seating requires more floor space per drink served but creates a mood and draws a crowd that might not be captured if only bar seating is provided. These lounge areas are popular before meals but can also encourage diners to linger after their meal. In some restaurants, dance floors or areas for entertainers to perform are important inclusions in cocktail lounges. Dancing or entertainment can capture diners who might otherwise leave the restaurant for an after-dinner drink.

Food Service in Bars

Food service in bars has become an increasingly popular option for many types of restaurants. At the tapas bar, for instance, food and beverage sales go hand-in-hand. In these situations, designers must consider the proximity of the bar to the kitchen.

As many customers have cut back on the numbers of drinks they consume, the sale of appetizers and hors d'oeuvres has become important to the restaurant's bottom line. In addition to increasing bar revenues, sales of appetizers in the bar area can decrease the time guests spend at dinner tables and thus increase table turns.

Design Decisions

In summary, the following points should always be taken into consideration when planning a bar design.

A high-visibility bar can help draw patrons into the restaurant.

The choice of partial, full, or no barriers between bar and dining room depends upon type of restaurant and the desired ambiance. Some type of sound control from bar to restaurant is almost always desirable.

If the bar offers food service, then it should be located near the kitchen.

If the bar provides beverage service to the dining room, the server's pathway between the two areas should be short and simple. If a separate service bar is located in the kitchen, the bar can be located further from the dining areas.

The bar pickup service area should be located away from areas where people congregate.

Sound and video systems should be integrated into the design scheme, not slapped on as an afterthought. Music and video can help to create an exciting bar area.

If live entertainment or dancing is planned for a lounge area, then extra floor space must be allocated.

Light, noise, and hard materials contribute to the animated, high-energy environment typical of today's gathering places. The type of restaurant should dictate the type of bar.

DESTINATION RESTROOMS

A visit to the restroom is a common part of the restaurant experience for most patrons, yet restroom design is often neglected. When the budget runs rampant due to unexpected costs, ownership tends to pull back the funding for restroom décor. In the worst scenarios, impractical design contributes to a messy, dirty environment that may lead customers to believe that the kitchen is dirty too. An attractive, clean restroom that carries through the design scheme of the restaurant speaks volumes about the caring attitude of management.

Architectural reference books and local building and sanitation codes mandate the size and number of water closets required in restaurant restrooms. However, they do not emphasize the importance of restrooms to the overall success of the restaurant, nor do they discuss the ramifications of design and décor.

Privacy of both sight and sound is an important consideration for any restaurant restroom. Vanity screens or some sort of labyrinth must be installed to ensure that sight lines into the restrooms are limited from exterior view. Mirrors must be carefully placed so as not to interfere with people's privacy in any way. Adequate ventilation is another absolute requirement. Exhaust fans in restrooms should be strong enough to create a negative pressure that draws air in from the dining room, through the restroom and out the vent. Some restaurateurs may opt for air-freshening units, but these can't surpass the effectiveness of plain old fresh air.

In any restroom a sufficient number of water closets (and urinals in the case of men's restrooms) are needed, with easy-to-use-and-maintain latching mechanisms. Easy-maintenance sinks and counters are also essential, along with soap dispensers that are easy to fill and keep clean. All too often, the spout of a soap dispenser hangs over the counter and leaves trailings of soap that must be wiped up frequently to maintain clean appearance.

Lighting plays an important role in restroom design. In fast food and other foodservice environments that use fluorescent lighting in the front of the house, fluorescent lighting is acceptable. However, in a softly lit tableservice restaurant, where incandescent lighting provides a flattering glow, the blue-hued glare of fluorescent tubes in the restroom can be shocking enough to ruin an evening.

Clean-looking restrooms are comforting to restaurant guests as they imply that the rest of the restaurant is also clean. Nonporous, easily cleanable materials are one of the best ways of ensuring that a trip to the restroom is not a turnoff. Tiles, vinyl wall coverings, and other practical materials can help the restaurateur maintain a spotless restroom with minimal effort. These applications don't have to look institutional; today manufacturers offer textures, colors, and designs that carry through a fashionable look.

Women's Restrooms

As reported by the National Restaurant Association, the average woman takes eight to ten minutes on a trip to the bathroom. Men take an average of four minutes. The time difference points up some important design considerations. Men generally use bathrooms for totally utilitarian purposes. Women, on the other hand, use bathrooms to perform a multiplicity of functions that include but are not limited to make-up retouching, coiffure correction, perfuming, wardrobe adjustment, and conversation. All of these activities require extra space and specialized elements. A make-up table or cosmetics shelf across from the sinks is an inexpensive yet helpful addition. Mirrors over the sink and over the make-up area should be high-quality polished mirror that does not cause any distortion. Wherever possible, a full-length mirror by the exit door is a welcome addition.

Although hand dryers should be included in every restroom—just in case the paper towels run out—they should be supplemented with paper towels and adequate waste disposal containers. Restrooms are frequently used by smokers and should contain wall-mounted ashtrays to keep the floor clean and prevent the disposal of cigarettes in a way that may lead to a fire.

A final inclusion, especially important in restaurants that cater to singles, is a place for women to talk within the restroom. This may be one and the same with the make-up area or separate from this area, but it should be large enough so that several conversations can be conducted. When separated from the water closet and sink area, these spaces can have a much more residential feeling, with touches such as a carpeted floor to diminish sound levels.

Men's Restrooms

As mentioned above, men take a more utilitarian approach to restrooms. However, such added amenities as a shoeshine are appropriate in certain settings. A hanger in the water closets is appreciated for hanging suit jackets. In fast food restaurants or diners where laborers often lunch, two soap dispensers—one with mild soap and one with abrasive soap for deep cleaning—are an added benefit.

Vanity screens are frequently placed between urinals. Wall-mounted screens must be firmly secured, or else within a short time they loosen, fall from their place, and leave unsightly holes in the wall. All too often vanity screens are placed too closely together and oversized men inadvertently loosen the screens as they push past them. Another disadvantage of the screens is that they are frequently splashed and rust quickly.

Customized Restrooms

The same attention to design detailing in the dining room can be carried over into the restrooms for a very pleasing effect (fig. 3-26). In a seafood restaurant, faux portholes can filter light into the space. In upscale restaurants with contemporary design, the standard vitrified china can be replaced with stainless steel. In some restaurants, a floral display in the restroom adds a residential touch that can downplay the institutional elements in the space.

This customization can go beyond the standard applications to little elements that are peculiar to a specific type of restaurant. Consider the restrooms in a barbecued ribs restaurant. A toothpick dispenser and hot towel dispenser in the restrooms become conversation pieces and are very helpful to guests. An area map and distance chart on the wall in roadside restaurants is helpful to travelers. In many restrooms, pay phones and/or vending machines can generate revenues for the owners and are useful for the guests.

As mentioned earlier, restrooms should be seen as an integral part of the whole restaurant. When well designed, they become a positive addition to the restaurant. When dealt with as an afterthought, they can appear incongruous and may be a reason not to return to the restaurant.

SUMMARY

Front-of-the-house design involves a delicate orchestration of spaces that works to create a total experience. From the moment the customer first sets sight on the building to the moment when he or she steps back into the outside world, design should be part of an integrated plan. Each design decision should reflect thoughtful problem solving that is sensitive both to the needs of the operation and to the design idea. Once the design team understands the basic principles, they can begin to make specific design decisions.

3-26. *Restaurant bathrooms should be as carefully designed as any other part of the space.*
(Joseph Durocher photo)

4

DESIGN IMPLEMENTATION: BACK TO FRONT THROUGH MANAGEMENT'S EYES

In the process-oriented approach to restaurant design, solutions are arrived at by analyzing the functional needs of a given operation. In order to understand the principles of kitchen design, therefore, we systematically move through the back of the house from an operational point of view, starting with the receiving of unprocessed food and ending with the plating of prepared food for service. This technique enables the designer to fill in the floor plan with appropriate work stations and equipment because each space or functional area in the back of the house has certain operating characteristics that translate into design features. These areas are discussed individually, but in the final design they must be integrated as a whole (fig. 4-1).

KITCHEN SUPPORT AREAS

Receiving

The receiving area should be accessible to the loading dock and the storerooms wherever possible to facilitate a smooth flow of food from delivery to receiving to storage. To facilitate access to this area, doors should be wide enough to accommodate pallets and hand trucks. Ideally, the loading dock leads directly to the receiving area, which is adjacent to the various

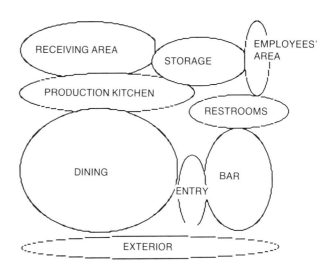

4-1. *A bubble diagram is a useful aid when sketching out the relative placement of restaurant spaces (Debra Durocher drawing).*

storage areas. In some restaurants, the purchasing agent's office is located near the receiving area, but for reasons of internal control the purchasing function is frequently handled from an office that is separate from the receiving area.

Receiving area floors must be smooth so that handtrucks or flatbed trucks can be moved about easily. Because all foods must be carefully inspected when they arrive, the area should be well lit. The optimum light scheme would supply overall lighting with fluorescent tubes and task lighting with incandescent fixtures.

Scales are most important in this area, as many foods are purchased by weight. In operations in which large quantities of meats are purchased, built-in floor scales are ideal: pallets, loaded with boxes of meat, can be rolled onto the floor scale and easily weighed. Weighing individual boxes of meat or other items purchased by weight can be done with a free-standing floor scale or table scale.

Although trash is frequently removed through the receiving area, in many locales building and health codes mandate a separate area to handle trash. Ideally, fresh foods should not travel through the same spaces as trash, nor should they be stored in the same area.

Storage

The storage areas should be located to be easily accessible from both the loading dock and the production areas. If they cannot be placed conveniently between these two areas, then they should be closest to the production areas because this proximity saves more labor time. Generally, food is received in large quantities and placed on rolling stock for transport to the storage areas. On a given day, a typical restaurant receives three to ten deliveries. The production personnel, however, may have to draw goods from the dry, refrigerated, or frozen foods storage areas thirty to a hundred times each day. In a complex food operation with more than one kitchen, the storage areas should ideally be placed near the most active kitchen.

Proper shelving systems are needed in every storage area. Fixed shelving units have been the standard of the industry, along with dunnage racks for storing large, bulky items.

Good shelving should be as flexible as possible by providing a means to change the height of each shelf. Under ideal conditions, shelving should minimize the need for costly aisle space. This is accomplished by placing the shelves on wheels, an especially useful feature in refrigerated or frozen food storage areas. Shelf depths and overall height should match the products to be stored on them and the size of the people who will be drawing goods from the shelves.

The amount of shelving in dry or refriger-

ated space is a function of the menu, the frequency of delivery, the state of the foods as they are purchased, and the number of meals to be served. Frozen foods that are ready for cooking require the least amount of storage per customer served. Fresh food, as it comes out of the ground or off the hoof, requires greater storage space. Total storage per person served can range anywhere from 1 to 2.5 cubic feet, with the mix between dry and refrigerated and frozen storage being a function of the menu and management policy.

Lighting and ventilation in storage areas is typically poor. High temperatures can shorten the shelf life of certain foods, and poor lighting levels lead to inadequate cleaning and poor management of these areas. Incandescent lights that can be turned on and off without decreasing bulb life should be used in all storage areas.

As indicated earlier, storage is generally divided into three major areas: dry goods, refrigerated, and frozen. The size and location of each of these areas are greatly affected by the menu, limitations of the architecture, and purchasing and receiving procedures.

DRY GOODS

Dry goods are frequently broken down into four categories: dry and canned foods, disposable paper goods and other nonchemical supplies, cleaning and chemical supplies, and spirited beverages. Each category is ideally assigned its own storage space. In addition, breakout pantry closets adjacent to production areas are frequently stocked with a par inventory of commonly used foods. Well-designed kitchens have par stock areas of dry goods for each production section.

Storing items separately is important for practical as well as required reasons. Chemical supplies should always be placed in their own storage areas as they could potentially contaminate foods or paper goods. Food goods—which are prone to theft—are often kept separate from paper goods. A fourth dry storage area is required when alcoholic beverages are served. At times spirits are kept in a locked cage within the confines of the dry foods storage area, but most frequently they are kept in their own area under the supervision of the beverage department.

Special humidity and temperature-controlled spaces are needed to store fine wines, and draft beer requires refrigerated storage.

REFRIGERATED FOODS

Refrigerated storage units come in differing sizes and must be matched carefully to the operation. Generally a mix of walk-in refrigeration, reach-in refrigeration, and undercounter refrigeration is used in restaurant kitchens.

Walk-in refrigerators should be utilized for extended-term storage of bulk foods or for short-term storage of batch-prepared foods. Such refrigeration systems are expensive and take up a great deal of space in the operation. In certain locations, locating walk-ins outdoors limits construction costs and thus saves money.

The walk-in floor should be insulated. In new construction, insulation can be installed under the tile floor. In a retrofit, insulation can be installed over the existing floor. A ramp must be provided either inside the walk-in or outside the unit so that staff can easily roll carts in and out of the refrigerator.

Reach-in refrigerators come in many configurations. One example is given in figure 4-2. Many questions must be considered before arriving at the right design for a given operation. For example, on which side of the door should the hinges be installed? The directional flow of materials to and from the work station should influence this decision.

Should each section of the reach-in have a single door or two half-doors? This is primarily a question of convenience and energy savings. Single doors allow the user to view the contents of the entire refrigerator by opening just one door, but as that door is held open, more heat infiltrates into the unit than in a half-door system. Should shelving be fixed or roll-in? Only single-door refrigerators come with roll-in shelving. Should refrigerator doors be solid or see-through? Solid doors provide the best insulation, but with see-through doors the kitchen staff can view the refrigerator stock without opening the door.

Options significantly increase the cost of reach-ins, but they are sometimes useful. Doors placed on the back and front of the unit allow the refrigerator to be shared by more than one

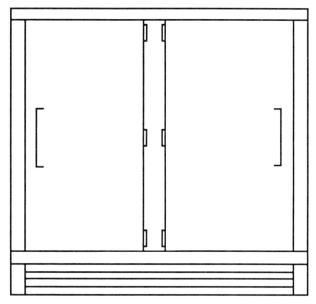

4-2. *A double reach-in with hinges on the center post can easily service two work stations (Lori Durocher drawing).*

work station or to function as a pass-through. Options such as locking systems, types of finish, interior lighting, and integrated thermometers must be chosen or rejected based on the needs of the operation. Locking systems, for instance, are imperative in complex operations, but a family-owned and operated restaurant may not need them. A stainless steel surface looks great when first installed, but cleaning and maintaining that high sheen can become problematic. An integrated thermometer is an excellent addition that makes sense only if a night watchman periodically checks on the temperatures.

Two types of refrigeration units in this category are refrigerated drawers and undercounter refrigerators. Refrigerated drawers are often used near grill areas for holding meats and toppings, or installed near a broiler station for holding seafood. The drawers are easy to access and clean.

Undercounter refrigerators are typically part of sandwich stations or are placed under grill or broiler units. Generally, they function in much the same way as refrigerated drawers except that they are not as accessible.

FROZEN FOODS

The configurations of frozen food storage units is similar to refrigerated units except for the addition of chest storage, which is generally reserved for ice cream. Unlike walk-in refrigerators, walk-in freezers must have insulated floors. In addition, unless insulation is inlaid in the floor slab, a ramp must also be provided. Wherever possible, the door of the walk-in freezer should open into a walk-in refrigerator to improve the operating efficiency of both the refrigerator and the freezer. A heater strip is an excellent addition around the doors of any type of freezer, as it prevents the buildup of frozen condensate.

Reach-in freezers can be configured in the same way as reach-in refrigerators. An important consideration with freezers, however, is infiltration heat loading. Half-doors will help to alleviate this problem.

Roll-in freezers are particularly helpful in banquet-preparation areas, where roll-in carts with preportioned desserts can be held for service. Chest-type freezers are perfectly suited to ice cream storage because their minimal temperature variations lengthen shelf life.

Office and Employee Support Areas

Restaurant offices are more functional than they are decorative. Space and equipment are needed to complete paperwork and to store records, product information, and reference books. Sufficient lighting and an adequate supply of outlets are necessary. If computers are to be installed, a separate electrical supply to the office should be provided.

Restrooms and locker rooms are typically underdesigned and poorly maintained. Employee morale can be positively affected if the locker rooms are well ventilated and lighted and the lockers are large enough to hold clothes and other personal belongings. An appropriate number of urinals and toilets should be provided, with extra toilet facilities for women. (This provision will help to keep the lines shorter in the restaurant women's room.) In addition, space should be provided adjacent to the hand sinks for staff members to place toiletry items. In many cases, the restroom facilities are shared with the customers. For clean, efficient operation, air dryers should be provided as a backup to paper towels.

Tile flooring with a floor drain is ideal for restrooms. This treatment facilitates easy cleanup if a backup occurs or if the area needs to be sanitized. Glazed tile or vinyl wallcovering is the preferred surface for walls because it will hold up better than painted, metal, or sheetrock surfaces. Adequate ventilation and lighting are also essential to a well-designed restroom.

Some operations provide an employee dining area. In such cases, durability is a key factor in the design. Tables and chairs take a greater beating than those in the customer dining rooms and therefore should be constructed to withstand the extra abuse. However, this area should receive esthetic attention; employee morale can be greatly boosted by a comfortable, attractive dining room that reflects managerial caring. Ventilation should be adequate to handle heavy smoke loads as oftentimes employees are allowed to smoke only in the employee dining areas.

KITCHEN

A well-designed kitchen integrates several areas within one space. Fabrication, preprepration, preparation (hot foods, bake shop, dessert, and salad), holding, assembly and service, and sanitation are all commonly incorporated into a kitchen design. Each of the areas is driven by the menu and designed for the preparation and service of different items. Each must function individually yet also work in concert with other kitchen areas.

Work stations are the building blocks of kitchen design. A work station is the space—flooring, work counters, production equipment, storage equipment, utilities—where a particular set of tasks is completed. Generally, the station is designed for one worker.

When several work stations are grouped together to accommodate similar types of preparation tasks, they are called a work section. These sections are grouped into work areas, and the areas make up the kitchen.

To understand the process of designing a successful work station, first identify the task. Figure 4-3(a) diagrams a single-sided work station where a sauté cook stands at the range and sautés food to order. In real life, however, no work station is as simple as this design. One needed component, for example, is refrigeration for holding the uncooked portions of meat. To resolve this, as shown in figure 4-3(b), a mobile refrigerator was added to the station. However, the station is still inadequate. Go further and think of it as a 360° circle, with multidirectional characteristics as seen in figure 4-3(c). The worker sautés meat on the range, reaches around to pick up a serving plate, places the portion on the plate, and then turns to finish off the plate with vegetables and a garnish from the steam table.

In figure 4-3(d), the complete work station appears in elevation from the worker's perspective and shows the range with an overshelf where plates can be held, plus an undercounter refrigerator. Note that the overshelf eliminates the worker's need to turn around for plates and the undercounter refrigerator does not block the aisle.

The workings of the complete station are most easily understood when the station is thought of in three dimensions. The sauté cook can easily reach the meat in the refrigerated drawers. After it is prepared, the plates are within easy reach, and the vegetables are ready for service on the steam table. This is not the ideal sauté station for every restaurant. Rather, it is a station designed for a specific purpose at a specific location. The key is that the station design is based on a single worker.

Continuing with a hypothetical kitchen design, imagine that a broiler station is installed to the right of the sauté station, with an open-grate gas broiler for broiling steaks and chops. As with the sauté station, a mobile refrigerator is needed to hold the uncooked steaks, along with a steam table and clean plate storage area.

To the right of the broiler station, imagine that a fry station is installed. Two deep-fat fryers are specified for frying prebreaded seafood and French fries. Storage space for plates, a steam table area to hold vegetables, and a freezer to hold the seafood and fries are necessary components of the station.

Together, these three work stations comprise a hot food a la carte section. When they are grouped together as separate entities, each with its own steam table and refrigerator, however, the end design is unwieldy and costly. In

COUNTER TOP RANGE

A

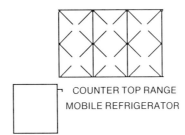

COUNTER TOP RANGE
MOBILE REFRIGERATOR

B

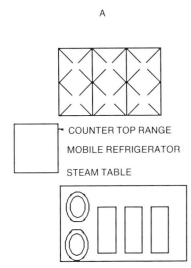

COUNTER TOP RANGE

MOBILE REFRIGERATOR

STEAM TABLE

C

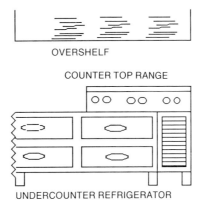

OVERSHELF

COUNTER TOP RANGE

UNDERCOUNTER REFRIGERATOR

D

4-3. A work station is built beginning with a basic piece of equipment, then additional pieces are added. For example, starting with the basic range (A), a rolling refrigerator is added to the left of the station (B). Next, a steamtable and plate lowerator (C), are added to make use of the full circle around the worker. In (D), the elevation shows how the refrigerator could actually be placed under a counter top range to save floor space and improve flow (Debra Durocher drawing).

this case, three refrigerators and three steam tables are not necessary. One solution (fig. 4-4) is to place an undercounter refrigeration unit where it is accessible to the range and broiler stations and place the freezer under the fryers. The drawers in the undercounter refrigerator and freezer are easier for the cooks to use than units with hinged doors. On the front side of the section, a single steam table unit with plate lowerators on either end has been added. Between the broiler and the fry station, a spreader plate has been installed for safety; it also functions as a work surface.

Of course, there are some compromises. The broiler and fry cooks have to reach a bit further for the accompaniments on the steamtable, and the cooks have to lean over to take food out of the refrigerated and frozen drawers. However, the section can be easily worked by three people or, during slower periods, by one or two people. This task-oriented design is a wise financial investment because it contributes to efficient job performance.

As kitchen design progresses, work stations and sections are designed for each area of the kitchen. The final step is to assemble all of the sections into an overall floor plan.

Relative positioning of the various sections affects the overall efficiency of the kitchen. Designers need to study the general plan to determine the best location of the various sections in relation to each other and to the service areas. This analysis can best be accomplished through a series of bubble diagrams that roughly plot out the relative position of the various areas of the kitchen.

For example, the bubble diagram in figure 4-5(a), an a la carte restaurant in which the servers must make several trips to the kitchen to service each table, has three glaring errors: The dish machine should be placed where the bake shop is located; the beverage station should be located where the walk-in refrigerator is located; and the cold food should be located where the dry good storage area is located.

The corrected design appears in figure 4-5(b). The solutions may seem obvious, but inefficient designs are often developed because care has not been taken to think through the floor plan from an operational perspective.

The placement of work sections becomes even more important in a complex foodservice system with many points of sale serviced from a single kitchen. Careful attention must be paid to the service systems at each point of sale. If a tableservice dining room and banquet room are to be serviced out of one kitchen, for instance, the dish machine should be closer to the dining room than to the banquet space. The service staff take more individual trips to the dish machine from the dining room than from the banquet space. Similarly, the hot foods station is usually situated closer to the dining room because staff travel back and forth from the hot food station to the dining room more often than they do to the banquet space.

Careful thought must be given to each station and section that will make up the final design. In the worst scenario, a station is completely forgotten. Such a situation can lead to a costly renovation of the kitchen long before it should be necessary.

All too often, kitchen designers go halfway. They think through functions performed in the kitchen and pull them together into well-integrated sections but then fail to properly relate these sections to each other. A typical example of this occurs when a separate bakeshop is set

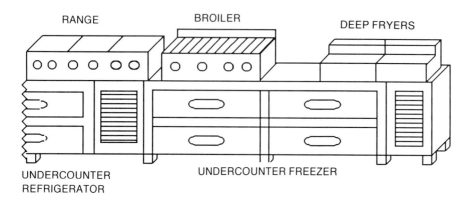

4-4. *An undercounter refrigerator under the range top serves the range and broiler station, while the undercounter freezer serves the fry station and broiler station (Debra Durocher drawing).*

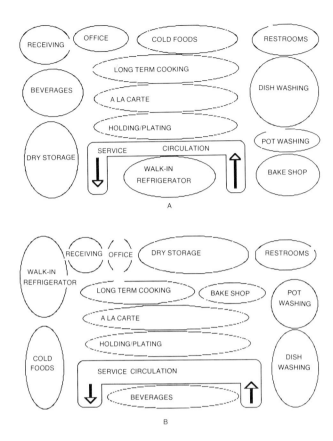

4-5. *The detailed bubble diagram (A) puts the cold food, beverage, and warewashing areas too far away from the service staff. The revised layout in (B) is the same size but shuffles the spaces to improve the flow of workers and materials (Lori Durocher drawing).*

up, requiring its own ovens, in a restaurant whose roasting ovens are used for only a portion of each day. If the bakeshop had been located close to the roasting ovens, then the baking and roasting could have been done in one set of ovens rather than two.

Some would argue that bake ovens are different from roasting ovens. Crisp French bread, for example, needs a steam-injected oven. However, roasts, pies, and cakes can all be cooked in a steam-injected oven if the steam is turned off.

Flexibility is the key to planning both equipment and work stations. What serves as a sandwich station for lunch can double as a dessert station for dinner if the space is properly designed.

Kitchen Area Guidelines

Remembering the basic equipment needed for each work station is easy, for example, a broiler

in a broiler station and a range in a sauté station. However, general requirements must be integrated into every station design for it to function effectively. These requirements include ambient and task lighting; refrigerated, frozen, or ambient temperature storage for holding unprepared food; disposal or trash cans; ventilation, consisting of exhaust air in heat-producing and warewashing areas as well as make-up air; special floor finishes such as floor drains for ease of cleaning and floor grates wherever stationary equipment is cleaned with water; hand sinks, soap, and toweling; and plumbing for clean water and waste water.

Although no two sections are exactly alike, table 4-1 lists *stations* as they would typically be incorporated into various *sections*. In some high-volume operations, two or more of the same type of station may be needed in a given section.

TABLE 4-1   TYPICAL STATIONS INCLUDED IN SAMPLE SECTIONS

Hot Foods Section
    Broiler station
    Fry station
    Griddle station
    Sauté station
    Sauce station
    Holding
Salad and Dessert Section
    Salad greens cleaning
    Salad preparation
    Dessert preparation
    Frozen dessert preparation
    Holding and service
Bakery Section
    Mixing station
    Dough holding and proofing
    Dough rolling and forming
    Assembly work station
    Baking and cooling
Banquet Section
    Steam cooking
    Dry heat cooking (roasting, broiling)
    Holding and plating
Short Order Section
    Griddle station
    Fry station
    Broiler station

Hot Foods

Hot food production is broken down into two areas: dry heat cooking and moist heat cooking. Dry heat cooking areas incorporate ovens, ranges, griddles, broilers, tilting fry kettles, and deep fryers. Moist heat cooking areas include steamers, steam-jacketed and trunnion kettles, and occasionally ranges.

Both dry and moist heat areas incorporate equipment that can be used for either quick or extended cooking. Extended-cooking units should be grouped together and quick-cooking equipment should be grouped together. Figure 4-6 shows a general area plan common to many hot food production areas. Here, roasting ovens, ranges, steam-jacketed kettles, and tilting braising pans are placed on the back of a half wall with the sauté, fry, grill, broiling, and pressure steam equipment placed on the action side of the wall close to the service area.

The ovens, kettles, and tilting braising pans seen on the back side are used to cook large batches of food over long periods of time (fig. 4-7). A cook can place a roast in the oven and leave it unattended for an hour or more, de-

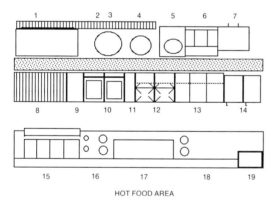

HOT FOOD AREA

4-6. *A hot foods area is composed of a long-term cooking section and an a la carte section. Included in this hot foods area is: (1) tilting braising pan; (2) drain trough; (3) 60-gallon steam-jacketed kettle; (4) 40-gallon steam-jacketed kettle; (5) 20-quart trunnion kettle; (6) flat-top range; (7) double-deck convection oven; (8) char broiler; (9) spreader plate; (10) double deep fryers; (11) spreader plate; (12) open-top range with overshelf; (13) flat-top range with overshelf; (14) double reach-in refrigerator; (15) sandwich station; (16) plate lowerators; (17) steam table; (18) service pickup shelf; (19) microwave oven (Lori Durocher drawing).*

pending on the mass of the roast. After browning, meat can be left to simmer for a stew in a steam-jacketed kettle, or veal shanks can be left to braise in a tilting braising pan. An advantage to extended cooking is flexibility in terms of the amount of time that foods can cook. Simply put, a beef stew can simmer for sixty minutes or eighty minutes with little discernible difference in the final product. A spencer roll (the boneless, closely trimmed rib eye roast used frequently for banquets) can roast for an hour and thirty minutes or an hour and forty-five minutes with little variation in the final internal temperature.

However, the equipment on the front, action side of the line is designed for quick cooking of food, oftentimes made to order. Unlike extended cooking, quick cooking requires precision timing. If deep-fried scallops cook a few minutes too long, they are overcooked. A broiled strip steak cannot be left alone. It must be turned and cared for not only because of flare-ups when fat drips into the broiler but also because the windows of time to cook a rare, medium, or well-done steak are narrow.

The high-pressure steamer—even though it is a moist heat cooking piece of equipment—is also placed on the front line because it cooks vegetables quickly in small batches on an as-needed basis.

The relative positioning of each of these pieces of equipment has practical as well as esthetic considerations (fig. 4.8). If at all possible, the high-rise pieces of equipment should be grouped together and the low-lying pieces should similarly be grouped into one area.

Station Options

The selection of different pieces of hot food equipment depends heavily on the menu items and their style of preparation. Flexibility is important, but a completely flexible kitchen poses problems for the production staff. Following is a brief guide to the generic needs of each hot food station.

BROILER STATION OPTIONS

Gas, electric, and charcoal are the major heat source choices. Each has specific cooking char-

4-7. *In the kitchen of Zincs, Chicago, the long-term cooking area is used for moist-heat cooking and baking. (Joseph Durocher photo)*

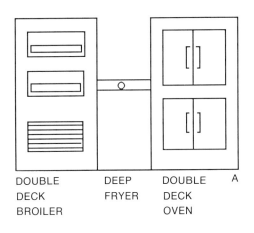

DOUBLE   DEEP   DOUBLE   A
DECK   FRYER   DECK
BROILER   OVEN

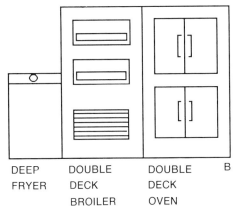

DEEP   DOUBLE   DOUBLE   B
FRYER   DECK   DECK
                BROILER   OVEN

4-8. *When a deep fryer is sandwiched between tall double-deck broilers and ovens (A), it is more uncomfortable to use than when tall equipment is only on one side of the fryer (B) (Lori Durocher drawing).*

acteristics. Total British thermal unit (BTU) heat output also affects cooking times.

In gas and electric broilers, the heat source can come from above as in a radiant broiler or from below as in a charcoal broiler. The flavor, texture, and appearance of the final product are affected by the choice of top heat or bottom heat equipment. Top heat broilers can be used for browning off the surface of foods or broiling delicate cuts that need to be cooked on a sizzle platter. Charcoal broilers—specifically mesquite—are high-heat, high-smoke broilers that need careful attention during the cooking process and create sufficient smoke that special attention has to be given to the ventilation exhaust.

Broilers are available as single and double decks. With gas and electric broilers, two cooking levels can save floor space and be supervised by a single broiler person.

FRY STATION OPTIONS

Both gas and electric fry units are available. The heat source and the distribution of heat to the fat kettle are both critical factors. The key concern is recovery time—the time required for the fryer to come back up to temperature after foods are placed in the fry kettle. Quick recovery time limits the amount of fat that is absorbed into the food.

The size of the fat kettle (the unit that holds the frying medium) helps to determine the amount of food that can be cooked efficiently at one time. A general rule of thumb is that one pound of product can be cooked in 5 to 8 pounds of frying medium. Floor-model fryers generally have large kettles and therefore great output capacity. Tabletop models that can sit on top of an undercounter refrigerator are space-savers, but their smaller fat kettles translate into smaller food quantities. The heat source, shape of the fat kettle, frequency of filtration, amount of food cooked, and care in handling of the fat all affect how fast the fat breaks down.

In some operations, one fryer is used for cooking all fried foods, including potatoes, fish, and onion rings. However, such a practice can lead to flavors carrying over from one product to another. Thus, the number of fryers should be based on a concern for product quality as well as for the volume of business expected.

GRIDDLE STATION OPTIONS

Gas or electric griddles can be specified. The evenness of heat dispersion, the BTU rating, and the speed of heat-up time are important considerations when choosing which type of heat source to order.

The choice of surface materials on the griddle also affects heat-up time and evenness of heating, as well as ease of cleaning. Stainless steel surfaces clean to a high gloss and thus are quite appropriate in areas where guests can see the griddle surface.

The size of the griddle obviously affects the amount of food that can be cooked on it at one time. When several different types of foods are cooked on the griddle simultaneously, temperature controls that can vary the temperature across the surface of the griddle are important.

SAUTÉ STATION OPTIONS

The designer must consider the total heat output of the sauté station burners, which can run on gas or electric heat. Three types of ranges are generally used for this station. The flat-top, sectional range usually has three sections, each of which can be heated individually. The ring-top range has a flat surface similar to the sectional, but with center rings that can be removed to allow gas-fired flames to come in direct contact with the sauté pan. The open-top range has two to eight open burners, with grates over them in gas ranges.

The open-top range is an immediate heat source. Flat-top and ring-top ranges, however, need heat-up time no matter what the heat source. A nice feature of the gas-ring range is that the center rings can be removed, thus allowing the range to give immediate heat through a central burner while the rest of the flat surface is also being heated. The sectional flat top allows the greatest flexibility, because sections can be turned on as needed.

Flat- and ring-top ranges are the equipment of choice in restaurants where substantial sautéing is mandated by the menu. The real advantage to the flat-surface ranges is that cooks have greater flexibility in the selection of pots and sauté pans. If the kitchen does not include a griddle station, then the flat-top range can be used to hold many more egg pans than could be held on an open-top range. Additionally, the intensity and evenness of the heat given off by a flat-surface range is superior to that of an open-top range.

Kitchen designers should keep in mind that range tops are subjected to considerable wear and tear. Generally, the materials used for sectional or ring tops is heavy gauge and can withstand a beating. However, in some open-top ranges, the burner spiders are so lightweight that they bend or bounce out of place when a heavy pot is set on the range.

Several equipment options are available for the sauté station range. Frequently the range comes with an oven situated under the range top, but this space is often used by cooks for pan or hand tool storage. Because the ovens are below the range, they are difficult to reach and can restrict flow behind a busy a la carte range. Another option, the salamander, is a top-mounted minibroiler that is best used for browning the tops of casseroles or sandwiches. It is a useful option if the kitchen has no other way to top-brown food but does not do the job of a full broiler. Perhaps the most useful and inexpensive option is a simple overshelf that can preheat plates and hold sauté pans.

SAUCE STATION OPTIONS

In some facilities, the sauce and sauté stations are one and the same, with chefs preparing stocks and sauces in pots and pans on a flat-top range. Other kitchens add a separate station with its own equipment to prepare such items as soups, stewed foods, and stocks in addition to sauces.

One of the most frequently used alternatives to making sauces on the range top is the steam-jacketed trunnion kettle. This piece of equipment ranges from a 32-ounce oyster cooker for individual portions to huge 40-quart units. At times a battery of two or more 20-quart trunnions are set up in a sauce station. The steam-jacketing envelops half to two-thirds of the kettle interior. Fully-jacketed kettles may heat faster, but they also bake sauces onto the sides of a half-filled trunnion, waste product, and make a mess to clean up.

Gas, electric, and central steam are the heat sources for trunnion kettles. Although direct steam is the fastest source of heat, gas and electric trunnions can reach much higher temperatures—up to nearly 300° F, as compared to about 220° F for direct, low pressure steam. In some circumstances, the gas or electric trunnion can double as a deep-fat fryer.

When steam is the heat source for the trunnion, it comes from either a self-contained steam generator or a central steam facility. Central steam is usually not available in free-standing restaurants, so the only option is to install a self-contained steam-generating system. However, in facilities with steam readily available throughout the building, central steam is an excellent, inexpensive heat source.

Trunnion kettles are lined with stainless steel or aluminum. Stainless is the preferred material because it never reacts negatively with food products.

Once prepared, sauces or sauced items need to be stored for service. In some operations they may remain in the trunnion or in a pot on the range. However, a hot water bath (bain marie) or steam table is helpful when holding many containers of different sauces for service. The major disadvantage is that water evaporating from the bain marie can add to the humidity discomfort level in the kitchen (fig. 4-9).

4-9. *An a la carte section needs a steam table or, as seen here, a bain marie to hold sauces and batch-cooked vegetables.* (Joseph Durocher photo)

HOLDING OPTIONS

Any of the previously mentioned pieces of equipment in the hot foods section can be used to hold foods. A dry or wet steam table is frequently utilized. Generally a single steam table with room for six to twelve inserts is sufficient, but the size of the steam table should always closely match the menu and the expected volume of the operation. The only additional specialized piece of equipment that can be included for holding food is a heated holding-warming cabinet.

Salad and Dessert

Salad and dessert sections vary greatly depending on the menu offerings and styles of service in the restaurant. In an a la carte restaurant, salads and desserts may be prepared and plated as ordered. In large-volume operations, the preparation and plating is likely to be accomplished prior to the serving period and stored for wait person pickup. In restaurants offering banquet service, additional preparation equipment, rolling stock, and storage space are required for both the salad station and the dessert station. However, some general requirements and considerations are worth noting.

SALAD STATION OPTIONS

Salad greens must always be carefully washed for service. A two-compartment sink with sideboards is well suited for this job. One of the compartments can be filled with water for cleaning greens, and the second can be used for draining washed greens. The sideboards are necessary to hold unprocessed greens and washed greens (fig. 4-10).

In many restaurant operations, reach-in refrigerators are used for holding washed salad ingredients. For banquet service, a walk-in refrigerator is helpful. The reach-in refrigerator must have tray slides to hold the sheet pans that most often become the shelves in a refrigerator. Sheet pans are also used to rack up portioned salads when salads are dished up in advance of service.

When the salad station does double duty as a sandwich station, slicers are frequently incor-

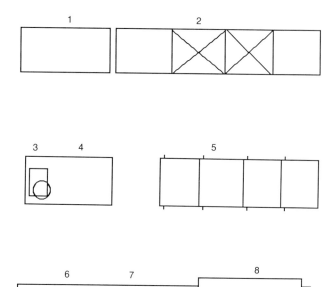

COLD FOOD SECTION

4-10. *A well-planned cold food station incorporates: (1) storage shelving; (2) salad wash sinks with sideboards; (3) food cutter; (4) work table; (5) four-door, pass-through reach-in refrigerator; (6) work counter with pickup overshelf; (7) slicer; and (8) sandwich station (Lori Durocher drawing).*

porated for salad and sandwich ingredients. A vertical cutter-mixer is also useful in this station when large amounts of tossed salads or chopped salads are prepared. Perhaps the most commonly used and versatile piece of equipment for cutting, chopping, and mixing in the salad station is the tabletop chopper with assorted attachments.

DESSERT PREPARATION

Desserts, including frozen concoctions, are often prepared in the salad and dessert section of the kitchen. In other kitchens, dessert preparation—making, mixing, and other preparatory steps—takes place in the bakeshop, with only the plating done at the dessert station.

As with salads, desserts need plenty of refrigeration. Frozen desserts require an ice cream chest and, if preportioned, a reach-in freezer. Soft-serve machines are required where soft ice cream is served and are also helpful in dessert stations where large numbers of frozen cakes, pies, or parfaits are offered.

Work counters, shelving, and other storage areas are vital to both salad and dessert sections. Rolling stock is very helpful for moving trays, clean dishes, and raw materials about the kitchen. In general, flexible equipment capable of preparing a wide range of products is the key to success in salad and dessert sections, as they are often used to prepare an assortment of ever-changing offerings.

Bakery

The bakery section may be a stand-alone section of the kitchen or one that is shared at certain times of the day with other production areas. In most kitchens, this area is broken down into four primary stations. First, the mixer station includes the mixing and support equipment needed for the preparation of batters, doughs, and toppings. Second, the dough-holding and proofing station is a passive area where doughs are held, generally under controlled temperatures, while they await the rolling and forming process. Third, in the dough-rolling and forming station, bread or pastry is rolled or formed as needed, sometimes by mechanized devices and sometimes manually. Fourth, cooking and subsequent cooling of baked goods takes place in the baking station. The bakery section may also include a finishing and decoration station, depending upon the volume and type of products being prepared.

MIXER STATION OPTIONS

Generally mixing is done mechanically. In a low-volume operation, however, this process may be done manually. Floor-model mixers are appropriate for heavy dough products, and table-model mixers are appropriate for pastry and batter products or small batches of bread doughs. In some cases, a vertical cutter-mixer may be used for mixing.

As part of the mixer station, storage of and ready access to raw materials is essential. Materials may be stored in rolling storage bins or refrigerated storage when necessary. Storage for mixer attachments and spices is also important and oftentimes integrated into a baker's work table, which is an essential part of this station.

DOUGH-HOLDING AND PROOFING STATION OPTIONS

Yeast-raised product generally goes through two proofing steps. The first step is a bulk proofing of dough as it comes from the mixing station. A second proofing is required after the dough goes through the forming station. Although dough can rise at ambient room temperatures, the additional heat and moisture in a proof box speeds and improves the process. After pie pastry or puff pastry is mixed, it is generally held in refrigerated storage to improve workability. In the case of batter products, holding or proofing is not necessary.

DOUGH-ROLLING AND FORMING STATION OPTIONS

Puff pastry dough goes through several rolling and folding steps, which are separated by time periods in a refrigerator. Rolling equipment is frequently used for pizza dough and pie pastries in large operations. Dough divider-shapers are frequently used in this station when volume warrants their purchase. Hand-operated dividers are relatively inexpensive and worth the investment when even a few dozen rolls per day are baked.

BAKING STATION OPTIONS

Designers should consider the various uses of the bakeshop ovens before deciding on equipment specifications. If the bakeshop will be used in the early hours of the day for the preparation and baking of breads and pastries and during the afternoon and evening for banquet preparation, then multipurpose ovens are needed. Roasting ovens—ovens with greater height in the oven cavity—are similar to bake ovens yet can hold large top rounds and other wholesale cuts of meat with ease. Another option is the convection oven, which is quite effective for baking. Although there is additional shrink loss, it can also be used for banquet roasting. Another alternative is the cavity oven. The standard cavity oven, which is placed under a range top, is acceptable for roasting but generally is not used for baking. However, the rotary oven, which holds foods on arms that rotate like a Ferris wheel inside the oven cavity, is sometimes used as a bake or roast oven in large-volume operations. A recent entry to the oven market is the combination oven, a dry convection oven and convection steamer in one unit. As a baking oven for pastry, this oven functions in the same way as a standard convection oven. On the oven mode with steam turned on, the oven is perfectly suited to baking crusty French bread.

If the space is to be a dedicated bakeshop, then the best choice is a deck oven, with steam injection capabilities for times when crusty breads are baked. No matter what oven type, sufficient rack space is needed to cool baked goods and to hold them for service.

In bakeshops where special confections and toppings are made, additional stations are required. A candy station, for example, needs a range top and in some cases a trunnion kettle. Designers need to know early in the planning phase if these specialty items are going to be offered on the menu.

Banquet

A banquet section is required only in a restaurant in which banquet service cannot be accomplished from other production stations. Meal preparation for small private parties, for instance, does not require a separate banquet station. However, when banquet business typically exceeds by 25 percent or more the ongoing volume of the restaurant, then designing a separate banquet section in the kitchen makes sense.

Steam equipment for banquets consists of large steam-jacketed kettles—over ten gallons—for soup, sauces, and stewed items, plus large-volume, low-pressure steamers. As with the a la carte section, the steam equipment can use central steam or be self-contained. Due to the large volume of food cooked in this area, floor drainage is necessary for the disposal of waste water. This can be accomplished through the installation of a floor grate and drain that runs the entire length of this section or by a recessed floor with drain holes.

One or more tilting braising pans can be helpful in large banquet operations. The flexibility of these pieces of equipment makes them ideally suited for numerous types of preparations, a requirement oftentimes placed on the banquet production department. As with the steam equipment, floor drainage is necessary for cleaning. Therefore, braising pans should be located close to the steam equipment.

The roasting station in many operations is one and the same with the bakeshop. The ovens selected for most banquet operations should be capable of roasting or baking a wide range of products. Oftentimes, a mix of ovens—deck and convection—are chosen to increase flexibility.

Banquet food can often be held in the same equipment that is used for proofing breads. In some cases, special equipment is needed to hold plated dinners for delivery to locations that are remote from the kitchen.

A plating station or area is essential for quick service to a large banquet. It can consist of a simple countertop or, in operations serving many banquets, a special banquet-plating cart. If plating and holding equipment is purchased for banquet service, the pieces should be as portable as possible. Portability allows the equipment to be removed from the plating area when not needed, to improve traffic flow in the kitchen.

Specialty Sections

Sometimes specialty sections must be incorporated into the design of a kitchen. Fabrication sections for meat, poultry, or seafood preparation may be required in certain designs. In others, parts of the production kitchen are moved within view of the guest. All specialty sections should be identified during the initial planning phases of a project because they mandate special treatments.

DINING ROOM SUPPORT AREAS

This section deals with three support areas that are primarily responsible for bridging the gap between the back and front of the house: display kitchens, service stations, and warewashing areas. Although the display kitchen is actually an extension of the back of the house, its design has a considerable impact on the ambiance and operation of the front of the house. Server stations situated in the dining areas enable the wait staff to take care of tabletop needs without traveling back and forth from the kitchen. Warewashing, which in a loose definition incorporates pot washing, is physically placed in the back of the house but greatly influences the efficient operation of the front of the house.

Display Kitchen

Today the display kitchen has become the hallmark of many fine restaurants and gathering places. The significance of display kitchens is that the functioning of the kitchen is within view of the customer. In some cases, all of the preparation is done where the customers can see it. At the other extreme, all of the prepreparation and par cooking is done in the back kitchen and the display kitchen becomes nothing more than a finishing station.

The designers of any type of display kitchen must consider the sight lines from the customer's vantage point (fig. 4-11). In restaurants where the guests have a full view of the entire display kitchen, every item must be well placed and kept very well ordered. In restaurants where diners have only a partial view of the display kitchen, the hidden areas, such as the undercounter spaces on the front line, need not be kept in perfect order. From a design perspective, the full-view kitchen should use undercounter shelving with cabinet doors, but open shelving would be fine for the partial-view kitchen.

All display kitchens benefit from a clean, well-organized appearance. In an enclosed kitchen, many indiscretions can be overlooked, but when a guest sees a roast chicken fall to the floor in a display kitchen, putting it back in service is not so easy. The area needs an adequate supply of hand- and tool-washing sinks to keep it spotless. Although much of the preparatory work is accomplished in the back-of-the-house prep section, last-minute manipulations always require cleaning, be it a roast tenderloin that is carved and sauced as ordered or the occasional spill from an overfilled soup bowl.

PRIMARY PRODUCTION DISPLAY KITCHEN

Traditional American diners and the primary production display kitchen go together like ice cream and pie. The short-order cook stands

4-11. The display kitchen at Scoozi, Chicago, designed by Aumiller Youngquist Architects, is a working kitchen used for pizza preparation. Some guests enjoy watching the pizza preparation process close-up. (Joseph Durocher photo)

with his back to a counter—flipping eggs and flapjacks, toasting bread, frying potatoes, and making sandwiches—all the while watching over the meatloaf baking in the oven below the range top that holds a pot of boiling potatoes. At breakfast and other meals, customers sit on counter stools to order and eat their food and to chat with the short-order cook, in much the same way as people talk to the bartender before going home at night.

With the advent of fast food operations, the production display kitchen expanded into another type of restaurant. In fast food operations the QSC—quality, service, cleanliness—mandate was forced by display kitchens. When the kitchen is in full view of the customers, production and service workers are compelled to keep the kitchen area clean and to handle food products properly.

Until the 1980s, however, when consumer concern and awareness of food mushroomed into a national obsession, production display kitchens were not deemed appropriate for serious restaurants. Not so long ago, the worst seat in the house was next to the swinging doors that led to the kitchen. A view inside would have been considered less than elegant.

Today, the production display kitchen is an integral part of many types of restaurants. In cafeteria-style steak houses, diners order their steak and watch it cook while they select the accompaniments for their meal. In many pizza parlors, customers are entertained by the dough twirling pizza cook as he creates their pizza. In numerous upscale tableservice restaurants, customers are paraded past the open kitchen where they can preview the type of food they will be ordering and then catch glimpses of the ongoing cooking as they wait for their meal.

In fact, the primary production display kitchen has become popular in all sorts of establishments, and the best seat in the house has become one that affords patrons a good view of the chefs at work (fig. 4-12). In gourmet establishments, gleaming copper pots and colorful tiled walls frame display kitchens through open or glass windows. In noncommercial cafeterias, people would rather wait in line at the short-order station to watch their burgers and sandwiches grilled and sliced to order than save time

4-12. *At Kuleto's, San Francisco, designed by Pat Kuleto Consulting and Design, the entire finishing kitchen is on display to the guests, including the wood-fired charbroiler and rotisserie.*
(Joseph Durocher photo)

by picking up batch-processed, preprepared food.

There is really no common formula for figuring out which food items, equipment, or even type of restaurant benefits from a production display kitchen. In each kind of restaurant, a feeling of involvement and intimacy with the kitchen is created for the customer. In the most successful display kitchens, a feeling of theatrical performance enthralls the customer.

To be most effective, nearly all of the prepreparation should be completed away from the display kitchen. Such operations as chopping, slicing, and pounding need to be done out of sight of the diners. The preprepared raw materials are then assembled for cooking in view of the customer. As with any a la carte range in the back of the house, efficient prepreparation is the key to success. For example, a well-designed pizza display kitchen requires rolling and turning the pizza, covering it with sauce and toppings, and slipping it into the oven. Thirty to sixty seconds are needed to assemble the product and then twelve to fifteen minutes to bake it. In the case of a sandwich station on a cafeteria line, when all the ingredients are ready for use, thirty seconds or less is required to assemble condiments and fillings on the chosen bread.

Backup raw materials must be close at hand for a production display kitchen to work effectively. Pass-through refrigerators from the prepreparation kitchen and undercounter refrigeration facilitate an efficient flow from back to front of the house. Under ideal conditions, each display kitchen has its own refrigeration and other storage areas.

Cleanliness is of vital concern in a production display kitchen. Clean-looking employees, equipment, walls, and floors are all important. Easily cleaned surfaces and convenient waste disposal areas help to maintain cleanliness, as does upgraded ventilation to minimize grease buildup and carry-over of odors to the dining room.

Stainless steel has been the preferred material in back-of-the-house kitchens, but display kitchens sport tile, plastic laminates, and other less institutional-looking materials to effect a more interesting environment. The appearance of the cooking equipment is another concern.

A stainless steel top for the griddle gives a clean look when eggs are cooked in front of the guest. Compact, tabletop, automatic lift fryers reflect a simplicity of design that is in keeping with display cooking, in contrast with the heavy-gauge, black-enameled surfaces of an open-top range with oven. When tabletop equipment is used, the undercounter area can be filled with refrigerated storage space.

Another type of equipment worth noting is the rotisserie. Here, cuts of meat are roasted on what is technically a vertical broiler unit. The pieces of meat revolve on a skewer in front of the heat source, thus ensuring even cooking and browning and a well-textured surface. The most elaborate of these rotisserie units are fitted with black iron, brass, and stainless steel and actually become a décor element. Some units are fired with hardwood charcoal. Unlike its companion units fueled with easy-to-adjust gas or electric burners, the charcoal units require constant attention in order to keep the temperature regulated.

A consideration with all rotisserie units is the amount of heat they give off. In New York City's Amsterdam restaurant, rotisseries roast all meat in a display kitchen that is visible from every part of the dining room. However, the units are sectioned off by see-through barriers that help block heat transmission. Patrons, therefore, can enjoy the view without sweating through their meals.

FINISHING AREA DISPLAY KITCHEN

When a display kitchen is used as a finishing kitchen, it functions like a cafeteria line when the line personnel plate up previously prepared foods. This same technique may be used in a tableservice restaurant but with an extra bit of flair. For example, imagine that the waiter orders sole mornay through the open window of a finishing area display kitchen. What patrons see is the previously poached sole (which is also used for the sole diablo) portioned into a casserole dish, then covered with mornay sauce, placed under a cheese melter for a few moments, removed, garnished with previously chopped parsley and a wedge of lemon, and set on an underliner. The total time required for assembly is less than thirty seconds. The time from placing the order to its being ready for pickup is less than five minutes. Although no real cooking takes place in the display kitchen, guests have the perception that their food is being cooked right in front of them.

The finishing kitchen may also make use of microwave ovens or compact tabletop convection ovens. The microwave oven can be used successfully in many different types of display kitchens. It is excellent when coupled with a service system in which foods are held hot, assembled, and then placed in the microwave to bring them up to serving temperatures. For example, a milk-based chowder may be held at lower than serving temperatures to keep it from breaking. When ordered, it is portioned into a soupbowl and then brought to serving temperature in a matter of moments in the microwave. The technique is also used quite successfully in Mexican restaurants, where ingredients for tacos and other items are held hot, assembled, and then heated in the microwave oven for service. However, not every item is suited to microwave heating, and attention must be given to the menu before this type of oven is specified.

The tabletop convection oven can be used effectively for heating casserole items that are held cold for service. In some operations that have gone to a cook-chill system, the contents of sealed pouches holding the special of the day are slipped into a serving dish and rethermalized —literally reheated—in a convection oven or in some cases a microwave oven.

SERVICE-ONLY DISPLAY KITCHEN

Another type of display kitchen is the service-only display kitchen. This type of kitchen is nothing more than a plating area. In some cases it is actually a server plating area or service buffet. As with the other two types of display kitchens, it assists servers in speeding food to their waiting guests.

In many instances, certain elements of the meal come from a service display kitchen and other elements come from a back-of-the-house kitchen. Soups and preplated appetizer items are often served up from the display kitchen. An antipasto bar can be displayed for guest viewing but for server access. The food setup in a tapas bar, where items are displayed and subsequently portioned by the service staff, is another example of a service display kitchen. This type of display kitchen has less drama, but the guests still benefit from a feeling of involvement, and the servers are helped in the performance of their duties.

TAKE-OUT DISPLAY KITCHEN

Today the take-out (and take-home) market can generate significant incremental sales for the restaurant. Display kitchens are a tremendous merchandising aid to encourage take-out business. Diners are intrigued by seeing items prepared before them as well as foods on display in refrigerated cases. When they decide to order food for take-out, patrons should be able to purchase fully prepared fare that is properly packaged for off-premise consumption.

To effectively capture the take-out market, care must be exercised in the selection and placement of equipment in the display kitchen. In standard restaurant layouts, the back-of-the-house kitchen is oftentimes placed in the rear of the space, with the display kitchen located between the prep kitchen and the dining room. When the display kitchen is used to service carry-out orders as well as the dining room, it should be situated in a location convenient for both purposes. But most importantly, the display kitchen must be placed so that take-out patrons do not track through the dining room. The ideal floor plan allows the display kitchen to service the dining room, act as a merchandising area for carry-out food, and be close enough to the bar so that while take-out fare is being prepared, incremental drink sales can be realized.

Planning for carry-out service must be integrated into the initial design process to ensure that adequate storage space for take-out containers is included in the design. Payment for carry-out items should also be considered when planning the design, and the production staff should not be required to handle money. Cashier stations, for example, can be positioned so that the dining room cashier also functions as an order taker and cashier for take-out.

Service Stations

Service stations, also referred to as server stations or wait stations, are often viewed by designers as a necessary evil in the dining room. They are necessary because they enable wait-people to provide efficient service, but evil because they have no inherent esthetic appeal and can be an ugly blot on an otherwise "pure" design. However, service stations need not be intrusive obstructions in the dining room if they are carefully conceived and developed in the early stages of the design process (fig. 4-13).

Service stations should be designed as functional appendages of the back of the house. No matter where they are placed, they must be well stocked with all of the backup supplies needed to service the dining room. In tableservice restaurants, that may include fifty or sixty backup or reset items. In a fast food operation the service station may include nothing more than a bottle of spray cleaner, toweling, and extra trash bags.

The esthetic design of service stations

should be well integrated with the front-of-the-house design. For example, the service station may be a finely crafted piece of furniture that blends well with the overall décor and helps to divide the bar area from the dining area. In New York's Nishi Noho (discussed in chapter 5) a large structural element in the center of the room serves as a comprehensive service station and as an architectural focal point. Inside this station, backup linen and tableware, along with water and hot beverages, are readily available to the servers. In Aurora (chapter 6), the service station is integrated into the service pickup area immediately adjacent to the kitchen, with only minimal supplies of tabletop items on gueridons located in the dining room. Common to these two restaurants are service stations that effectively support front-of-the-house functions, yet do not detract from the overall design scheme.

4-13. *This maitre d' stand and service station at Rosalie's, San Francisco, is well integrated with the decor. Unlike many service stations, however, it does not hold back-up supplies to reset tables.*
(Joseph Durocher photo)

On the contrary, they sometimes become integral components of the architectural idea.

The purpose of the service station should be to improve the speed and efficiency of service. This is particularly important in large operations where servers must travel long distances from the kitchen, and in operations where several small dining rooms are serviced from one central kitchen. There are no set rules for what should be incorporated into a service station: The station merely needs to improve speed and efficiency of service, plus function as a backup to assist in the quick resetting of tables during peak demand periods. In some tableservice restaurants, service stations incorporate an ice bin, water station, coffee and tea burners, roll warmer, and all of the elements required to reset tables and hold dirty tableware and linen.

The design of any station should rely on management philosophy, the menu, and the type of service. If standard operating procedure after seating a guest is to ice a glass, fill it with water, present warm rolls, and then finish the meal with a bottomless cup of coffee, then a well-equipped service station is absolutely essential.

Warewashing

As mentioned in chapter 1, the placement of the warewashing equipment can significantly affect the efficiency of a restaurant. Placement is simple in a single dining room restaurant: just as the server enters the kitchen. When operations have multiple points of service with a central warewashing station, however, the location of warewashing equipment is a trickier question.

In a complex operation, the placement of warewashing is affected by the number of trips and the volume of tableware brought to the warewashing station. Consider a hotel where banquets are served from one side of the kitchen and the dining room is served from the other side. Dishes are hand-carried to and from the dining room. However, service to and from banquet areas is accomplished by carrying dishes on sheet pans that are set on tray stands. The sheet pans are then removed to the service corridor and placed on mobile racks that are wheeled to the dish area. In this case, although the greater volume of dishes comes from the banquet area, warewashing should be located closest to the dining room because the wait staff makes more frequent trips to and from the dining room service areas. If the use of bus buckets is integrated into dining room service (thus limiting server time running back and forth from dining room to warewashing), then the location of the warewashing system could change. Considering very specific operational systems is essential when making decisions about the location of warewashing.

Placement of warewashing in other than tableservice restaurants is also important. To be most effective, the warewashing in a cafeteria should be located somewhere near the exit from the cafeteria. This may necessitate separating the warewashing section from the kitchen. The alternative may be to install a costly conveyor system or to use mobile carts where users deposit their trays, with filled carts transported to the warewashing facility.

When planning a bar operation, glasswashing is particularly important. Consideration must be given to the noise and space required for an undercounter glasswasher, versus a hand-washing system, versus transporting the glasses to and from a remote warewashing facility.

Closely aligned with the warewashing area is the pot-washing station. Although sometimes the pot-washing station is separated from the dish machine, most operations keep the two areas together because of cross-over staffing between the two stations. Further, in large operations with a sanitation supervisor, supervising the staff is easier when the stations are closely linked. Another reason for placing the two operations together is that in some locales the pots must be sterilized and the dish machine is the best place to accomplish this function. In certain situations the pot-washing process is mechanized through the installation of a motor-driven device that grinds the dirt off the pots. In other operations in which the volume of pots and pans is substantial, a pot-washing machine may be installed along with the standard three-compartment sink required by most local boards of health.

Environmental Conditions

The lighting, ventilation, spacing of equipment, types of surfaces, and sound levels all have an impact on the effectiveness of production staff in the kitchen. These environmental factors can also affect employee turnover rates, which in turn affect the bottom line.

VENTILATION

The ventilation system is composed of exhaust and make-up air. Exhaust air is generally removed from those portions of the kitchen where smoke, heat, and steam are created. Building codes in most communities require that ventilation hoods be installed over all heat-producing equipment. Further, the codes require that fire-detection and -extinguishing systems also be installed as part of the ventilation system.

The amount of air that is removed from the kitchen affects the comfort level of the employees. However, for every cubic foot of air removed through the hoods, make-up air must be provided. Make-up air can come from ducting that dumps treated air into the kitchen, the dining room, or both areas. A negative pressure should always be maintained in the kitchen (more air drawn out of the kitchen than is being supplied by make-up air ducts in the kitchen) to ensure that smoke and grease are kept from the dining room.

There are two schools of thought about adding make-up air to a kitchen. The first is to add the air evenly throughout the entire kitchen. The second is to add the air where it is most needed. Fresh air is dumped near the dish machine, in the fabrication area, over the bakeshop, or in other areas where heat builds up. In certain newer hood systems some of the make-up air is added right at the face of the hood. This limits the amount of air that is drawn across the vertical face (fig. 4-14) of the hood. A flow of air that becomes too strong is discomforting to the cooks. In any event, a minimum of conditioned air should be drawn out of the dining room. Dining room air is filtered, heated, or cooled and therefore very costly if too much is exhausted through the kitchen exhaust system.

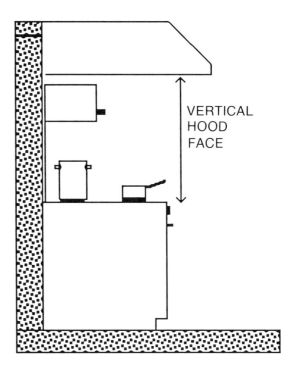

4-14. *Exhaust air must pass across the vertical hood face at sufficient velocity to trap smoke, heat, and airborne grease (Joseph Durocher drawing).*

LIGHTING

Direct lighting in the back of the house is very desirable but must be carefully engineered. Although sufficient light is needed to differentiate between a piece of flank steak and a piece of skirt steak, too much light can create glare that ultimately leads to eyestrain. When properly angled, however, direct task lighting is practical and energy-efficient.

To ensure that dinner plates look their best, using incandescent lamps in the food production area can be very helpful. The kitchen at New York's Le Bernardin (discussed in chapter 5) is lit solely by incandescent lamps. The result is that the food is viewed under the same type of light by the chef as by the diners. Historically, mood lighting was not important in most kitchens, but its role in display kitchens is very important. Theatrical spotlights, for example, are used to highlight the work surfaces in the display kitchen of the Rattlesnake Club Grill in Denver, which was mentioned earlier. Here, the lighting scheme provides adequate illumination for the cooks and a focal point for guests to view their meals being prepared.

ACOUSTICS

Kitchens can be very noisy places to work. Too much noise can cause discomfort and create unsafe working conditions, and high noise levels may obscure communications between production and service staff. Ultimately, this unfortunate process leads to guest dissatisfaction.

Noise can be controlled through the careful selection and placement of noise-producing equipment, as well as the installation of acoustic treatments. If a dish machine is placed, for operational reasons, near the entry of the kitchen, then acoustic controls are needed to prevent the carry-over of sound into the dining room. Acoustic ceiling tiles are commonly specified in kitchens. However, sound-absorbing insulation in the wall between the dish area and the dining room may also be called for. To limit the sound of the dish machine from traveling to the rest of the kitchen, a wall separating the dish area from the remaining back of the house can be helpful.

SUMMARY

An operational and managerial understanding of all kitchen requirements is essential before a successful design can be implemented. Perhaps management should draw up a wish list of desired features and equipment. In any case, the kitchen designer ought to ask many specific questions regarding back-of-the-house procedures. Will management serve frozen green beans, or will storage and processing space be needed for fresh beans? Will pies and cakes arrive from the local bakery, will frozen pies have to be baked off, or will raw ingredients have to be stored in order to bake breads and pastries from scratch? The answer to these and countless other questions all markedly affect the space and equipment needs of a restaurant kitchen.

5

DESIGN APPLICATIONS: MINI CASE SOLUTIONS

In previous chapters, the basic principles of front- and back-of-the-house design were discussed. Once these are understood, then developing individual solutions for special problems becomes possible. This chapter presents a selection of interesting design solutions that have been included in some of today's restaurants.

They have been culled from hundreds of such solutions to demonstrate the diversity of problem solving involved with restaurant design. However, the design of a restaurant does not begin with the reinvention of the wheel. Good design follows basic principles, and good designers and restaurateurs learn from experience.

UPDATING THE HOTEL RESTAURANT

AMERICUS   Sheraton Washington Hotel, Washington, D.C.

Designer Brad Elias of the New York–based Hochheiser-Elias Design Group was faced with a typical hotel restaurant design problem: The space looked beautiful but didn't sell. The Americus restaurant was one of just two eating establishments in the 1,200-room Sheraton Washington, and its upscale appearance supported its role as the hotel's signature restaurant. Yet its formal design, with a long entry corridor, formidable maitre d' stand, secluded cocktail lounge, and cold marble esthetic, was not attracting enough business. It was "a setting that called for evening gowns and tuxedos," explained Elias, and it was turning off the many hotel guests who wanted a less formal place to relax and socialize after spending long days in meeting rooms.

The old floor plan is illustrated in figure 5-1. On the left-hand side, a long, enclosed, bottleneck corridor led to a formal marble reception area and maitre d' station. Patrons had to walk 20 yards through this corridor, climb two steps to the reception area, and then go

another 5 yards past 6-foot-high partitions that blocked the view of seated diners before they reached the maitre d'. A grand piano located at the end of the entry corridor was audible in the dining room but contributed very little to the enjoyment of drinkers, because the small, secluded bar was stuffed into a back corner of the restaurant. The outer wall of the restaurant that ran along the atrium consisted of a decorative, two-story chrome cage that further diminished the restaurant's eye appeal and did nothing to baffle noise from the meeting room floor below.

Elias recommended a redesign of the entire area. His new design was based in part on trends in the restaurant marketplace—specifically the "craze for grazing, excitement and noise"—and in part on the fact that this was a convention hotel with a lot of guests who wanted to socialize and had no place to go except Americus. In design terms, this translates into lightening up the décor as well as the menu and using popular materials such as wood, tile, brass, and neon.

The designer's philosophy was that "if the

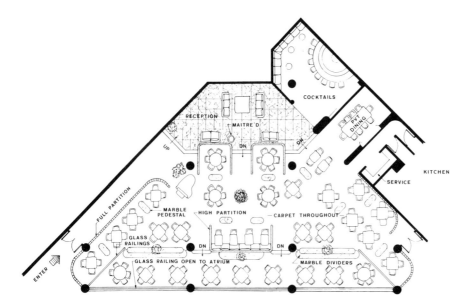

5-1. *The existing floor plan of Americus restaurant before renovation illustrates the formal environment. Note the bar tucked into the far corner of the room (Brad Elias, Hochheiser/Elias Design Group drawing).*

restaurant is positioned to attract the local market, then it will attract the hotel guest as well. Our goal was to achieve a broader appeal that could conceivably help support a profitable operation."

The solution shown in figure 5-2 fits within the physical dimensions of the original restaurant. However, it exhibits a spatial flow typical of popular free-standing restaurants. The bar area, which sets the tone for the experience, was moved from the back of the operation to a prominent position at the entryway. The bar increased in size as well, from fourteen to forty-seven seats. This new, highly visible area helps to pull guests out of the lobby and adds significant revenue to the hotel. The grand piano was also moved to a position within the bar and lounge to add audio excitement to the bar experience, and its carry-over sound reaches out into the lobby to attract guests into the restaurant.

In general, the removal of barriers to sights and sounds throughout the restaurant was crucial to the success of the design. The former six-foot-high partitions were replaced with low mahogany and lacquer panels capped in brass that allow diners a modicum of privacy but prevent total isolation. The cage separating the restaurant from the atrium was replaced with panels of chrome, brass, and glass.

Because sound plays such an important role in the success of today's bars, hardwood floors and tiles replaced carpeting in Americus's bar area. To boost food sales at the bar, a raw bar and oyster stew station were added and placed right in the front of the area for visual appeal. Food served at the bar counter proved to be a popular option for single diners.

In the dining area, twenty-eight seats and two additional service stations were added (the old design had only one service station). Smaller tables pushed closer together create a sense of vitality that was previously missing and help to foster the see-and-be-seen ethic of popular free-standing restaurants. New materials such as mahogany, black lacquer, brass, etched glass, and richly colored fabric animate the formerly flat room. Platform seating levels and custom-designed, rose tortoise glass light trees contribute dimension and sparkle.

In summary, Americus was redesigned into a more casual, comfortable, yet still elegant environment with an active bar area. It reflects Elias's philosophy of marketing by design, which grew from his dual education and experience in both the marketing and interior design professions. At Americus, according to the designer, this philosophy resulted in a threefold increase in business for the restaurant.

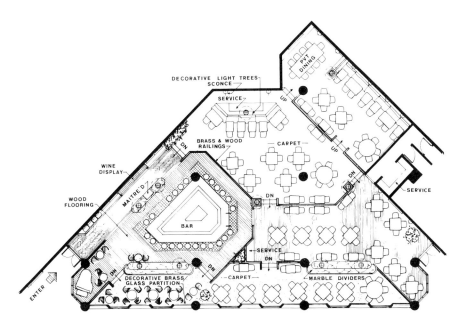

5-2. *The revised floor plan of Americus restaurant after renovation shows the new spatial arrangements, including a much larger bar located just inside the entryway (Brad Elias, Hochheiser/Elias Design Group drawing).*

POPULAR PLACE TAKE II

THE BREAKAWAY Fairfield, CT

New York–based architect David Spiker helped create a restaurant success in 1980 and was called upon in 1984 to work some magic again. His original renovation of The Breakaway, a structural makeover that involved $65,000 worth of new construction, had transformed a run-down roadhouse into a successful sandwich shop. The design worked exceedingly well but four years of wear and tear on the inexpensive sheetrock, wood, and paint surfaces had taken its toll. The assignment for what Spiker calls "redo II," involved modifying the existing design to make it more durable and more upscale. In addition, the redesign was supposed to complement an expanded and upgraded menu.

The Breakaway's new menu offers full meal service, and management felt that patrons' expanded gustatory expectations called for a more refined design than Spiker had provided in the funky redo I. Redo II was a decorative, not a spatial renovation (fig. 5-3), achieved at a cost of $25,000 for construction and $10,000 for furnishings. Spiker used gypsum board, wood trim, plastic laminate, studded rubber tile, and paint to give the restaurant "a new set of clothes."

So the restaurant closed for a week, and off came the sixteen shades of paint that had helped create a playful ambiance in redo I. A much simpler palette graces redo II: Pale gray walls with black enamel trim provide a quiet backdrop for deep blue, green, and red accents. The oversized red-and-gray checkerboard rubber floor tiles help absorb noise, as does the heavily padded, navy pin-striped chair and banquette fabric. Highly graphic artwork and mirrors detailed in a gridlike pattern add color and depth to the newly sophisticated space.

5-3. *Breakaway's new materials and finishes were chosen to match the upscale market and menu. (Peter Paige photo)*

BRINGING THE ROOF DOWN

ALO ALO   New York, NY

Bringing the roof down is exactly what designer Adam Tihany had in mind when he designed this stylized stage set. Faced with a room that had floor space for ninety-five diners, Tihany was charged with the creation of an intimate, café-style restaurant. Because the space had 40-foot-high ceilings, the designer's first idea was to build a mezzanine, thus providing extra seating and helping to achieve a cozy cafe atmosphere with lower ceilings. This solution, however, was prohibited by New York City building codes.

Instead, Tihany creatively addressed the spatial problem by "lowering" the ceiling with custom-designed light fixtures. The large pink discs with inverted pyramid shades resemble flying saucers, and they give the feeling of a lower ceiling without affecting the kinesthetic sensation of height that enhances this design (fig. 5-4).

The whimsical attitude of the light fixtures is reinforced with papier-mâché restaurant caricatures designed by artist Stephan Hansen. Along with the light fixtures, they provide interesting visual focal points in this chic Italian bistro.

Tihany not only used lighting to lower the ceiling height but also turned a potential liability into a functional advantage by building a "wine cellar in the sky" that is accessed by a spiral staircase. Situated on the north wall of the restaurant, well above eye level, this novel application became a great merchandising tool to show off the owners' wine collection. It also utilized what would have been nonfunctioning space at ceiling level.

The designer was challenged by other spatial considerations as well. Sitting at the base of a new high-rise building, the restaurant space "was basically a glass box with a curved corner," according to Tihany. He located the bar area just inside the glass-fronted entryway, where it provides an excellent venue from which window-shoppers can check out the scene before entering the restaurant.

The design of the glass racks above the front bar illustrates an attention to detail that makes a big difference to the functioning of the bar area. This placement eliminated the need for a true back bar, which would have limited the movements of the bartenders in a very small space. Unlike the configuration of many bars, where glassware hung over guests is stained with cigarette smoke that has lodged in their inverted bowls, Alo Alo bartenders hang their glasses above a protective Plexiglas shelf that prevents the glassware from getting smoked.

5-4. *The ceiling heights at Alo Alo were scaled down with saucer-shaped hanging light fixtures that enhance the restaurant's whimsical attitude.* (Peter Paige photo)

BRAND SPANKING OLD

CONNIE'S PIZZA   Chicago, IL

Chicagoans have enjoyed Connie's Pizza since the early 1960s. By the mid-1980s, the restaurant was packing in customers every night, and the dozens of delivery trucks that whisked steaming-hot pizzas to local residences couldn't keep up with the orders. When the owners decided to open a much larger restaurant at a new site, they charged Donahue Designs with creating a design that would keep the old customers, appeal to new customers, and support the burgeoning home-delivery business.

Senior project designer Robert Donahue helped the owners search for a site close to the original store in the deteriorated warehouse district on Chicago's South Side. They settled on a 2½-acre site that was strewn with scrap metal and old buildings and constructed a new Connie's there that is eight times larger than its predecessor. Opened in 1986, it houses a 300-seat restaurant, a take-out section, a drive-through, and a delivery operation, and it blends so well with its gritty surroundings that it could play

one of Al Capone's storehouses in "The Untouchables" (fig. 5-5). The building is entirely new construction carefully detailed to duplicate a turn-of-the-century warehouse: A 28-foot ceiling with exposed joists and beams, exposed brickwork, and a wooden floor with cork chips embedded between the planks are just a few examples of the attention to "historic" detail.

In fact, the restaurant's facade appears and feels so authentic that building inspectors "were confused by the apparent adaptive re-use of buildings they couldn't remember previously seeing," said Robert Donahue. Yet the entire structure was made from new materials, save for a few barrels, hinges, scales, and a single steel truss that was woven into the roof structure.

Connie's several dining areas sit on different levels and comprise 7,800 square feet of the total 15,000-square-foot building. The visual effect of the front of the house evokes a period piece without kitsch. Guests walk onto the "loading dock" and then through the large

5-5. *The exterior of Connie's looks so original that building inspectors thought it was a restoration.*
(Steinkamp/Ballogg photo)

5-6. *The interior of Connie's was carefully designed to replicate a classic Chicago South Side warehouse.*
(Steinkamp/Ballogg photo)

wooden "warehouse doors." They move past the "foreman's office," marked by a vintage time clock, which is actually a private dining room that sits ten people at a round mahogany table "reminiscent of the days of bosses and back-room deals," described Donahue. Restaurant patrons continue on to the waiting room where they sit on sacks of "flour" loaded onto "pallets" if they have to wait for a table. As guests progress through the space, they are led into one of five dining areas: the "central clearing house," "lower receiving area," "wine room," "olive room," and "cold storage vaults."

An important difference between this re-creation and some other pseudo-historic restaurants is the exceptional workmanship of old-world craftsman Tony Locania. Although he constantly reminded construction management that he was working too hard, Locania frequently suggested ideas that improved the authenticity of the extensive masonry work found throughout the space.

Furniture design also evidences a rare attention to detail that helps to foster Connie's historic flavor. Donahue and his team created a chair that is a composite of three antique barrister chairs; to perfect it for today's fussy customers, they had people of every shape and size test models for comfort before deciding on the final design. Although the turnaround time at Connie's is relatively short, Donahue still felt that comfortable chairs were important. The chairs sit at oak tavern tables with brass toes and baked-enamel tops bordered in ebony, satin-wood, and mahogany inlay. Center-cut hardwood end grain flooring was used throughout the restaurant, just as it is still used in warehouses today (fig. 5-6).

Despite the grand scale of this pizza factory, the architecture of the space does not feel overwhelming. Few customers know that well over a thousand deep-dish pizzas are created each day in this brand spanking old restaurant.

CUISINE SOUS CLOS

HEATHMAN RESTAURANT   Heathman Hotel, Portland, OR

Jerry Marlow, one of the owners of the art deco Heathman Hotel, aspired for the renovated hotel to be the best little hotel in town, . . . one that shoots for the top of the market." With that mandate, Carter Case Architects and interior designer Andrew Delfino set out to create a hotel restaurant that would appeal to diverse markets: business travelers during the week and local clients on weekends. They also wanted an upscale ambiance that matched the formality of the 160-room hotel above. "The challenge," said architect Carter Case, "was to create a space that would feel timeless and sophisticated, and have high street visibility." Case therefore utilized classic materials such as teak, marble, granite, and stainless steel and an illumination plan that created "indirect layers of lighting" to evoke a quietly elegant atmosphere.

One of the important solutions in the space was the creative use of plate glass to allow a feeling of openness (fig. 5-7) yet afford a level of intimacy that befits the type of restaurant. Glass dividers, placed along the backs and sides of banquettes, help to increase the feeling of privacy. Most significant, however, was the installation of a plate glass window wall between the display kitchen and the dining room. Diners benefit from the visual experience of viewing the kitchen while the sounds and smells of the kitchen are kept behind glass. The formal setting of red marble, highly polished wood, beige travertine, and other rich finishes is enlivened but not bothered by the casual feeling of an open kitchen.

The window wall between kitchen and diners also minimizes the problems of balancing ventilation between back and front of the house, always a challenge with display kitchens. Unlike kitchens left completely open to the dining room, the Heathman display kitchen does not have to draw off conditioned air from the front of the house, which is ultimately an energy savings. In essence, it provides a visual treat without many of the accompanying operational headaches common to open display kitchens.

5-7. *The glass-enclosed open kitchen of the Heathman Hotel Restaurant affords diners an exciting view yet minimizes ventilation problems common to open kitchens.*
(Steven Cridland photo)

HOTEL FAST FOOD

LE CAFE   Hyatt Regency, New Orleans, LA

The prototypical hotel coffee shop, with its plastic booths and bright-orange-and-green color scheme, has disappeared from all but the most stalwart properties. In its place, cafes of every sort—from pricey, elegantly designed establishments serving gourmet power breakfasts to fern-filled overpriced eateries serving nothing more imaginative than frozen hash browns—have sprung up in hotels across the country.

Yet hotel guests still need a moderately priced eatery that provides them with a quick bite to eat. Given an ever-growing labor shortage, moreover, hotel management likes customers to do some of the work.

Le Cafe (fig. 5-8) provides a design and operational solution that may signal a new direction for some hotel eateries of the future.

Chicago-based Banks/Eakin Architects devised Le Cafe as an eighty-eight-seat, self-serve deli cafe where diners can order at the sandwich-beverage station and then take their food to a cafelike setting located in a former disco. The architects incorporated some cues from fast feeders in that they kept light levels high and specified long-legged, high-backed, bentwood cafe chairs that keep diners from lingering over their meals (regardless of their padded seats.) In addition, Le Cafe operates like a fast food eatery in that diners carry their own orders to the table. The lighting, use of mirrors, and aqua, white, and red color scheme help to brighten a formerly dark room. This was an inexpensive transformation of a dated space into a revenue-producing foodservice area.

5-8. *Le Cafe provides hotel guests with a self-serve, fast alternative to the traditional coffee shop.*
(Orlando Cabanban photo)

LANDLOCKED LUXURY LINER

SEAFOOD SHANTY Langhorne, PA

The Langhorne Seafood Shanty was designed from the ground up by Rhode Island–based DiLeonardo International. Owner Joe Gentile wanted a design that heralded a new image for his carefully expanding chain. The new design was instituted in part to justify an increased check average that was mandated because of the rapidly escalating cost of seafood. Gentile recognized that the higher check average was central to his continued profitability, and he felt that the new design would help him meet his goal by offering more perceived value to customers.

DiLeonardo International accepted the challenge—as they had with previous Seafood Shanty operations—and created an upscale, sophisticated theme that avoided the typical trappings of a seafood restaurant. Gone are the plastic lobsters and wooden traps. In their place are references to the good life on the sea.

Beginning with the exterior architecture, the design gives cues that communicate the idea of a luxury cruise ship. The approach of the building is heralded by a 40-foot-high mast topped off with a blue neon running light. Blue neon is also used as a trim around the upper edge of the building. The structure has few right angles—as is often the case in cruise ships—and even the exterior corners are rounded (fig. 5-9). As guests approach the front door, they traverse

5-9. *The 40-foot-tall mast—capped with a band of blue neon—creates the first subtle suggestion of the nautical theme at Seafood Shanty.*
(Warren Jagger photo)

a wooden boardwalk. Once past the entryway (fig. 5-10), diners encounter a 16-foot-long display of fresh fish that previews the menu and emphasizes the idea of fresh, high-quality fare.

The service areas are divided into three "decks"—the bar, the main deck dining room, and the upper deck captain's dining room. This spatial arrangement helps to create a feeling of movement because diners have to walk up and down the levels as they move through the space. The 17-seat bar is on a raised level that visually flows into the main deck dining area. The 207-seat main deck provides the liveliest see-and-be-seen dining, although the designers broke it into three sub-areas to afford a modicum of privacy. The 60-seat upper deck offers a quieter, more intimate milieu. In contrast to the sound-reflecting wooden floors on the main deck, the upper deck is fully carpeted and fitted with soft banquettes and padded armchairs to dampen the sound (fig. 5-11).

Throughout the restaurant, various treatments evoke the luxury liner concept. For example, simulated metal ceilings complete with "rivets" echo the bulkheads found in a ship. Wood veneer wall coverings recall the solid wood millwork found in the dining rooms of vintage cruise ships. Blue tiles mirror the color of the sea and also help to define traffic patterns.

5-10. *The Seafood Shanty entrance is marked by a progression of spaces. After walking down a wooden gangplank, patrons pass through a small vestibule into a waiting area where a fresh seafood display previews the menu to come.* (Warren Jagger photo)

5-11. *On the upper-deck dining level, smoke stacks banded with blue and red stripes lend the feel of an oceangoing liner.* (Warren Jagger photo)

CREATING A MULTIFUNCTIONAL SPACE

DINING ROOM AND MEMBERS' LOUNGE   The Art Institute of Chicago, Chicago, IL

The Chicago Art Institute, originally opened in the 1890s, was enlarged in the mid-1970s to include the addition of a members' lounge and grand hall for afternoon tea. This space had only a very small plating pantry, quite suitable for the service of beverages and finger sandwiches.

However, demands on this type of space soon grew to exceed its capabilities (a common occurrence in institutional settings). By the early 1980s, daily luncheons and evening banquets, prepared in the general kitchens two floors below, had transformed the space into a restaurant and banquet facility. Serving hundreds of banquet guests from a makeshift servery and providing the Art Institute's very sophisticated membership with the haute cuisine menu they desired became impossible. The space was severely underutilized and the Art Institute was missing out on potential profits from events such as parties, receptions, and dinner dances.

These were the challenges facing the team of architects and designers at Norman DeHaan

Associates when they tackled the careful restructuring of this cathedral-like space in 1985. The charge was to work within the existing room and maintain the integrity of the 6,300-square-foot space that in places rose to a ceiling height of nearly 35 feet. Added to the spatial considerations were the operational demands on a room that was to be used for high-quality tableservice dining at lunch, lectures, afternoon tea, evening buffets, and late-night dinner-dance fund-raisers. The room had to meet the esthetic and service needs of a diverse group of highly educated, well-traveled, demanding patrons: visitors, members, trustees, and donors.

The designers' first step was to convert the pantry into a full-service finishing kitchen. With the exception of salads, luncheon dishes are cooked to order in this compact kitchen. For banquet service, however, many dishes are still preprepared in the main basement kitchens and then transported to the new finishing kitchen for final preparation. The key to the kitchen de-

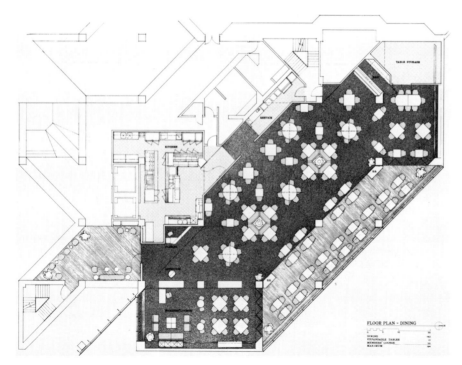

5-12. *The Chicago Art Institute's floor plan can be changed to accommodate banquets, receptions, and other uses. Here it is set up for dining (Norman DeHaan Associates drawing).*

sign here is the operational decision to preprepare recipe ingredients in the main kitchen. Were it not for this decision, the finishing kitchen would not have been large enough for banquet service. In the final design (see floor plan, fig. 5-12), only the equipment used for the cooking and assembly of a la carte foods was incorporated into the new kitchen.

With the finishing kitchen as a support base, the redesigned restaurant can offer up to 194 luncheon guests a varied, high-quality menu that changes every two months, accommodate up to 256 guests for a banquet, or hold a reception for 350. A table-storage area, banquet service bar, and service station were all added to the room to improve the effectiveness of the banquet operations. During lunch, the chef is always on call to prepare last-minute special dishes for trustees or other important clients.

With the exception of three columns, the entire dining room consisted of one large, freespan space. The architecture, which followed the geometric patterns of the physical building shell, was dramatic, but it lacked focal points to attract diners to the center of the room. Patrons wanted to sit only by the windows. Principal-incharge Norman DeHaan faced the challenge of providing visual focal points by suspending five custom-designed dropped chandeliers from 8-foot-square mirrors, as can be seen in figure 5-13. Besides functioning as decorative elements, the lights create sparkle, especially as they reflect in the ceiling mirrors, and balance the scale of the high ceiling.

Another technique the designers used to break up the overscaled space are banquette islands located at the center of the room. During lunch, the banquettes—centered around large floral arrangements—offer what has become a popular seating choice. During group functions when more floor space is needed or sightlines have to be kept open for lectures or visual presentations, the banquettes can be easily disassembled and stored.

With some of the world's finest art located in galleries just a hundred feet away, DeHaan and his associates strove for an interior design that would complement the artistic milieu. They enhanced the room's dramatic architectural features with stepped tiers of upholstered wall panels that aligned with the various beams, soffits, and ceiling planes. These fabric-wrapped panels work with the carpeting, upholstered chairs, and an acoustical ceiling to maintain quiet in the room. Such a serene atmosphere is very much in keeping with the hushed hallways of the Art Institute. Most important, the use of the room increased significantly with the new finishing kitchen and redesigned dining area. According to Robert J. Wiedenbeck, associate director of the Department of Special Events, the space was booked nightly for special functions subsequent to the redesign, and members reacted enthusiastically to the new look of the room. The entire project, including kitchen design, cost approximately $750,000.

5-13. *Custom-designed chandeliers diminish the vertical expansiveness of the space and add sparkle to the room.*
(Van Inwegen photo)

STUDENT CENTER SERVERY

UMPHREY LEE STUDENT CENTER   Southern Methodist University, Dallas, TX

This ground floor cafeteria, situated in a neo-Georgian building on the lush suburban campus of Southern Methodist University, was serving up to 1,500 meals per day in facilities originally designed to serve 900. It required a comprehensive renovation that addressed both cosmetic and functional concerns, and in 1986 a redesign of kitchen, servery, and dining areas totally transformed the outdated cafeteria into an upscale dining environment. Designed by architects Harwood K. Smith & Partners (HKS, Inc.), who renovated dining areas in a postmodern mode befitting the building's classical shell, the redesigned cafeteria generated a 400 percent increase in cash sales during its first year of operation. Among its many well-designed features, the spacious scatter-system servery, designed by HKS and Birchfield Foodsystems, is especially noteworthy.

With a bright red color scheme, vivid posters of larger-than-life fruits and vegetables, and eye-catching food displays highlighted by overhead, incandescent spots, the servery design actually seems to stimulate the appetite (fig. 5-14). It is anchored around a shopping mall concept developed by Director of Dining Services Merle Parker. Parker visited numerous facilities across the country—not just noncommercial cafeterias but hotels, restaurants, and shopping malls—and became convinced that students would enjoy shopping for food in the same way they shopped for clothes. Similar to a retail food court, the servery at Umphrey Lee offers patrons various food options located at separate stations. Instead of moving linearly through a line, people travel around the servery at their leisure, survey the day's offerings, and then make their choices. Generous circulation space permits this system of perusal.

Many serveries, even those organized in a scatter system, are dominated by stainless steel equipment. At Umphrey Lee, the servery space stands on its own as good design. The room's visual focal point is a large, vivid red salad bar that sits in the middle of the space. Its red color

and overhead lights are a great foil for fresh, brightly colored vegetables.

At both the salad bar and other food stations, angled sneeze guards anchored by red piping replace traditional glass shelves. These innovative units serve a dual purpose. First, they are functional. One of Merle Parker's pet peeves is the overshelves in cafeteria lines that cause all sorts of problems, such as gooey pie fillings sticking to the upper shelf, that the angled sneeze guards eliminate. Second, they are neat graphic elements that help to unify the room. Commonly regarded as purely functional, the sneeze guards are transformed into an important design statement.

5-14. *The bright red self-service salad bar is the focal point of the Umphrey Lee scramble servery, designed by HKS, Inc. and Birchfield Foodsystems.* (*Rick Grunbaum photo*)

24-HOUR DINING

MANUFACTURERS HANOVER TRUST COMPANY OPERATIONS CENTER   New York, NY

How can an underground, round-the-clock cafeteria serving more than six thousand people each day work both as a practical feeding facility and as a relaxing, low-key environment? This was part of the problem that faced Carson, Lundin & Thorson Architects when they were called upon to update the space in 1985. Seventeen years earlier, the same architects had designed a sleek, high-tech cafeteria that had become outdated both visually and psychologically. Corporate management wanted "an entirely new and much more peaceful design," explained Senior Associate-in-Charge Donald Chapman, "one that offered a restful alternative to employees' intense working environments." Functionally, the layout had to support a constant flow of food production and customer feeding. Esthetically, the design had to lure diners down an escalator and into a windowless, low-ceilinged space.

In order to lead people down to the cafeteria from the lobby (and vice versa), the escalators joining the two floors are banked with banners of silk-screened landscapes that change with the seasons. The banners enliven an otherwise sterile journey and hint of seasonal menu changes. In the dining area, the architects achieved their goal by toning down the design with more subdued lighting, installing a new acoustic ceiling for noise control, and bathing the atmosphere in pastel hues that support the newly refined ambiance. They devised a cut-out wall treatment of light blue "waves" that seem to float on the horizon and help to expand the sense of space. Black-and-white checkerboard tile traffic paths establish circulation patterns from serving lines to carpeted dining areas. The absence of prints, accessories, and potted plants also helps to instill an open feeling in the windowless rooms (fig. 5-15).

The new cafeteria is a complete departure from the old design. What had been an intense, energized environment became quiet, muted, and restful. The result, one year after the redesign, was an increase in customer participation of more than 25 percent.

5-15. *The checkerboard tile floor establishes traffic flow in this gigantic underground cafeteria at the Manufacturers Hanover Trust Operations Center. (Norman McGrath photo)*

FAST FOOD GROWS UP

MCDONALD'S   New York, NY

Several design firms proposed grandiose art deco schemes for the design of a—gasp—McDonald's located in the Time & Life Building at Manhattan's revered Rockefeller Center. After all, the building is an art deco landmark; therefore, the restaurant should have an art deco theme as well. However, designer Charles Morris Mount had a different idea. His concept was not to emulate the building's style but merely to allude to it. He felt that any attempt to compete with Rockefeller Center's vintage design would be a poor imitation of the real thing.

Mount's reasoning struck a chord. He was awarded the commission after he sketched his ideas on a paper napkin. With project director Kate Goldman, he then embarked on a project whose slick, curvilinear interior offered full-grown businesspeople an opportunity to go to McDonald's without their kids.

What sets this McDonald's apart from other upscale fast food designs of the late 1980s is its attitude as an urban gathering place. The market here consists primarily of a breakfast and lunchtime business clientele who work in the Rockefeller Center complex. Although Goldman remembers that on opening day in 1985 incredulous passers-by just wouldn't believe that the glitzy restaurant was really a McDonald's, it soon became a popular place not only for a quick bite but also for informal business meetings.

This McDonald's is well liked by a clientele of young urban professionals because it provides the same kind of see-and-be-seen atmosphere as their favorite grand cafes. The curving facade, embellished with touches of glass block, allows an unobstructed view inside. A tiled entry runway, whose drama is enhanced by a mirrored ceiling and wall, plus low-voltage, incandescent track lighting overhead, offers a theatrical arrival and a path to the order counter

(fig. 5-16). Carpeted seating levels are quieter but still give diners a view of the action at the serving lines. Pale blue, aqua, gray, and salmon color accents contrast with shiny stainless steel. The restaurant has no applied decoration—no plants, no artwork, and no accessories—which reflects the clean architectural approach popular in many independent restaurants. Sweeping curves reference the feeling, not the re-creation, of art deco.

Food at the Rockefeller Center store is the same as at any McDonald's. The interior, however, sizzles with urban chic. Altogether, this design takes its inspiration from the market, not from the menu.

5-16. *The glitzy, mirrored entry runway at this McDonald's leads patrons down a tile-paved promenade to the order stations.*
(© Norman McGrath 1986)

COOL VICTORIAN ICE CREAM

THE GREAT MIDWESTERN ICE CREAM COMPANY   Columbia, MO

The Lawlor/Weller Design Group was faced with the challenge of creating the first in a series of dessert restaurants to be built throughout the Midwest. The owners wanted a design that would have a "strong sense of place" yet attract a wide market. Ownership further required that natural materials be used wherever possible "to give the friendly air of Midwestern hospitality."

Anthony Lawlor and Susan Weller responded by developing a design that "aimed to strike a balance between the copies of ice cream parlors of the 1890s and the neon and tile gelaterieas of the 1980s." The first Great Midwestern Ice Cream Company was located in a former printing plant of brick construction, but the design idea was to incorporate elements that could easily be transferred to other types of buildings, including new shopping mall construction or other styles of older buildings.

Two themes unify the design solution. First, elements of Victorian architecture typically encountered in a Midwestern town are utilized throughout the fifty-seat, two-level space: The town gazebo, front porch railings, and trellis archways all help to achieve the welcoming Midwestern atmosphere desired by the owner. Second, a chair rail design pulls everything together and unifies all shapes and forms into a coherent whole (fig. 5-17). In addition to serving as a decorative wall design, the geometric chair rail motif is an equipment skirt in the serving line, forms the trellises that arch overhead, and bridges the lower and upper levels as the stair railing and guard rail. One noteworthy point is that the arched trellis, which works well in this old building, can also be used quite effectively in modern open spaces such as shopping malls to delineate the confines of serving and eating zones while maintaining a feeling of openness. What makes this solution impressive is how a practical application such as the chair rail can also work as a unifying design element. At the

Great Midwestern Ice Cream Company, a simple geometric form creatively applied pulls the place together—without becoming overbearing.

5-17. *At the Great Midwestern Ice Cream Company a simple visual motif, used for chair rails, arched trellises, and other surfaces throughout the space, unifies this Victorianesque interior.*
(John Keller photo)

YES, VIRGINIA, THIS REALLY IS MCDONALD'S!

MCDONALD'S Larchmont, NJ

Principal-in-charge Brad Elias of the Hochheiser-Elias Design Group had three mandates when he embarked on the design of one of thirty units showcased by McDonald's for the company's thirtieth birthday in 1985. First, he was to provide a contemporary, innovative interior that could be used as a prototype for future stores. Second, he had to work within McDonald's strict maintenance and durability standards. Third, a neutral backdrop was requested, so that when the facility became worn a fresh look could be created just by changing the artwork, upholstery, and wallcovering.

Before embarking on the decorative scheme, the designers had to solve some problems caused by the architecture of this new,

120-seat unit. Two important features—a greenhouse dining area and recessed skylights in the 10-foot-high ceiling—had to be dealt with before they could work as architectural assets.

The problem with the south-facing greenhouse was heat and glare. When the sun beat down, this area became uncomfortably warm, and the brightness was so intense that people couldn't see. What Elias and his team came up with to ease the situation was a black solar screen that covered the entire greenhouse roof. They then draped white fabric panels over the black screen to create a checkerboard pattern, a decorative motif that was used throughout the store's interior. The practical result of this ap-

5-18. *Gridlike dividers, levels, and skylights define several different dining areas in the Larchmont McDonald's. (Peter Paige photo)*

5-19. *Wooden park benches offer diners a desirable alternative to the molded-plastic seating of yesteryear.*
(Peter Paige photo)

plication was that harsh, hot sunlight was diffused into a soft glow as it shone into the room.

The second architectural problem was singularly unattractive skylights. These were "recessed deep into the ceiling, broken up by structural beams, and looked like tiny slashes high up and far away," said Elias. In order to make the skylights appear larger, the designers angled back the surrounding ceiling area and covered it with checkerboard tiles. They also mirrored the beams and installed trough planters between them. Finally, the entire skylight was edged with exposed lamps. The effect, as can be seen in figure 5-18, is impressive.

This inviting design reflects many current directions for fast food interiors, but it is also eminently practical. All materials and finishes can be easily cleaned, and the atmosphere is quietly upscale rather than outrageously trendy. The classic black-and-white checkerboard motif is warmed by parklike wooden benches and decorative "street lamps" (fig. 5-19). Platformed dining areas, counter seating for singles at both bar height and dining height, a wide mix of seating types, resin-covered fabric tabletops, and a complex lighting scheme are all hallmarks of popular, full-service restaurants brought into this fast food milieu.

DOUBLE-BARREL DINING

ED DEBEVIC'S SHORT ORDERS DELUXE AND SHAW'S BLUE CRAB   Deerfield, IL

Local zoning codes place many restrictions on restaurant design. In the case of this Deerfield, Illinois, location, zoning ordinances prohibited building more than one structure. What owner Lettuce Entertain You Enterprises was granted was a permit to build one 450-seat restaurant, but the market was unlikely to support such a large establishment.

Therefore, in order to take full advantage of the site yet still meet local codes, the owners decided to construct a dual-concept building that housed two entirely different operations. They retained Aumiller Youngquist Architects for exterior, interior, and kitchen design.

According to the architects, their biggest challenge was to give "separate, yet harmonious identities to the restaurants." Operationally, they were very different. Ed Debevic's Short Orders Deluxe, which had opened in other Illinois locations with great success, is a light-hearted 1950s diner fantasy. Shaw's Blue Crab, with a higher check average, is an upscale dinnerhouse. Paired together within the one Deer-

field building, they share a common entry area and guest bathrooms, but all other sections of each restaurant are kept separate.

The exterior architecture and shared entry area posed the greatest design challenges. Zoning ordinances, in addition to mandating a single building, were extremely restrictive regarding exterior signage. Therefore, the architects had to create an exterior identity for each restaurant, and off-road visibility, with architectural treatments. They used a cream-colored, glazed concrete block as the base building material to unify the architectural statement. To hint that there were two separate entities within, Ed's exterior was trimmed with a turquoise-green band of color and Shaw's was trimmed with a deep red color. In addition, Ed's front was shaped like a dining car, a signature element in all Ed's units; Shaw's front was distinguished by a tower and a partial overhang over an existing pond to give it a wharflike appearance (fig. 5-20).

Inside, the architects carried through the

(A)

5-20. *The Shaw's Blue Crab facade (A), overlooking a pond, is but half of the dual-restaurant building. The other half houses Ed Debevic's (B), an entirely different concept with a 1950s diner front.*
(Steinkamp/Ballogg photos)

color differentiation in the shared lobby to help distinguish between the two restaurants. Each dining area is treated entirely separately, although each harkens back to the past. Ed Debevic's sports the soda fountain, diner car, and open kitchen of vintage diner design in a whim-sical recreation of the 1950s esthetic. Shaw's Blue Crab reflects a more subdued design approach, with painted brick, warm woods, and muted colors that evoke a 1940s East Coast urban crab house.

(B)

TUBE STEAK CHIC

CHICAGO DOGS   Chicago, IL

In 1985, the price of a corner hot dog and Coke in the typical American town cost $1.70. Ron Dickstein, the owner of Chicago Dogs, found that he could more than double his take to a check average of $3.75 per head—if the hot dogs were sold in a chic setting.

This fifty-seat fast food eatery is surrounded by several competing stores in a shopping center in the affluent Chicago suburb of Highland Park. The only sure way for Dickstein to realize his high check average and to attract his market share was to augment the dogs with a high-end design scheme. He retained the firm of Aumiller Youngquist Architects to "create a design atmosphere which was sophisticated enough to attract the upscale suburban clientele yet funky enough to bring in the teenage crowd," said architect Keith Youngquist.

The designers had to overcome two constraints common to restaurant projects: time and money. With 2,000 square feet of raw space, an all-inclusive $100,000 budget, and a mere three months until opening day, they went into high gear immediately. Because Aumiller Youngquist could provide turnkey services including engineering and kitchen planning, they were able to consolidate efforts in the front and back of the house. Their first move after arriving at the spatial plan was to design the kitchen lineup and order $35,000 worth of kitchen equipment to allow sufficient lead time for delivery and installation. Next, they considered front-end furnishings and finishes, rejecting those that couldn't be delivered on schedule and "building as many items as possible ourselves, in the field, to save time," explained Youngquist. In the end, the job came in on time and on budget.

The design of Chicago Dogs gleams a sleek black and white with a clean, stylish look that appeals to well-off clientele of all ages. First impressions are created by the large black-and-white floor tiles and corniced columns that direct traffic flow into the space (fig. 5-21). In a somewhat unusual layout, patrons flow through

5-21. *Columns are a focal point in Chicago Dogs. They divide seating areas, create a traffic path to the service station, and house trash receptacles. (Courtesy of Photo Images)*

the middle of the room, with the columns separating them from dining areas on either side, to one of two cash registers where they place their orders. Not only do the columns act as directional signals but also each has a trash enclosure and tray receptacle built into its back side.

Aumiller Youngquist selected all the elements for their durability and ease of maintenance. Booths, banquettes, and stools are covered with wear-resistant black Naugahyde; chairs are stacking metal with "very durable" paint; tabletops are plastic laminate finished with black metal bases; the base of the serving counter is a matte black laminate impervious to dirt and stains. The entire restaurant can be wiped down very quickly with soap and water, and every item contributes to the spotless black and white esthetic.

The result of Dickstein's 1985 investment of $100,000 was a projected yearly gross of $350,000 in 1986.

THEATER AS RESTAURANT

TWENTY:TWENTY   New York, NY

Big, theatrical, stage set restaurants have become common on the urban landscape, places that attract affluent, well-dressed young restaurantgoers who dine out as much for entertainment as they do for food. What distinguishes Twenty:Twenty, housed in a cavernous cast-iron building at 20 West Twentieth Street in New York, is a unique architectural layering of space devised by the designers, Haverson/Rockwell Architects. The dividing of the whole makes Twenty:Twenty different from many of its competitors.

Haverson/Rockwell organized this space like a theater, and the restaurant experience is a carefully controlled production with a cast of players that includes the diners themselves. Guests make their entrance at center stage and then move either down to a large, ground floor orchestra pit at right, or up to one of five saw-toothed balconies at left (fig. 5-22). Unlike most theaters, however, the higher the seating level, the higher the status. The most desirable seats in Twenty:Twenty are at the front of the elevated balconies, where patrons have a grand view over black, wrought-iron railings. Lit with concealed white neon tubes, these dining plateaus seem to float. Their stepped facades and zigzag configuration divide the huge room into a fascinating progression of vertical spaces.

5-22. *The architects of Twenty:Twenty took full advantage of the vertical grandeur of this old industrial building by creating saw-toothed seating balconies. (Joseph Coscia, Jr., photo)*

HAVE IT YOUR WAY

BURGER KING RESTAURANT #4348   Edison, NJ

Joseph D. Anghelone is President of New Jersey–based Consumer Food Services, one of Burger King's largest franchisees. Anghelone believes that fast feeders should adapt their designs to their customers and be flexible enough to target special customer groups. This philosophy is evident in the design of such CFS units as Governor's Island Burger King—the first and only fast food restaurant at a Coast Guard base, which serves pizza and beer as well as the regular menu selections—and the country's first Whopper Express, located in downtown Manhattan. At the Whopper Express, giant graphics of mouthwatering food items and a slick, high-tech interior whose only seating is stand-up counters spell success for this limited menu concept. At unit #4348, featured here, Anghelone specified Burger King Corporation's Image 87 concept in order to appeal to a wide customer base.

Detailed plans for Image 87 were developed at Burger King Corporate Headquarters and made available to franchisees for both retrofits and new construction such as #4348, which opened as one of the first new-image units in 1985. Upgraded architectural and interior décor elements, as well as new operational design components, were included in the plans (fig. 5-23).

In design, the building encompasses an open atrium interior with exposed wood trusses that give the room an airy appearance, plus a greenhouse dining area. Interior finishes were upgraded from standard Formica to "real" materials, including oak and brass.

From an operational perspective, there were two major design changes. First, a multiconventional lineup, which is basically a post-and-rail serpentine queue system, was installed. Instead of choosing from several registers as

5-23. *Burger King's Image 87 building features an updated wood-and-brick facade that incorporates a greenhouse into one of the walls. (Consumer Food Services, Inc. photo)*

they did in the old design, customers queue up in the same fashion as a bank line, with two or three cashiers at the end waiting to take their order. Second, a self-service drink bar was installed adjacent to the final pickup station (fig. 5-24).

According to Anghelone, customer satisfaction with unit #4348 has been excellent. Truly a market-driven design, it attracts a wide spectrum of clients, including a substantial business lunch crowd. "Everybody's preference nowadays is for a lighter, upgraded environment," noted Anghelone, "and businesspeople really like the alternative of having a quicker, more casual lunch than in a sit-down, full-service restaurant. When they have informal meetings, they especially like the option of getting another fast cup of coffee at the drink station." In fact, the drink bar is popular with all patrons because it allows them to participate in the fast food process and really "do it their way." They can regulate the amount of ice in their cups, for example, or mix decaf with regular coffee. Patrons also like the new multiconventional

lineup, because they don't have to bother trying to figure out which is the shortest line, and the new system is just as fast. Interestingly, Anghelone kept one element in #4348 that became obsolete in most other units—a free-standing salad bar. Because the restaurant is located in the same strip plaza as a health club, "unbelievable" numbers of women come to Burger King after their workouts and use the salad bar. Anghelone recognized that this market group would not respond as well to prepackaged salads.

As for the upgraded décor, Anghelone admits that it requires additional maintenance. The windowed greenhouse needs continual upkeep, as do the brass, the oak, and the abundance of live greenery. "We have to have an attendant out on the floor all the time, polishing the brass, dusting the wood, and so on. But the new design is worth it," said Anghelone, "because it keeps all our traditional customers and also attracts new customers. The income from the extra customers offsets the cost of the extra maintenance work."

5-24. *The self-service beverage bar allows patrons to participate in the fast food experience and "have it their way."*
(Consumer Food Services, Inc. photo)

HEY, THE STREET IS CROOKED

ZIG ZAG BAR & GRILL New York, NY

In 1986, the firm of Janusz Gottwald & Associates Architects was retained to design a limited bar and grill restaurant for father-and-son restaurateurs Stanley and Allen Bernstein. Architect Janusz Gottwald and designer Laura Gottwald were in charge of both exterior and interior design for what they described as a "nontrendy, neighborhood place that wasn't a period re-creation, but that gave people the feeling of having always been there." After traveling with the Bernsteins to dozens of bars and restaurants throughout New York, they knew that the owners wanted a comfortable environment for casual dining and drinking, so they used a lot of mahogany, including reconditioned solid mahogany tables and diner seating circa 1935, to evoke a warm, familiar atmosphere. Narrow bands of art deco pressed-tin trim, which Laura Gottwald found in an architectural salvage store, gleam like silver ribbons against the rich, red mahogany.

The Gottwalds also wanted the design experience to be somewhat unusual, with a "twist of surprise" that would distinguish it from the run-of-the-mill pubby bar-restaurant. Their solution was to give the ordered grid pattern of New York City's Chelsea district a new wrinkle. Both exterior and interior of Zig Zag Bar & Grill are a bit out of kilter, loaded with subtle angles and gradations so that perpendicular surfaces appear oblique—and vice versa. The trickery begins at the entrance, with a front wall angled fifteen degrees from being parallel with the street. This angling effect continues throughout the entire restaurant (fig. 5-25). Although the room is shaped like a rectangle, it appears to be a trapezoid that grows progressively wider. Its visual—and social—focal point is a zigzag-shaped bar that runs along one side of the restaurant like a jagged lightning bolt. In addition to carrying through the visual motif, the bar's saw-toothed configuration encourages mingling because people like to congregate at each angled nook. At lunch the space appeals to local businesspeople, and with the change of a tape, turn of the volume control, and transfer of management from father to son it becomes a meeting place for the younger hip crowd in the evenings.

Mirrors were used extensively throughout the restaurant to create more optical playfulness. For instance, one catches a glimpse of an interesting person in the mirror, yet with a quick turn of a head the image is gone because the mirrors are also placed on angles and the resulting reflections play tricks on the eye. A trip to the restroom evidences an extension of the design theme there as well, with mirrored walls set at differing angles to cause multiple reflections everywhere in the space.

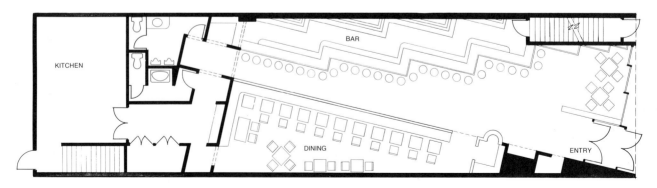

5-25. The floor plan of Zig Zag illustrates how Gottwald created spatial illusions starting at the entrance, where the front wall angles fifteen degrees from the normal straight grid (David Hoggatt drawing).

BLACK AND WHITE AND FULL OF LIGHT

BATONS   New York, NY

Number 66 West 11th Street in New York City has lived as Enrico and Pagliari, an Italian dinner buffet house; as Christy's, a laid-back, family-run restaurant with a menu to match; and in its most recent re-creation as Batons, an ultra-chic hangout created by the New York firm of Sam Lopata, Inc.

Batons is a study in stylized starkness, as can be seen in figure 5-26. Almost entirely black, white, and gray, the space has a hard-edged personality tempered by the incessant activity of a large open kitchen. From the bare concrete floors, to the sheetrock walls airbrushed with textured gray swirls, to the black,

5-26. Sam Lopata designed Baton's skylit dining room as a perfect setting for urban stargazing.
(Peter Paige photo)

three-legged armchairs, to the white-and-black, custom-designed light batons, the place was reborn with the energy that draws fashionable New York restaurant devotees.

More than a black-and-white stage set, Batons is a carefully crafted reaction to spatial constraints. Lopata was faced with a confiningly low seven-foot ceiling at the entrance of the space that could not be raised. He reacted to this situation with two design techniques. First, with lighting design consultant Ken Billington, he developed a lighting application that consists of zigzag light bands recessed into the ceiling (fig. 5-27). Streaking overhead like bolts of lightning, they temper the effect of the low ceiling because they are inset rather than hung. Second, Lopata opened up the space so that arriving guests can view the cocktail lounge, the bar, the display kitchen, and the entry to the back dining area as soon as they step inside the space. By reducing the visual barriers, he not only created the impression of spaciousness but also fostered the see-and-be-seen atmosphere so important to Batons' success.

This philosophy of spatial openness went so far that when the space was first opened, Lopata placed the maitre d' stand not in its customary spot inside the front door, but back at the edge of the rear dining area. Guests were not greeted when they entered the front door; rather, they were allowed to flow into the unobstructed space and had a long walk through the cocktail lounge and bar area before reaching the maitre d' stand or the coat room. A spatial arrangement found often in European cafes, it unfortunately did not work for the American market. People got confused when they entered the restaurant and looked around for assistance instead of moving forward to the maitre d' stand. The maitre d' stand was subsequently moved to a more visible spot at the front entry area.

The maitre d' placement notwithstanding, Batons' spatial arrangement helps to establish the tony attitude of a hip urban gathering place. The placement of the cocktail area and bar directly inside the front doors allows bar patrons ample opportunity to view the arriving guests, and vice versa. Additionally, the spatial juxtaposition of the bar with the display kitchen creates a truly special bar experience. Here, the bar sits directly across from the large open kitchen,

so bar patrons have a direct sightline to the chefs at work. In between the bar and the kitchen is the main access corridor, which leads from the front entry and cocktail and dining area straight through to the skylit main dining room at the back of the restaurant. The walk through this area, with the buzzing, well-dressed bar crowd to the left and the exciting, slightly frenetic open kitchen to the right, sizzles with energy.

The lighting solutions exhibited in this restaurant are most noteworthy and help to create the esthetic signature of the place. Ken Billington's firm had extensive experience in theatrical lighting and brought special drama to many of Sam Lopata's designs. At Batons, the innovative ceiling lights consist of low-voltage fluorescent tubes inset into the 7-foot ceiling. They cast a relatively dim ambient light into the cocktail area and contribute a clean, chic look to the space.

The second lighting solution was a whimsical one. In the bar area, black iron and glass cocktail tables plug into floor sockets and provide a rosy uplighting that animate the tables' high-tech personality.

The third lighting solution plays the most important role in this daring design, however, and in fact gives the restaurant its name. Placed throughout the space are tall, fluorescent sticks of light resembling oversized batons. A modern-day reinterpretation of the classic floor lamp, the fixture consists of fluorescent tubes wrapped with black strips. Each baton fits into a base unit that allows it to be angled to different positions. These unusual light sculptures slash through the space like Darth Vadar's light sword. A neat geometric interplay is created as their vertical lines bisect the low, horizontal space.

5-27. *A lightning bolt streaking overhead was intended not only to add vitality to Batons' bar but also as a practical lighting solution for a low-ceilinged room.*
(Peter Paige photo)

MEET ME BY THE RED TOMATO

SCOOZI   Chicago, IL

Restaurateur Rich Melman presented a real challenge to architects Bill Aumiller and Keith Youngquist when he brought them to an old Zebart garage on Chicago's West Side and asked them to help him create yet another successful restaurant for the Lettuce Entertain You group. Melman's concept guideline was to create a huge "Italian tapas bar" and restaurant with an interior design that supported the concept. Working with Jordan Mozer & Associates and Glossbert Associates, the architects created a layered look for the space that evokes a working class atmosphere. Replete with old Italian imagery, it feels as if it had been there forever.

Exterior architecture forms a vivid first impression (fig. 5-28). Mustard-colored awnings sweep down to windows filled with colored bottles. Huge posterlike murals of Italian products are painted onto the stone building facade. Over the entry door hangs a giant red tomato that "became Scoozi's signature," said Bill Aumiller. The timeworn theme of Scoozi's design is even carried out onto the sidewalks, where the concrete was torn out and reapplied in a roughshod fashion.

Inside, the walls became sketch pads for the artist "who once occupied the space," and then an oversized mirror was hung over part of one of the sketches by a "subsequent occupant." A "window" was closed up with the brick wall of the adjoining building. The plaster on the walls is cracked (actually it was cured to make it crack), and the exposed pipes were painted to make them look rusted. The floors are covered with eighteen different tiles and three different marbles bound together with black grouting, as well as with mahogany intentionally interspersed with mismatched woods.

As each of these detailing elements was added to the restaurant, it was checked against a story line that guided the architects and the owners in the creation of the concept. The resulting interior—albeit carefully orchestrated—looks like a mélange, a message from the many past lives of this space.

5-28. *Despite the building's timeworn appearance, the red tomato signals the place to be for Chicago's svelte set.*
(Joseph Durocher photo)

DRAGON DANCE

SHUN LEE WEST   New York, NY

Just a single design element in this Chinese restaurant reflects its Oriental cuisine, but it is quite a conversation piece. Ringing the plush black and pale pink dining room is a seven-headed translucent dragon whose wheat-colored body and glowing red eyes are lit from within by flickering interior lights (fig. 5-29).

Despite the dragon and the ethnicity of the staff, Shun Lee's design could very well come from any corner of the planet (or beyond). In fact, the stark entry where a monolithic maitre d' station stands guard feels futuristic, as does the rather elegant ambiance in the dining room. Designed by Stanley Jay Friedman, Inc., the interior matches the high check average rather than reflecting the clichés of Chinese restaurant design, an appropriate treatment for the 1986 redesign of this popular restaurant located near New York's Lincoln Center.

In Shun Lee's dining room, the designers created a sunken seating area rimmed by booths and banquettes on the platform above. All diners are surrounded by the multiheaded dragon, a sculptural wall application that gives new meaning to the concept of indirect lighting. Bathed with uplighting that washes the pale pink walls and glowing from within due to hundreds of tiny lights strung throughout its body and heads, the dragon transformed a nice room into a special room.

In addition to its visual appeal, Shun Lee reflects thoughtful integration of functional details. Wait stations, for instance, are custom-built into the walls and so unobtrusive that diners sitting next to them are barely aware of their presence. The black vinyl fitted covers on tabletops allow waitpersons to change tablecloths without disturbing the visual integrity of the space because the black coverings are invisible against the room's black backdrop.

5-29. *A glowing, red-eyed, multiheaded dragon is Shun Lee West's single decorative embellishment in the dining room.*
(Elliott Kaufman photo)

THE BEST BACK OF THE HOUSE

LE BERNARDIN   New York, NY

Pierre Franey, noted food writer and former chef at Le Pavillon, said in 1986 that Le Bernardin's kitchen was "the best in the United States and one of the best in the world." The 1,100-square-foot kitchen is the core of this gourmet seafood restaurant that serves up to 150 meals a seating.

Other restaurants can serve that many meals from a 350-square-foot kitchen. What then is so special about this seemingly oversized space? The answer lies with the owners, Gilbert and Maguy Le Coze, both of whom are accomplished chefs. Their orientation is to the back-of-the-house environment and the food that is created there. What they wanted was a kitchen design that functioned perfectly for a made-to-order menu that is always prepared with fresh ingredients. Gilbert Le Coze worked closely with architect Philip George and food facility consultant Frank Giampietro on the planning and design of Le Bernardin's kitchen.

What is so special about this kitchen is that it provides a working environment for the chefs that is psychologically pleasing as well as extremely efficient. Open spaces between workers eliminate the cramped feeling so common to many kitchens. Well-designed flow patterns of raw and finished foods limit the cross-flow that typically causes cooks' nerves to frazzle during busy production times (fig. 5-30). Throughout the entire kitchen incandescent lighting is used. Not only is the soft lighting much easier to work in than that provided by harsh fluorescents, but it also gives the cooks a better image of how the food looks to guests.

One layout item of note is the hot food section that is located not against a wall, as is customary, but as a center island (fig. 5-31). There, in the midst of the kitchen, the back-to-back ranges allow easy pass-through space for chefs. The stoves are fronted with stainless steel; almost everything in the kitchen, including countertops, are made of easy-to-clean stainless steel.

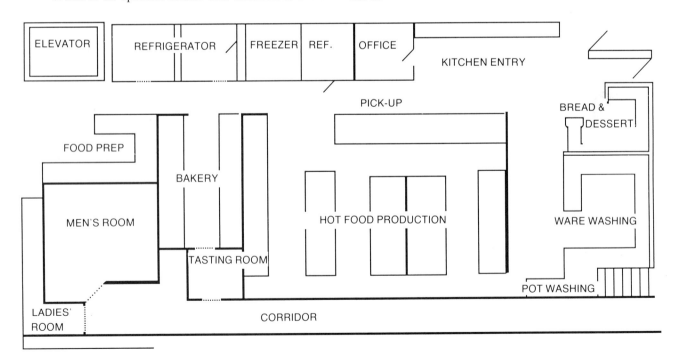

5-30. *Le Bernardin's kitchen floor plan illustrates space planning that maximizes productivity and minimizes cross-flow of work and materials.*

Most important, Le Bernardin's kitchen was designed to have a place for everything and everything in its place. A separate area was provided for the preparation and storage of baked goods. Adequate storage for refrigerated ingredients is located at each of the work stations, ensuring that the foods are stored under ideal conditions even as they wait to be cooked. Typical of the attention to detail in this immaculate kitchen is a drain in the sink where kitchen staff shuck oysters, so the oysters do not sit in water and lose flavor.

Adequate space is also included in the kitchen for the service staff. With perhaps a dozen service people in the kitchen at one time, additional space in the entry area limits the chance of accidents. Further, the kitchen layout allows waitpersons to pick up plated dishes without having to walk through the kitchen and disturb the flow of back-of-the-house workers.

Another spatial inclusion not frequently seen in American kitchens is the tasting room. The room serves as a quiet place for the chefs to taste and discuss their creations. It also provides a unique marketing opportunity for service to VIP guests.

5-31. *The extensive use of easy-to-clean stainless steel, a mirrored, acoustic ceiling, and soft, incandescent lighting creates a good working environment.* (Peter Paige photo)

SERVICE STATION ARCHITECTURE

NISHI NOHO   New York, NY

Japanese restaurants are generally quite small. In New York City, where rental costs are astronomical, they often verge on the miniscule. An exception to this tradition is Nishi Noho, an establishment located in downtown Manhattan's Noho district close to Soho and Greenwich Village, which opened in 1985. It might be one of the world's largest Japanese restaurants, but the space does not seem overwhelming because designer Charles Terrel divided the room with barriers, floor levels, and light zones that diminish the feeling of expansiveness.

One of the most significant architectural and functional elements in the restaurant is a large faux-concrete unit (fig. 5-32), resembling a mobile trailer that is parked in the middle of the dining area. The blocky, rectangular structure has a hollowed-out interior that provides a service and cashier station for Nishi Noho's wait staff.

This ingenious architectural element answers needs that are too often overlooked in large restaurants, where servers must walk long distances through front-of-the-house dining areas in order to reach their customers. At Nishi Noho, Terrel's response was to enclose the corridor that leads from the kitchen to dining areas with the faux-concrete structure and to line this structure with backup supplies for tables, plus cashier and beverage stations. Thus, the visual and sound distractions inherent to open service stations are eliminated. Additionally, backup supplies are readily available for servers to reset the tables.

5-32. *A major design element of Nishi Noho is a faux concrete bunker that hides extensive service-support facilities.*
(Joseph Durocher photo)

POST-MAYAN INDUSTRIAL

CINCO DE MAYO   New York, NY

Gone are the days when the only way a restaurant said Mexican was to put out sombreros, cacti, and brightly colored blankets. Gone, too, are the days when the only Mexican foods gringos ate were tacos and tortilla chips. In recent years, as the American craving for Tex-Mex restaurants and their expanded menus has grown exponentially, the design challenge has become saying Mexican without screaming olé.

One answer, as Frederic Schwartz of Anderson/Schwartz Architects discovered when he designed New York City's second Cinco de Mayo restaurant in 1986, is to do as the Mexicans do. Go where the Mexicans go. Find indigenous places, not buildings contrived to appeal to the tourists, and observe their use of finishes and materials. Study Marjorie Ingle's book, *Mayan Revival Style*, for its explanations of Mexican forms and colors. By doing just that, a whole new palette of colors, finishes, and materials helped to create an expressive yet non-gimmicky interior (fig. 5-33). For a total budget of $100,000, Anderson/Schwartz created an atmosphere that evokes Mexico without shouting clichés.

Materials used throughout the bar and lounge and the ninety-seat dining room are commonly found on pickup truck bumpers and shanty rooftops, as well as in chic New York restaurants. The bar front and the head rest of the banquettes were fashioned of corrugated steel. Diamond-plate steel sheets were attached to the bar ends and used as trim over the cushioned banquette backs. The bar top is zinc, and the foot rail is a fat steel tube. Rough-and-ready looking, these surfaces are "authentic to the core," said one diner who grew up in Texas, just north of the border.

The green, blue, yellow, terra cotta, and red paint used on furniture and surfaces in Cinco de Mayo were custom-mixed by the architects to match paint charts the owners brought back from a trip to Mexico. Colors were often juxtaposed in traditional Mexican fashion, such as walls painted terra cotta at the base and creme yellow on top. In the main dining area, a pair of giant structural columns were covered with a swirling "sand painting" that reflects all the colors of the restaurant.

5-33. *Creative use of indigenous materials and colors at Cinco de Mayo adds an air of authenticity to this upscale Mexican restaurant.* (*Elliott Kaufman photo*)

SOUTH-OF-THE-BORDER SNEEZE GUARDS

MRS. GARCIA'S   Los Angeles, CA

The owners of Mrs. Garcia's wanted to open a Mexican fast food restaurant where the concept of good, fresh food cooked in view of the customers would be central to the design. In response to this mandate, the design firm of Rockefeller/Hricak created "Mrs. Garcia's house," using architectural elements to define a progression from the street through the "house," (the cooking area) to the "courtyard" (the seating area). Vibrant colors and bright lighting evoke the festive hues and bright sunlight found south of the border.

A special solution in this tiny, twenty-six-seat restaurant is the atypical sneeze guards designed by the architects. Sneeze guards are mandated in all food operations where guests are allowed to serve themselves. In Mrs. Garcia's, Rockefeller/Hricak's creative response to this requirement looks like a couple of elegant, suspended storm window sashes, as seen in figure 5-34. The sneeze guards not only meet board of health regulations, but they fit with the design idea of Mrs. Garcia's home and the De Stijl-inspired scheme of bright colors and right angles. This clever response to a code requirement—one which often results in standard sneeze guards that detract from the design—illustrates how a potential liability can be turned into an architectural asset.

5-34. *Rather than specify off-the-shelf sneeze guards, architects Rockefeller/Hricak fashioned protective windows for Mrs. Garcia's that carry forward the design theme. (Christopher Dow photo)*

CREATIVE CAFETEERING

MAMA MIA! PASTA   Chicago, IL

Cafeteria designs often fail to consider the problems busy executives or students face when trying to balance a tray along with their books, papers, and magazines. The problem is not as acute in old straight-line cafeterias where guests place their reading material on a tray, rest it on a tray rail, and slide it along in front of them as they move through the lines. In the new scramble cafeterias, however, patrons must carry their trays—laden with food—from station to station.

At Mama Mia! Pasta, Banks/Eakin Architects developed a cafeteria design that shines with creativity throughout and eliminates many of the problems faced in other cafeteria service operations. Careful design attention makes possible a little more, a little better service. Mama Mia! Pasta, opened in May 1984, is basically a double-loaded, straight-line cafeteria. Although much preparation is done in the kitchen, the vitality of the operation is helped with ongoing cooking performed on the serving line. What really separates this cafeteria from all the rest is the tray rail that rests on the service side, rather than the customer side, of the line. Guests place their orders at the head of each line (fig. 5-35) and follow the tray as the staff slides it along and fills orders in front of them.

From the replaceable carpet tiles that restaurant personnel change themselves to the smooth, curved forms of the servery, bar, and dining room, Mama Mia! Pasta is special to look at. The undulating-wave pattern of the dining room ceiling relates to the cafeteria's location on the Chicago riverfront and anchors this area with a strong visual signature. Another design feature that helps the crowded cafeteria to maximize its return is the dining counter that runs along the entire length of the restaurant facing out onto the river. This type of seating is ideal for single diners and is part of the total 160 seats that turn over up to six times during a typical lunch period.

5-35. *Service staff—rather than guests—moves orders along the tray rail in Mama Mia! Pasta, thus providing a little more service to the lunchtime crowds. (Orlando Cabanban photo)*

NEW WAVE VERNACULAR

BOARDWALK FRIES AND CLAUDIA'S Horton Plaza, San Diego, CA

The fries are great: cut in the store, fried in front of the waiting guests, and served au naturel or with a choice of toppings. Nevertheless, the architecture is what brings people into the space for the first time. The golden french fries that literally burst out the front wall of the tiny Boardwalk Fries take-out in Horton Plaza, San Diego's popular outdoor mall, unite with snappy exterior signage and neon lighting to create a compelling visual image that is hard to resist.

Boardwalk Fries is one of three installations designed by Grondona/Architects in the Horton Plaza. Because they did not want their designs either to compete with the shopping center's pronounced postmodern esthetic or to become invisible against the candyland backdrop, the architects conceived of their projects as "art installations." Indeed, the highly graphic facade of Boardwalk Fries, with giant French fries made of styrofoam that explode from their rear container (fig. 5-36) right through to the front of the store, works as a zany sculpture in its own right. There is no question that this three-dimensional artwork pulls people into Boardwalk

5-36. *The theme of Boardwalk Fries is graphically displayed by this giant cup of styrofoam fries mounted on the interior wall.*
(Joseph Durocher photo)

Fries: During one two-hour late-afternoon period on a weekday in 1987, at least four people were always inside Boardwalk Fries waiting for their orders—people who had stopped to look at the fries in disguise before entering.

Right next door to Boardwalk Fries, Grondona created another phenomenal success: Claudia's (fig. 5-37), perhaps the best place anywhere to buy a cinnamon bun. Like Boardwalk Fries, Claudia's was conceived as an art installation, which helped to distinguish it from the surrounding field of fast feeders. More than a static artwork, this fanciful storefront offers the pedestrian a wild experience of sight and smell.

What first catches the eye is a three-dimensional object that looks like the frame for a hot-air balloon, with a "big, humongous crown" (in the words of one young observer) sitting on top. If that wasn't enough to draw in customers, the architect appealed to the sense of smell by turning the base of the frame into the outlet for a scent-blower that emits the irresistible aroma of freshly baked buns. A Rube Goldberg type of contraption pumps smells into a collection funnel, through a transmittal duct, and then to the front of the store (fig. 5-38). The tantalizing aroma that continually wafts out of Claudia's is enough to turn even the most diehard health food fanatic into a serious cinnamon bun addict.

Grondona's idea was that "exposing the whimsical working parts of a happy cinnamon roll bakery, complete with streamlined 'scent blower' and exploded flour on the walls, challenged the passerby to participate." This idea of a participatory design experience was crucial to his concept.

Claudia's was a hit with the public and received a lot of recognition from the architectural profession as well. In 1987, the fast food bakery garnered a prestigious award from the American Institute of Architects, who cited the "witty, mad collage of colors, shapes and images" and praised it as "a new high in olfactory architecture."

Creating highly original places like Board-walk Fries and Claudia's within a shopping center isn't easy. Horton Plaza's codes and regulations, involving such applications as building setbacks and awning projections, posed many constraints. Grondona tackled these challenges by careful design development, including paintings, models, and detailed drawings, and by organizing his own art installation group, called the "G-Force," for much of the manufacturing, painting and installation.

Grondona said that the design of Claudia's "was based on challenging the established icons of current fast food reality." Certainly both Claudia's and Boardwalk Fries exemplify a creative and exciting new approach to fast food design that harkens back to the heyday of vernacular architecture, when storefronts shaped like giant doughnuts or hot dogs or ice cream cones left no questions about the type of food. Claudia's, which one observer compared to "a bakeshop frozen in time one second after the roll maker exploded," and Boardwalk Fries, with its giant carton of golden fries jutting aggressively out toward the sidewalk, could well portend a new wave of irreverent yet functional fast food design.

5-37. *Grondona's fanciful storefront facades for Claudia's and Boardwalk Fries draw in the crowds.*
(Joseph Durocher photo)

5-38. *Inside Claudia's, the exposed workings of the cinnamon bun bakery send tantalizing aromas through the space.*
(Joseph Durocher photo)

HIGH-END HEAVY METAL

B. SMITH'S   New York, NY

This futuristic version of *West Side Story*, designed by Anderson/Schwartz Architects, contains three acts. Patrons enter via a set of angled stainless steel doors placed at the building's corner and move on to either the street-level restaurant (ahead), the platform bar (up a few steps to the right), or the second-floor rooftop cafe (up a flight of stairs beyond the bar at far right).

Act I is the bar, with a greater collection of various types of metal than a foundry (fig. 5-39). From the swirl-ground stainless steel bar with its steel bar foot rail to the brass hardware embedded into the ground concrete floor, the bar at B. Smith's provides not only a hip backdrop for a cool crowd, but also an impervious transition zone from the rough-and-tumble Eighth Avenue environment outside. In other words, the materials are very durable as well as great to look at.

These are practical, hard materials reminiscent of the urban streetside landscape. They were applied in many of the bar areas that typically show signs of wear and tear soon after opening day. The kick panel of the bar, for example, is immune to all but molybdenum-tipped army boots. The bar top was made of a welded and polished sheet of steel that is very easy to clean and sanitize, and there is no elbow pad under which dirt can catch or Bloody Mary mix turn sour. The polished steel drink rail—unlike some of its wooden counterparts—can withstand a great deal of abuse. Similarly, the polished concrete floor requires little ongoing maintenance.

Act II of B. Smith's is the dining room, which feels like an oasis of calm compared to the noisy bar and busy street beyond. In fact, most of the free-standing seating in this room rests on a carpeted island that is surrounded by a hardwood promenade. The promenade serves as a runway to showcase guests as they arrive in the dining room. The service staff also uses this wooden runway as a main circulation corridor from back to front of the house, thus keeping out of the way of seated diners. Barbara Smith,

5-39. *The architects of B. Smith's deliberately separated the sleek, hard-edged bar from the more subdued dining room.*
(Elliott Kaufman photo)

who along with the Ark Restaurant group owns the restaurant, softened the space with large clay vessels, peach and turquoise colors, and a vivid abstract mural. Open picture windows over the back bar link the two rooms and allow people on both sides to view an interesting architectural vignette, but not each other.

Act III at B. Smith's is a rooftop cafe and party area that opens onto an al fresco cafe. It is reached by a staircase at the far end of the bar, which carries through the high-tech esthetic with industrial safety metal railings, sparkling concrete treads, and backlit risers covered in sandblasted wire glass. Inside, the sole decorative application is a light sculpture that crisscrosses the ceiling like gossamer strands and is actually thin electrode wires that support the low-voltage lamps suspended between them. Outside on the rooftop, nothing distracts from the slightly seedy, quintessentially New York view.

Each of B. Smith's separate spaces offers a different type of experience, from the sleek excitement of the bar, to the comfort of the colorful dining room, to the privacy of the stellar rooftop cafe.

WILD WEST FACELIFT

CADILLAC GRILLE   Jackson, WY

Townships across the nation hold strong to their architectural heritage. That drive to maintain the past led to strict architectural guidelines and protective zoning covenants in the downtown commercial district of Jackson, Wyoming.

Such regulations dictated a vernacular approach to the design of a new facade for the Cadillac Grille restaurant. Formerly the Silver Spur restaurant, with neon lettering on the fascia and silver spur sculpture projecting from the roof, the building looked a lot like a tacky 1950s roadhouse when architect Daniel F. Williams of Atelier One Ltd. was commissioned to redesign it, concurrent with an interior renovation by Harold Tubbs. Williams completely redid the facade to create a period piece that harkened back to the golden days of the cowboys (fig. 5-40). It won a state Honor Award from the American Institute of Architects in 1985.

The architect replaced the old fieldstone facade with river cobble from a local quarry that curved in to the entry doors and a small amount of glass block to hint of the restaurant's art deco interior. The doors themselves were actually recessed three feet from the building exterior to provide for a sloped rampway that made the restaurant handicapped-accessible. California redwood—which requires little maintenance in the harsh climate—was used extensively to create the fascia and moldings of the new exterior. A vaulted redwood arch lends drama to the design. The town of Jackson provided an antique-looking wooden boardwalk that carried out the Western theme and complemented the rest of the remake.

5-40. *The streetscape of Jackson, Wyoming, is enchanced by the sensitive interpretation of Old West architecture used for the Cadillac Grille. (Ed Riddell photo, courtesy of the California Redwood Association)*

VERNACULAR CAPE

STARBUCK'S   Hyannis, MA

Cape Cod, the peninsula that juts out like an arm from the side of Massachusetts, has the feeling of a summer retreat all year round. Sand is everywhere, scrub pines abound, and the shapes and weathered wooden finishes of many of the buildings have come to symbolize the area's informal atmosphere.

One addition to the landscape in 1986 had all the trappings of a classic Cape Cod landmark. Starbuck's, designed by Walper Yarosh Associates, architects, and Rhode Island–based Morris Nathanson Design, Inc., grew from a summer hot dog stand into a 240-seat restaurant. The 6,055-square-foot building, although new, was very much in keeping with the time-worn Cape Cod vernacular (fig. 5-41).

5-41. *Starbuck's exterior design reflects its Cape Cod location.*
(*Warren Jagger photo*)

Spatially, Starbuck's is a big gathering place restaurant laid out in traditional form with a large, raised central bar that serves as the social hub. Surrounding the bar, although completely open to its vitality, are several dining areas, each of which has its own special orientation to the central core, as can be seen in the floor plan (fig. 5-42). Various seating levels help to break up the barnlike space and define the different seating sections.

Dining sections include a greenhouse area that, with its traditional wicker porch chairs, is a favorite spot for older clients who drop in for lunch or early-bird dinners. Later in the evening, diners who want more privacy frequent the two dining areas located to the right side of the bar and separated by a classic pine and maple front porch railing. These seating sections are more interior than other parts of the restaurant and have a relatively subdued ambiance suitable for dining as compared to drinking.

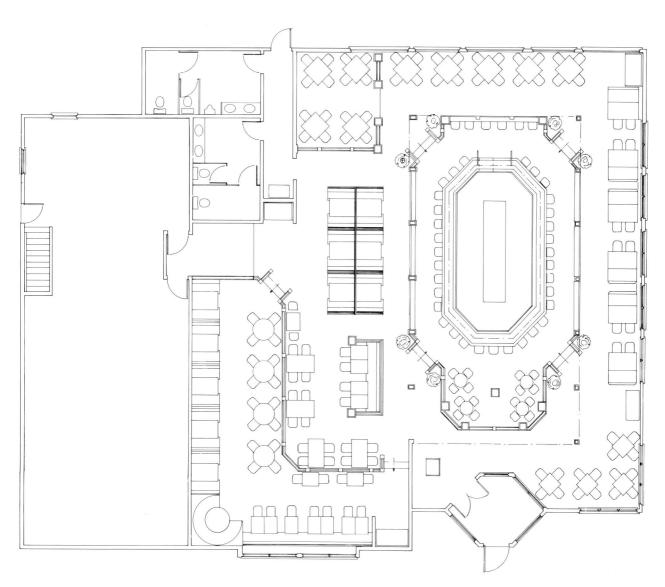

5-42. *The floor plan of Starbuck's shows the positioning of the several dining areas in relationship to the central bar (Morris Nathanson Design, Inc. drawing).*

An important element in Starbuck's design is the feeling of openness engendered by the pitched wooden ceilings supported by open trusses and the windows that encircle the raised roof of the bar area (fig. 5-43). However, when the house is not filled to capacity, guests can be concentrated in a given area to avoid the uncomfortable feeling of a big, empty restaurant.

The designers' selection of materials also plays an important role in this restaurant. Pine is the traditional wood of choice on the Cape; many of the cottages built in the 1950s and 1960s are trimmed with knotty pine. Morris Nathanson Design specified knotty pine throughout Starbuck's from the newel posts to the boxed-in posts and beams. Much of the wood was "pickled with white stain to create that weathered shingle effect, as if the salt air had been whipping through the beams for years," said project designer Blase Gallo. Such sensitivity to the local architectural vernacular helped to create a comfortable environment that draws a varied clientele from the surrounding communities.

5-43. *A vaulted ceiling above the platformed bar provides this bustling area with a desirable feeling of openness.*
(Warren Jagger photo)

MULTICONCEPT FRONT AND BACK

ZINCS   Chicago, IL

The Presidential Towers is a high-rise complex located on Chicago's West Side that includes 2,500 apartments, shops, and offices. In 1986, it became home for Zincs (fig. 5-44), a brasserie that connects three different concepts—a bar, an atrium cafe, and a formal dining room—to the atrium lobby of the Towers's entrance. Designed by Jeanne Hartnett & Associates, Zincs was meant to appeal to local residents rather than draw a destination crowd.

The forty-seat bar serves beverages and light snacks from a finishing kitchen. The cafe, situated in the atrium that connects the bar with the restaurant, has ninety-six seats. The cherry- and mahogany-paneled dining room accommodates a hundred diners, and a private dining room adjacent to the entryway seats forty-five.

Open passageways between the rooms create a free-flowing feeling between the spaces. The long, narrow bar area is distinguished by an undulating bar top with a bartender's station located behind each curve. The atrium cafe, with its terrazzo flooring, fountain, and plantings, has an al fresco atmosphere.

The dining room offers the most intimate dining experience but is visually linked with the cafe by a greenhouse that projects from the front of the dining room right into the cafe area. The greenhouse also provides a sound barrier that helps to maintain hushed tones in the dining room.

Designed by Pascal & Associates, the back of the house provides even more surprises. It seems grossly oversized for the restaurant's 280 seats: With its large steam-jacketed kettles, 60-quart mixer, and tilting braising pan, the kitchen resembles a food factory.

The kitchen of Zincs is just that, a food factory. The design was deliberately oversized so that the kitchen could offer catering services to the apartments in the towers, plus off-premises catering. The owners also wanted the kitchen to serve as a satellite kitchen for future restaurant or banquet outlets.

One unusual inclusion in Zincs's kitchen is a Cryovac system for sealing cooked, portioned meals. The pouches are either frozen or refrigerated and then reconstituted when needed. This system—relatively new to the United States but popular in Europe—increases the profitability of the kitchen. At Zincs, it maximizes the productivity of the cooks, minimizes waste, and allows the menu to be expansive without overtaxing the a la carte line.

5-44. *Zinc's bold signage gives the restaurant a strong presence within its high-rise atrium location.*
(Joseph Durocher photo)

LIKE IT'S ALWAYS BEEN THERE

REMI   New York, NY

New York's svelte Upper East Side is home to many chic neighborhood restaurants, but the hockey players' bar at 323 East 79th Street wasn't one of them. In fact, it was a dive, an anomaly in the upscale marketplace. When designer Adam Tihany transformed this storefront space into Remi in 1987, he tore it up inside and out and started from scratch. What he created was a restaurant that fit so well with the surrounding cityscape that it felt as if it had always been there.

Remi is the sort of elegant little bistro that offers patrons the intimacy of a small restaurant yet is also a place to see-and-be-seen. An upscale personality is established by the spiffy facade, with its blue-striped awning, brass-footed, cream-colored walls, and four long, narrow windows etched with the restaurant's "drunken sailor" logo (fig. 5-45). The windows allow passers-by to look inside the interior: At night, bathed in salmon light, the view beckons people in to a warm refuge from the city streets.

Patrons in the sixty-six-seat dining room cannot see out to the street, however, which effectively separates the cozy world of the restaurant from the impersonal urban landscape. Such careful design decisions typified Tihany's approach to Remi. He knew exactly the type of restaurant he wanted to create and used many techniques learned from his experience as a restaurant designer to achieve his goals.

One of Tihany's biggest challenges, for example, was to fit as many seats as possible into a very small space. The resulting seating layout has banquettes and free-standing tables hugging the room's cast and north walls and square four-tops in the center of the space arranged not in evenly spaced rows but instead placed diagonally, which increases seating capacity. Everyone is on display at Remi, but the lowered ceiling around the room's edges cossets the diners under it in a more private fashion than the wide-open central section. Rosy pink lighting flatters people's complexions. Judicious use of mirrored strips behind banquettes and mirrored panels at the back wall—which also has a windowed wall section looking into the wine room—expands the sense of space in the compact restaurant. After noticing a deafening cacophony of noise during the busy dinner hours, Tihany installed acoustic, fabric-wrapped panels in the coffered ceiling. As a result, the din turned into a lively buzz, just the right noise level for this well-tailored Venetian bistro.

5-45. *Remi's well-detailed exterior establishes an elegant streetside presence. (Joseph Coshia, Jr., photo)*

VICTORIA ATE HERE

CAFE MAJESTIC San Francisco, CA

Had Queen Victoria visited San Francisco, she would have felt quite comfortable dining in the Cafe Majestic, which re-emerged in 1986 in the renovated Majestic Hotel. Originally opened in 1902, the hotel had fallen into disrepair until the early 1980s, when a change of ownership brought the financial wherewithal to bring it up to snuff. Part of the project involved new life for the hotel dining room, which emerged as a gourmet restaurant in its own right.

The room that houses the Cafe Majestic was an empty shell when restaurateur—and former *San Francisco Chronicle* food and art critic —Stanley Eichenbaum and his partners began reconstruction of the space. San Francisco was glutted with fine restaurants, so Eichenbaum felt that both design and cuisine would have to be truly special to draw people to the Cafe Majestic. He worked with the hotel management's designer, Candra Scott, to turn the former Victorian bistro into a more refined, romantic restaurant than it had been in the past. Using antique pictures as a guide, the design team reconstructed the room into a turn-of-the-century retreat where décor, cuisine, and service combine to form a memorable experience. Eichenbaum meshed design with cuisine so thoroughly that he even adapted turn-of-the-century San Francisco recipes for modern-day tastes.

The entry through the hotel lobby takes diners past a horseshoe-shaped bar, fashioned of mahogany, that is the focal point of the lounge. The walls are decorated with hundreds of carefully mounted lepidopterans (butterflies) that provide color and an air of formality. Bar patrons can glimpse the dining room beyond either through the entryway or through a service station arch.

The feeling of grace and beauty is carried forward into the restaurant with the sweep of decorated arches and the stateliness of classical columns. Large clay urns and tall shutters along the windows further add to the grandeur of the space. Notwithstanding the highly decorative milieu, the light and airy feeling in the room is echoed in the finely crafted and garnished cuisine (fig. 5-46).

5-46. *The ornate detailing in Cafe Majestic was drawn from restaurant vignettes depicted on turn-of-the-century postcards. (Joseph Durocher photo)*

EVERY SEAT THE BEST SEAT

WILDFLOWER INN RESTAURANT   The Lodge at Vail, Vail, CO

Architect Warren Platner, whose design for New York's Windows on the World has become one of the city's foremost attractions, approaches projects from a multiplicity of viewpoints. Unlike many architects, he designs restaurants with decorative as well as architectural features and solutions, which may partly account for their popularity with the public. Moreover, he responds to the dictates of the market.

Platner described Vail, Colorado, as "a relatively modern American mountain resort, cheerful, airy and light in character." Notwithstanding the large numbers of both summer and winter tourists, the area is loaded with fine restaurants. When management of The Lodge at Vail retained Warren Platner Associates to add yet another gourmet restaurant to the scene, it meant plunging into an already competitive marketplace. Therefore, Platner developed the visual idea of wildflowers in response to the restaurant's mountaintop home, planned a design that would be equally comfortable for those who dressed for dinner and those who stayed in their daytime garb, and strove to create "a special restaurant with its own personality" to lure people away from the competition. Management supported this concept by approving a separate production kitchen for Wildflower, which helped the chef to produce special fare and the establishment to build its own reputation distinct from the hotel.

The restaurant is located in a new wing of the resort, with windows all round and mountain scenery on three sides. The space was organized with outlying seating bays that surround an interior seating section, as can be seen in the floor plan (fig. 5-47). Given the views, customers would naturally perceive the window seats as the best seats. Therefore, Platner and his designers paid particular attention to the interior portion and implemented a number of elements there to make seats every bit as special as those in the porchlike windowed areas. Window seats are all at free-standing ta-

bles, but in the interior room custom-designed alcove banquettes provide a more intimate dining experience (fig. 5-48). They are separated from each other by stone posts capped with big wicker baskets overflowing with silk flowers—diners there are sheltered by cascades of flow-

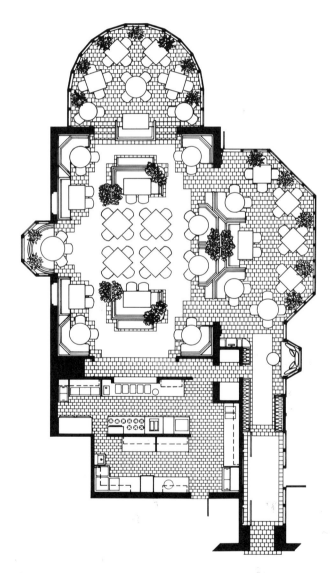

5-47. *Wildflower, with its self-contained kitchen and variety of seating areas, draws many of its patrons from outside of the hotel (Warren Platner Associates Architects drawing).*

5-48. *In the interior dining area, special alcove seating, profusions of silk flowers, custom tablelamps, and a view into the kitchen create a popular space.*
(Jaime Ardiles-Arce photo)

5-49. *Wildflower's maitre d' stand was artfully integrated by Platner and his associates into the wine storage area cabinetry that flanks the entryway.*
(Jaime Ardiles-Arce photo)

ers. In addition to the alcove banquettes, a few rectangular, free-standing tables in the center of the room were specified so that management could push them together to accommodate large parties. At those tables, Platner and his associates designed a very tall, decorative table lamp that rises high above the diners and gives the tables a special character. Moreover, the elevated inside room offers patrons their own special view into the partially open kitchen.

Wildflower's decorative motif is reflected in every design element of the restaurant: the custom-designed maitre d' stand (fig. 5-49), the silk-screened window shades, the painted woodwork, and the yellow ribbons hanging from silk lampshades. A pale yellow and white color scheme accented with multicolored flowers extends the Alpine atmosphere inside and effects a kind of lighthearted milieu that is comfortable for patrons in formal or informal dress. The consistency of the motif adds up to a place with its own identity. According to Platner, such attention to detail does not have to be expensive: painted woodwork, quarry tile floor, and standard roller shades, for instance, were not expensive purchases. In fact, the priciest items were the silk flowers. "We bought the finest artificial flowers available, because they were the centerpiece of the restaurant," noted Platner, "but we really didn't do anything economically extravagant."

ITALIAN ILLUSIONS

LAKESIDE DELICATESSEN Oakland, CA

When Ace Architects was retained to renovate the successful Lakeside Delicatessen in its hometown of Oakland, they had no idea that the design would become an imaginary re-creation of the space "as it should have been" in Roman times. But, faced with Lakeside's expansion into the adjacent store, the architects devised a creative plan based on discoveries of classical elements. A pantheon-like rotunda, a terrazzo floor design of the sea god Triton, and a columned arcade leading to an outdoor garden where Neptune brandishes his trident in a stonework fountain (fig. 5-50) contribute to the classic story line in this forty-seven-seat eatery.

The creative idea could never have been accomplished without careful planning because the owner could not afford to close down the existing delicatessen during the four months while the new one was being built. In order to keep the restaurant open for as long as possible, the architects organized the project into three phases. During phase I, the existing deli stayed open while the architects worked on the neighboring store. They built half the rotunda, and installed service counters, casework, and equipment. During phase II, the newly built adjacent store was open for business, serviced by the existing kitchen. Meanwhile, the existing front of the house was closed, and the architects completed the complementary half of the rotunda. Only in the third and final phase did the delicatessen close for just over two weeks, and the wall between the spaces was demolished. "We were greatly relieved," said project architect David Weingarten, "when the two halves of the rotunda matched!" In addition, over this short period the kitchen was upgraded, terrazzo and epoxy floors were installed, and final utility hookups were accomplished. The work required close coordination of the various building trades by the general contractor and cooperation from the many building and agency inspectors.

5-50. *Throughout the Lakeside Deli, classical columns are given a new twist.*
(Russell Abraham photo)

HOTEL? WHAT HOTEL?

KULETO'S San Francisco, CA

How do you create a hotel restaurant that has a different enough image from the hotel to make it seem like a totally separate establishment? Then again, how can you design that same restaurant so that it helps to sell the hotel? This was part of the challenge facing Pat Kuleto of Kuleto Consulting and Design when assigned to design a restaurant in San Francisco's Villa Florence Hotel, which was also designed by Kuleto.

Kuleto had a very long, skinny space in which to fit the bar and restaurant that would later bear his name. What he created was an establishment with its own identity, one that did not look like it was part of the hotel, yet one that blended unobtrusively into the hotel. He accomplished this tricky feat by designing two entrances, one through the hotel lobby and one from the street (fig. 5-51), and by dividing the room into a series of distinctly separate spaces.

The street entry leads directly to the bar, where stools and highboy tables provide seating for a mixed crowd of young professionals who frequent the place after work. Beyond a half-wall partition, seating is used by drinkers as well as diners during the busy cocktail hours (fig. 5-52).

Kuleto located a second area on a raised platform behind the bar and adjacent to a display cooking area where cooks grill meats and

5-51. *The exterior of Kuleto's is clearly differentiated from the entrance of the Villa Florence Hotel.*
(Joseph Durocher photo)

5-52. *The seating area adjacent to the bar provides a lively setting and a clear view of people entering and exiting.*
(Joseph Durocher photo)

fish over open flames (fig. 5-53). Some seating is provided at a sushi bar, and some at deuces across from the pickup station. Diners also have the option of more intimate seating areas in the secluded rear section of this seating area, at the back of the restaurant.

A third area of the room does not have the same tapas bar or bistro effect of the bar and dining sections just described. Here the glass-enclosed dining room is open to and actually juts out into the Italianate hotel lobby. This quiet, airy space offers the most private dining

and is the only area in the restaurant open for breakfast.

But how can three such distinct areas flow together and function well for the operator? What kind of design concerns have to be incorporated? Pat Kuleto's solution was to understand the restaurant business from the ground floor up and integrate that understanding into the design.

Kuleto had been a bartender, a restaurateur, manager, cook, and designer-consultant for more than 130 restaurants, and his breadth of experience went into each establishment. First, he looked at and got involved with basic concept development to determine what kind of a restaurant would work in a given space—that's the market study part of his work. He said that he would love to create a cutting-edge design, but instead most of his efforts focused "on spaces that looked new enough to draw people in, yet were timeless enough to stay in vogue when the fashions changed in a few years." The intended life-span of Kuleto's, for example, is fifteen to twenty years.

Second, Kuleto studied operational concerns and thought the design through from the worker's perspective. His design is sensitive to the needs of cooks, servers, and bartenders because he knows their jobs and because he worked closely with key staff members to make design modifications before the construction was completed.

The bottom line of this approach to design at Kuleto's is a 165-seat restaurant that successfully integrates the architecture of two distinct spaces—the restaurant and the hotel. Further, the relatively modest design investment of $850,000 (in 1987) produced a restaurant that was expected to gross nearly $4 million in its first year of operation.

5-53. *The cold food preparation area in the display kitchen provides an expanded back-of-the-house view for diners.*
(Joseph Durocher photo)

In the spare architectural interior of City Restaurant, Los Angeles, architects Schweitzer-Kellen used color on the tables and chairs to highlight the tabletop as a visual focal point. (Tim Street-Porter photo)

Claudia's highly graphic exterior in San Diego's Horton Plaza, designed by Tom Grondona Architect and the G-Force Art Installations, gives visual and olfactory cues to passersby of what they can expect inside. (Robinson/Ward photography ©)

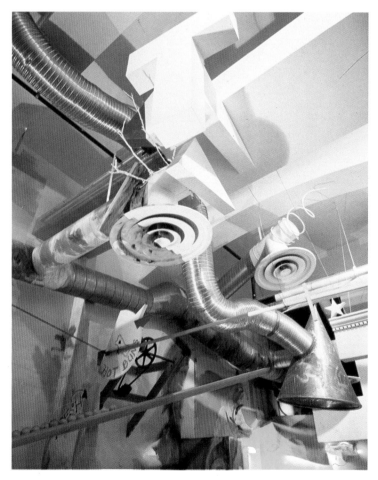

Grondona and the G-Force created a whimsical metaphor of the "exploded parts" of a cinnamon bun factory in Claudia's interior. (Robinson/Ward photography ©)

The former Tivoli brewery in Denver was transformed by Communication Arts Incorporated into the Rattlesnake Club, an ingenious blend of restoration and modern design applications. Seen here is the main dining floor, with its newly built mezzanine level. (R. Greg Hursley, Inc. photo)

At New York's America, MGS Architects took full advantage of the wide open industrial space to enhance the grand cafe environment. A central promenade capped with a stylized neon flag divides the seating areas and leads guests to the elevated bar. (Masao Ueda photo)

The raised deuces along America's north and south walls provide the most visible seating in the restaurant. Panoramic murals juxtapose "modern" America in pastels with fragments of Navajo Indian designs. (Masao Ueda photo)

This Seafood Shanty restaurant in Langhorne, PA,
was fitted out by DiLeonardo International with
furled canvas, banded columns, wood and metal
pipe rail, and blue tiling to evoke the feeling of a
cruise ship.
(Warren Jagger photo)

Architect Warren Platner utilized color and texture
to create a warm summerlike feeling in the
Wildflower Restaurant, The Lodge at Vail, CO.
(Jaime Ardiles-Arce photo)

The sizzling servery design at The Greenery, St. Vincent Medical Center, Toledo, OH, was a drastic departure from its institutional-looking predecessor. Morris Nathanson Design, Inc. used bright primary colors and reflective surfaces to help speed customers through the space. (Warren Jagger photo)

The main dining room at The Greenery was placed in what was formerly a courtyard sandwiched between two existing buildings. To create an open, comfortable atmosphere, Morris Nathanson Design specified skylights, greenery, and a zoned dimming system. (Warren Jagger photo)

Architects John Portman & Associates took full advantage of their famous "exploded architecture" technique in the creation of an atypical dining environment at the R. Howard Dobbs University Center, Emory University, Atlanta. The terraced dining levels provide a dramatic stage set for both student dining and catered functions. (Timothy Hursley photo)

Aumiller Youngquist, P.C. maintained the "trellislike" appearance of existing ceiling trusses, added bare bulb lighting, painted faded "frescoes" on the deliberately cracked walls, and utilized a mélange of floor tiles to create a rustic Italian theme at Scoozi, Chicago. (Steinkamp/Ballogg photo)

The raised seating platforms at Scoozi, with their extensive amounts of heavy woods, textured wall treatments and booth seating, provide an intimate environment quite different from the bustling core of the restaurant. (Steinkamp/Ballogg photo)

*The interior of Cardini, in the Los Angeles Hilton, relies
on classic architectural forms to shape dining bays. Architects
Voorsanger & Mills worked closely with fifteen other design
team members to create this atypical hotel restaurant.
(© Peter Aaron/ESTO photo)*

Architect Hervin Romney utilized vibrant colors to
transform an undistinguished 1930s building into a
signature art deco exterior for this Miami Beach
Burger King.
(Jose A. Fernandez photo)

Romney's unusual yet effective interior scheme
turned the Burger King building inside-out to give
customers the feeling of dining in an outdoor plaza
sparked with color and whimsey.
(Jose A. Fernandez photo)

Exquisite food presentation focuses attention on the tabletop at New York City's China Grill. Dappled gold wall surfaces warm up the contemporary design scheme by Jeffrey G. Beers Architects.
(Joseph Coscia, Jr. photo)

Paint charts, brought back from Mexico, were used by ASA Architects to formulate the palette of colors used throughout Cinco De Mayo, New York City. Corrogated metal and steel decking on the face of the bar also help to evoke the spirit of Mexico. (Elliott Kaufman photo)

The bar at Aurora, New York, designed by Milton Glaser and Phillip George, is the restaurant's centerpiece. Luncheon guests often choose to dine at the undulating marble countertop, crowned by a glowing multitude of bubble-shaped chandeliers. (Regina S. Baraban photo)

Stark white linen and the classic forms of glasses and flatware offer a perfect backdrop for a food-centered dining experience. Glaser incorporated his signature "bubble" motif in the design of china, produced specially for the restaurant. (Regina S. Baraban photo)

Zakaspace Designers artfully employed light, color, and texture to create a fanciful 1950s interior for Monday's at Printers' Square, Chicago. Photographic blow-ups above the bar reveal vintage glimpses of the city.
(Jon Miller, Hedrich Blessing photo)

Philip George designed Le Bernardin, located in New York's Equitable Center, in a luxurious, residential style appropriate to a four-star dining experience. (Peter Paige photo)

Working with co-owner/ chef Gilbert LeCoze and facilities consultant Frank N. Giampietro, George carefully designed every detail of Le Bernardins' spacious kitchen for environmental comfort and ease of operation. (Peter Paige photo)

6

DESIGN APPLICATIONS: MAXI CASE STUDIES

The creation of a restaurant is always a daunting experience. As we've established in earlier chapters, foodservice design is a complex, multifaceted process that brings together a range of disciplines and personalities. Anything can happen. Construction and renovation invariably uncover structural surprises. Prices of FF&E rise, and more monies must be found or budget adjustments made. The chef changes the menu, and kitchen design requires modifications. Unexpected construction delays throw the whole schedule off, forcing ownership to postpone opening and lose important revenue. Tempers flare, egos soar out of control. And sometimes, magic is created.

In the final analysis, each restaurant design has its own singular story. We've selected seven very different types of places to discuss in this chapter. Each case is presented in the same format, which clearly reveals the similarities and differences between them. What we've attempted to do is weave a narrative; uncover the human dynamics and thought processes which birthed each restaurant. The cases point out the delicate interactions between the many diverse personalities, and the complexity of the teamwork that is at the root of any successful restaurant design.

A NEW DIRECTION FOR HOTEL RESTAURANT DESIGN

CARDINI   Los Angeles, CA

The design of Cardini, a handsome Northern Italian restaurant located in the Los Angeles Hilton, was made possible by the leadership of one man who was tenacious enough to insist on an atypical hotel restaurant design and courageous enough to pay the price. Indeed, Henry A. Lambert, president of the Reliance Development Group who owned the hotel, functioned in the traditional role of patron for Voorsanger & Mills Associates Architects, designers of the restaurant. Without such strength at the helm, the architects could not have bypassed the corporate red tape inherent to complex hotel projects and departed from prototypical hotel restaurant design.

Lambert was the glue that held a very large team together and the catalyst for what became a synergistic team effort. At times up to seventeen people participated in the weekly design meetings, whose primary team members included Ed Mills, principal, and Konrad Wos, project director, from New York–based Voorsanger & Mills; Hilton General Manager Andre Schaefer, Food and Beverage Director Maurice A. Constantin; Senior Vice-President, Western Region, Hilmar Rosenast; and General Contractor James A. Amato.

Project Background

The Los Angeles Hilton opened as a Statler Hotel in 1949 with 1,228 rooms and suites. When the hotel was purchased by Reliance Development Group in the early 1980s, a total $60-million refurbishment of the hotel had already begun. Numerous other hotels had been built in the area of the Hilton, and its dated appearance kept it from gaining its fair share of the market. The first phase of the refurbishment was to modernize the public spaces of the hotel and to modify guest room configurations that reduced the number of sleeping rooms to only 910. The second phase of the project included the renovation of the existing Veranda restaurant, which, although it hadn't been substan-

tially updated for twenty-five years, was the best the hotel had to offer. In its place an entirely new restaurant, Cardini, was built and opened in 1985. The third phase of the project included repainting the exterior skin of the hotel and redesigning the courtyard and pool area adjacent to Cardini. These efforts were but a part of Hilton's billion-dollar restoration program of twelve of its aging properties.

Ownership did not expect Cardini to be a significant moneymaker for the hotel. Rather, the idea was for the restaurant to create an image that would help to elevate the image of the Los Angeles Hilton.

Design Description

FRONT OF THE HOUSE

Dramatic, Romanesque architecture forms the décor in this 160-seat restaurant whose floor plan echoes the layout of a typical Italian village (fig. 6-1). Cardini can only be entered from the

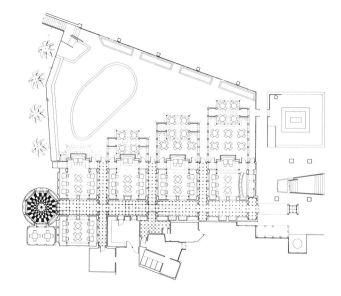

6-1. *The floor plan of Cardini clearly shows the individual dining bays that contribute to the success of the restaurant (Voorsanger & Mills Associates Architects drawing).*

hotel lobby. It is fronted by an outdoor terrace on its far side and a long circulation corridor along the inner wall. Highlighted with small niches displaying such items as exotic flowers, food displays, and Italianate carvings, this 100-foot-long columned corridor beckons patrons to enter the restaurant and provides a transition from the lobby environment. It is an impressive statement that leads customers to expect an impressive dining experience.

The entrance corridor (fig. 6-2) separates the kitchen (at left) from several small dining pavilions (at right) and ultimately leads to a semiprivate octagonal dining room that marks the south end of the restaurant (fig. 6-3). The square dining bays, each seating twenty-seven, are separated from each other by low dividing walls, structural columns, and secondary or side street corridors that house gueridon wait stations, the only backup for service supplies. Capped by vaulted wooden ceilings and brightened by a surprisingly warm, Mediterranean blue color scheme, the dining areas offer intimacy but not total seclusion: The open grid of the low dividing walls allows a clear sightline through the space.

6-2. The circulation corridor at Cardini separates the kitchen on one side from the dining room on the other side.
(Regina S. Baraban photo)

6-3. *The octagonal dining bay, with its sound-absorbing ceiling treatment, provides a quieter and more intimate atmosphere.* (©*Peter Aaron/ESTO*)

BACK OF THE HOUSE

Cardini's kitchen is hidden from public view to the left of the main corridor. The kitchen's placement causes some cross-traffic flow between guests and service staff, but because of the leisurely pace of the restaurant, this does not pose any operational problems. The kitchen is actually an extension of the main kitchen of the hotel. Although it is physically connected with the banquet and coffee shop kitchens, its equipment, operation, and staff are separate.

To the right of the entryway to the kitchen is the servers' beverage station. Here, the service staff draw their own nonalcoholic beverages, are supplied with alcoholic beverages from a service bar, and enter their orders at one of two service stations. In turn, these orders are printed out for the production personnel at the cold and hot food stations. Although these stations function well, Food and Beverage Director Constantin feels that the beverage area

would function even better for server maneuverability if the cold food station had also been placed here. Additionally, Constantin would have preferred that the cappuccino and espresso machine be staffed by a beverage person rather than used by all the wait persons.

Immediately behind the beverage station sits the dish machine, which is used exclusively for Cardini. The cold and hot food stations are lined up perpendicular to the main corridor. The cold station (fig. 6-4) is relatively small and capable of holding two workers during peak times. Food is stored in undercounter refrigeration and in a reach-in refrigerator to the left of the station. On the service side of the reach-in are sliding glass doors, and on the production side are right-hand-hinged swinging doors.

The plating area is comprised of steam table wells, a trunnion kettle, and overshelves with overhead calrod units to maintain the temperature of foods waiting to be served.

The hot food section is made up of several

6-4. *Kitchen staff relies on a fully stocked cold bain marie to meet demands during peak service hours.*
(Joseph Durocher photo)

stations. The boiler station is equipped with an undershelf and an overshelf for pan storage. Adjacent to this station is a double-cavity convection steamer used for vegetables and some seafood products. The menu relies heavily on sautéed items so the sauté station, with its twelve open-top burners, is one of the busiest in the kitchen (fig. 6-5). Below the burners is a set of three cavity ovens that do all of the roasting for the restaurant and at times hold food during service. Top-broiled or browned foods are finished in the salamanders over the sauté station. The pasta station is an extension of the sauté station and is nothing more than a series of pots on open-top burners. When Cardini first opened, Chef di Cucina Ruggero Gadaldi removed the automatic pasta heater and opted instead for the stove-top pots. With the addition of a wall-mounted, long-neck faucet, fresh water could be added to the pots as needed.

The pasta itself is made daily in a corner of the bakeshop. The bakeshop produces all of the rolls and desserts served in Cardini and also desserts for other outlets in the hotel. Most desserts served in Cardini are garnished with some form of chocolate: truffles, leaves, and curls. To produce these chocolate delicacies, a refrigerated chocolate room sits between the hot food kitchen and the bake shop. Chocolate carvings, used to garnish banquet buffets served elsewhere in the hotel, are also created in this room.

Cardini's chef sets his own product specifications, which then guide the hotel purchasing department in the selection of top-quality items. Chef Gadaldi specifies fresh, seasonal ingredients. Cardini's food is received and stored in the hotel's receiving and food storage areas.

Type of Restaurant

Cardini is an upscale, moderately expensive Northern Italian establishment located in the Los Angeles Hilton. It is a hotel restaurant that

6-5. *Pasta and sautéed foods, prepared on twelve open-top burners in the hot foods section, dominate Cardini's menu.*
(Joseph Durocher photo)

does not resemble a typical hotel restaurant either in appearance or in style of management. Organizationally, Cardini is part of the hotel's food and beverage department, but Cardini's executive chef does not report to the hotel's executive chef, who is responsible for banquets, as is generally the case. Rather, he reports to the food and beverage director. This chain of command is considered crucial for the smooth operation of a first-class restaurant.

The Market

Open five days a week for lunch and six nights a week for dinner, Cardini attracts a distinct customer group for each meal period. During the day, businesspeople frequent the restaurant. Ownership intended the restaurant to generate repeat luncheon business and it does: Food and Beverage Director Constantin estimated a hefty 75 percent of the lunch crowd has eaten there before; many dine at Cardini three or four times a week. Management's goal of becoming an established part of the downtown Los Angeles business community has apparently been realized.

Nighttime business presented a greater challenge. The owners anticipated an evening clientele of hotel guests, who form a reliable but relatively small market base. Because the Hilton is situated in a downtown business district—as compared to the more glamorous Beverly Hills or Santa Monica locations nearby—it was not expected to draw large numbers of destination customers for dinner. Still, ownership hoped that a good restaurant would attract some evening business. As it turned out, 1987 dinner business exceeded 1984 forecasts, according to Constantin, with an average of eighty-five to ninety diners nightly.

Cardini was designed to draw not only restaurant customers but hotel customers as well. The idea was to create a kind of ripple effect: Diners, impressed by both the environment and the cuisine at Cardini, would see the hotel in a new light. Luncheon regulars would recommend the hotel to their out-of-town associates and guests. People would book the hotel because they had heard of the restaurant. In effect, Cardini's reputation would help to sell hotel rooms. Additionally, good word-of-mouth regarding the restaurant would also boost banquet and convention sales.

In general, the design team anticipated an upscale clientele cognizant of both good food and good architecture. The lunch crowd, as hoped for, consists of well-dressed, fairly conservative businesspeople who speak softly and carry many gold cards. Cardini has developed a loyal following, particularly with architecture buffs. Formal business meetings are often held over lunch in the back (most private) room. Dinner clientele includes hotel guests and some destination diners; good reviews have probably helped the dinner business. Both lunch and dinner customers are mature and subdued, with men in suits and women in dresses.

When Cardini opened in 1985, Northern Italian cuisine was fairly new to southern California. The only direct competition consisted of Rex, an elegant and pricey Northern Italian restaurant nearby, which had an excellent reputation and a very high check average. The owners felt that the market could support a more moderately priced Northern Italian restaurant with first-class cuisine and service to match. Northern Italian cuisine had already established itself as a sure winner on the East Coast, and ownership perceived the West Coast as following the trend, especially given the success of the direct competition.

Secondary competition in this area of downtown L.A. was comprised of non-Italian restaurants that attracted a similar business clientele, and nighttime competitors consisted of similarly styled and priced restaurants located in trendier areas outside of downtown. The people who went downtown to work every day didn't want to travel back at night to go out to dinner.

During the day, however, downtown Los Angeles offered a steady and growing business clientele. In particular, Lambert was developing a large office building right next door to the Hilton that, when it opened in mid-1987, would provide a significant new customer base for luncheon at Cardini.

Cardini's location in downtown Los Angeles guaranteed a relatively savvy, ethnically diverse business crowd. California's year-long bounty of fresh vegetables and fruits as well as its pioneering spirit of culinary experimentation had bred a generation of well-informed diners with high expectations. The restaurant could not succeed without good food. Similarly, the abundance of dramatic architecture and high-design restaurants influenced Angelenos to be very selective about design.

Cardini's location inside a hotel, despite the fact that it guaranteed some evening business, was primarily an obstacle to be overcome. Although the hotel lobby had been renovated shortly before Voorsanger and Mills were brought on board, the 1950s-style building had little street appeal. There was nothing inherently interesting about the architecture. The restaurant did not have an outside entrance and could be reached only by walking through the hotel lobby. The existing kitchen was really a finishing area, with most preparation handled in the main hotel kitchen, a situation that General Manager Andre Schaefer found unacceptable for a first-class restaurant. Schaefer and Constantin bucked the system to redesign the back of the house into an autonomous kitchen and also developed a separate management team.

Cardini's design effectively upgraded its entire environment. Subsequent to their work on Cardini, Voorsanger and Mills were retained to redesign the terrace and pool area outside and to supervise the repainting of the hotel in a subtle gray-and-white stripe that obliterated the dated esthetic. Deep inside a hotel lobby is never the best location for a fine dining restaurant, but by creating something special out of something ordinary, the design team created a destination spot.

Economic conditions in Los Angeles were fairly stable during the development of Cardini. In general, the economic climate when Cardini was built looked quite positive from the developer's perspective, helped along by the ACRS (accelerated capital recovery system) benefits of the 1982 tax laws.

Concept Development

Cardini's concept stemmed primarily from Henry Lambert's philosophy of transporting New York thinking to Los Angeles, whose skyline in 1985 did not yet reflect the architectural flourishes of postmodernism so prevalent on the Eastern Seaboard. California has historically been receptive to all manner of new fashions, and Angelenos were thought likely to welcome the stylistic embellishment of postmodern architecture as a fresh idea.

Lambert's concept began with the decision to create a high-quality restaurant and then encompassed the postmodern esthetic. He retained Voorsanger & Mills, a respected firm at the forefront of architectural style, before he decided on the type of cuisine. Voorsanger & Mills developed the design concept as an expression of interior architecture that relies heavily on the interrelationship of texture, color, materials, and form.

Only after the design style and design firm were set did Lambert decide on the food. The decision to go with a Northern Italian menu was based both on food costs and on the market potential in downtown Los Angeles. As the concept evolved, it encompassed a smooth integration of food with design.

The Menu

Chef di Cucina Ruggero Gadaldi was brought on board four months before opening. By that time, Hilton management had given approval for Cardini to have its own kitchen and management staff, and the concept of Northern Italian food was established. Adhering to a philosophy that cooking be simple, with fresh, natural ingredients, Chef Gadaldi developed a light Northern Italian menu, distinguished by meats prepared in their natural juices, fresh herbs and spices, and innovative pastas such as black ravioli with tarragon and New Orleans shrimp and whole wheat fettuccini with fontini cheese, potato, white cabbage, butter, sage, and garlic. Gadaldi contributed to the kitchen design as well so that the kitchen staff could efficiently produce Cardini's menu.

Cardini's menu was not significantly altered during the first two years of operation. Items evolved, but Gadaldi's *nuova cucina* remained a winning approach. Due to the facts that the chef contributed to the kitchen and menu design prior to the restaurant opening and that the public had a predilection for Northern Italian food, stability reigned in Cardini's kitchen.

The Budget

Originally budgeted at $600,000, the total redesign, including kitchen and outside area, came to approximately $1.05 million. The kitchen line, installed during the last four months after Chef Gadaldi came on board, cost $200,000.

According to the architects, contractor James Amato of Environmental Planning Inc. did a superb job not only in terms of workmanship but also in terms of cost control. He built the dining bays one at a time so that the first became a kind of full-scale model. The first dining bay took ten weeks to build; the rest took four weeks each. During the planning process, Amato was able to suggest cost-saving measures that did not compromise the architectural idea, said project architect Wos.

On the one hand, because the restaurant was to function as the showpiece for the hotel, Lambert allocated the additional funds necessary to achieve the architectural plan. On the other hand, the architects relinquished some costly design applications that were not absolutely essential to the concept. In the end, everyone compromised, but no one sacrificed. "It could have cost less," said Lambert, "but it was worth it."

Style of Service

Cardini benefits from well-executed a la carte service. Dinner plates are set up for service in the plating area of the kitchen. All foods are assembled on the plates and covered with dome lids. The plates are then carried to service carts at the patio-side ends of the service corridors. Because of the use of banquette seating, this style of plate service works better than platter service and also speeds the artfully assembled plates to the guests. The waitstaff carefully set the plates in front of the guests. Plates with meat, poultry, or other protein foods are always positioned with the meat closest to the diner, a simple but important detail.

The service teams are set up so that one captain, one waitperson and one commis service each twenty-seven-seat dining area. The service is attentive without being overbearing, and the waitstaff often watch the room from the seclusion of the service corridors.

Speed of Service

The service is very leisurely. The waitstaff does not speed through the corridors as if they were in the hotel coffee shop. At Cardini, lunch typically takes sixty to seventy-five minutes and dinner up to two hours.

Per Customer Check Average

Cardini was conceived as a moderately expensive, fine dining restaurant whose per customer check average would be lower than the directly competitive Northern Italian restaurant located nearby. In 1987 the check average, excluding drinks, was $21.60 for lunch and $32.00 for dinner. Generous portions helped to achieve a good price-value relationship.

General Ambiance

What the architects worked to achieve at Cardini was a balance between the bustling, see-and-be-seen restaurant and the subdued establishment geared to quiet business meetings. They wanted patrons to feel private, yet not entirely cut off from other diners. The idea was a serene atmosphere that nonetheless was comfortably animated by people, sound, and all the life of a restaurant. Exciting architecture would create high expectations and a far-reaching reputation for the hotel.

Management Philosophy

More than anything else, the idea of Cardini as imagemaker for the hotel drove both ownership and management. The restaurant was intended to boost banquet sales and sell hotel rooms. Profit was not the motive. The goal was to give Los Angeles something new, something people would talk about for a long time to come.

The Design Team

Many players influenced the design of Cardini. As part of a complex foodservice system, the restaurant required years of complicated planning. Over those years countless meetings were held and battles fought, but the core design team emerged as a strong, united entity whose vision superseded individual egos.

Working with team leader Henry Lambert of Reliance Development Group were several Hilton executives, including corporate people and L.A. Hilton management. Here, we include interviews with the two Hilton executives who were most intensely involved with both the design and the ensuing operation of the restaurant: General Manager Andre Schaefer and Food and Beverage Director Maurice Constantin. From Voorsanger & Mills, both Partner-in-Charge Ed Mills and Project Director Konrad Wos were involved very early on in the conceptual phases. They subsequently retained foodservice, electrical, and lighting consultants to assist in design development and implementation. Among these were lighting designer Carl Hillmann and contractor James Amato. All of the people who contributed to Cardini's concept and design talked about an atmosphere of positive teamwork.

HENRY LAMBERT, DEVELOPER

As president of New York–based Reliance Development Group, Henry Lambert had a background not only in real estate but in the food business as well. As founder and operator of the successful Pasta and Cheese shop chain, he was well acquainted with the practical components of a foodservice operation. As a developer of hotels and office buildings across the country, he was committed to quality architecture. These two facets of his personality were clearly manifested in the design of Cardini.

Talking with Lambert in his sweepingly modern office at New York's Park Avenue Plaza, we saw him as an efficient businessperson with well-organized, clear objectives. Members of the Cardini design team credit him with a steadfast vision and commitment to a first-class restaurant, without which Cardini could not have been realized.

It all began, said Lambert, with his company's decision to purchase the L.A. Hilton and transform it from a faded 1950s hotel into a semi-luxury downtown property. "The existing restaurant was mediocre and yet it was the best restaurant in the hotel," noted Lambert. "I decided to change it into a 'new' restaurant that could possibly become a destination spot for both lunch and dinner. I realized that the chances of it being profitable were less than certain, but I still believed it was worth it because it would set the tone of the hotel."

Design was such an important ingredient in Lambert's marketing strategy that he identified the design style first. The next step was choosing the architect. Ed Mills had previously designed a private home for Lambert, so a trusting relationship between client and designer had already been established. "Voorsanger & Mills were a reasonable choice, given that they were on the cusp of postmodern architecture and that I was comfortable working with them," explained Lambert, who added that he felt he could "control the architects in terms of producing an economically viable design and a practical layout that would support the restaurant operation."

The food decision was based on marketing strategy and food costs. "Los Angeles in the early eighties had lots of flaming sword restaurants and informal bistros, but not many Italian restaurants," said Lambert. "In addition, our food costs and labor costs would be lower than in other types of restaurants." Of course, Lambert's background with Italian food was helpful to the restaurant's development.

After these basic decisions were made, many things occurred simultaneously. Lambert worked with Ed Mills and Konrad Wos on the restaurant design and with Cardini's management team to identify a food concept that would fly in downtown Los Angeles.

The end result, according to Lambert, "has created its mark and operates fairly efficiently." He saw the food as comparable to the best restaurants in downtown Los Angeles, subject to continual improvements. He is pleased with the architecture and believes that, albeit expensive, it fulfills its purpose as imagemaker for the hotel. "Cardini's interior," asserted Lambert, "will be regarded as a fine example of postmodern architecture for a long time. I think it has a shot at becoming a classic of its kind."

ANDRE SCHAEFER, GENERAL MANAGER

Concept and design development of Cardini can be traced, in part, to the efforts of General

Manager Andre Schaefer, who has since moved on to become general manager of Miami's Fontainebleau Hilton Resort. A twenty-two-year veteran of the Hilton Corporation, Schaefer was born into the hotel business in his native Luxembourg. He had an extensive food and beverage background and had been responsible for the opening of numerous Hilton hotels around the world.

As for the Los Angeles Hilton, Schaefer felt that the existing Veranda restaurant was tired and worn and could attract business only at lunch. He was supported by Henry Lambert in his belief that "a first class restaurant was needed to set the etiquette for the entire hotel." Further, "when people dine in a first-class hotel restaurant, they will leave talking about the restaurant, never about the hotel," observed Schaefer. "In this case," he continued, "the restaurant becomes the signature of the hotel."

Schaefer enthusiastically supported the concept of operational autonomy for a first-class hotel restaurant. Consequently, as noted earlier, Cardini has its own kitchen and an executive chef who answers directly to the food and beverage manager and general manager rather than to the executive chef overseeing the other restaurants and banquet operations. This concept was also carried forward into the front of the house with an autonomous maitre d'.

The result of Cardini's separatism was evidenced by a strongly united restaurant staff, said Schaefer. Further, he pointed out that organizational autonomy enabled the restaurant staff to react to changes in the marketplace far more quickly than if they were incorporated into a larger food and beverage organization.

Schaefer's ideal is a restaurant that manifests itself as "perfection in quality of food, service and décor." As to the question of what is most important to the success of a hotel restaurant, Schaefer replied that food, service, and design are all equally important, and each must be compatible with the others if the restaurant is to succeed. Financial success, said Schaefer, was incidental to Cardini. "It didn't really matter if this restaurant never became a profit center. The important thing was that when a potential banquet customer was entertained at Cardini, the hotel made the sale."

MAURICE A. CONSTANTIN, DIRECTOR OF FOOD AND BEVERAGE

Swiss-born Constantin began his career in food-service at age fourteen, when he decided to become a chef. Over the ensuing years, he traveled extensively and worked both front and back of the house in various operations. When he became food and beverage director at the Los Angeles Hilton, Cardini was in the planning process.

As the project developed, Constantin strongly supported the concept of an autonomously run restaurant with Northern Italian cuisine and set about "convincing everyone involved that we didn't need a pizza oven or veal parmesan." Constantin agreed with Schaefer that a fine restaurant in a hotel should be operated separately from other hotel foodservice. As food and beverage director for the entire hotel, he became involved as mediator between the hotel staff and the restaurant staff. "Part of my role," Constantin recalled, "was to act as the link between restaurant people and other hotel people. I was able to appease both sides when things got hot, and eventually we built a strong team for Cardini. Now, everyone is used to the situation and to each other, and things have gotten easier." Constantin observed that Cardini's status as part of the hotel offers some advantages, namely, engineering, maintenance, and other support services. The restaurant's sharp angles and soft colors require careful and continual maintenance, according to Constantin.

Another component of Constantin's job involved working with the architects on front-of-the-house design decisions that affected the operation. "I focused on the operation and the architects focused on esthetics," he noted, "and there were many compromises. The architects were flexible enough that they changed things as long as it didn't destroy the design idea."

The end result functioned quite well, according to Constantin, who cited the fact that staff could traverse the "side street corridors" without crossing in front of the guests and that the dining bays were the perfect size for a three-person team of captain, waitperson and busperson. Constantin also discovered that during slow periods the restaurant could feel half-full rather than half-empty if diners were seated in each section rather than filling up sections one at a time. He also found that the separate "rooms" helped to mute noise.

Conversely, the maitre d' cannot readily keep his eye on all the tables and efficiently supervise the room. There was one major design omission as well—the architects forgot about service stations. Responding to management's request, special gueridons were designed and placed in the corridors to provide the necessary service backup.

In terms of the tabletop, muted red showplates with finely drawn lines of black and white form an interesting contrast to the restaurant's soft blue backdrop. The selection was a team effort. "But Henry Lambert didn't want the plates to become the centerpiece, so we chose white dishes to highlight food presentation," noted Constantin.

In mid-1987 Constantin left Hilton to launch his own venture. At that time, he felt optimistic about Cardini's long-term future, as long as management did not require "too much of a profit." The restaurant was contributing sixteen to twenty percent of the hotel's total yearly food and beverage sales. "We were breaking even with beverage sales included," said Constantin, "and did not really anticipate ever making much of a profit."

Making a profit, as stated earlier, was not Cardini's mission. Most important, in Constantin's words, "was the contribution of the restaurant to the image of the L.A. Hilton. Our repeat business was terrific, and people were coming into the hotel just because they had heard of Cardini. The hotel's sales staff made extensive use of the restaurant, and it was a considerable boost to banquet business. Given our goals, the return on investment was just fine."

ED MILLS AND KONRAD WOS, ARCHITECTS

The practice of New York–based Voorsanger & Mills Associates Architects encompasses a range of building types, including some highly regarded restaurant and retail projects. Voorsanger & Mills approaches each commission as a fresh architectural challenge and does not fast-

track a restaurant design or any other project. The firm's maxim is that good architecture takes time to develop. Project architects often spend many months in the programmatic phase working out complex architectural solutions. In the case of Cardini, Partner-in-Charge Ed Mills and Project Director Konrad Wos both stayed intensely involved from conception to completion. Their design was widely praised by the press and won awards for interior, tabletop, and lighting design.

The architects were brought in by Reliance after previous owners had renovated the lobby and charged with the redesign of the hotel's fanciest existing restaurant. "The space and the food were both a disaster," remembered Wos, "and people weren't eating there for many reasons. The 200-seat restaurant hadn't been substantially changed since 1952, and everything was worn. There were kidney shaped seating booths, a waterfall, and lots of vegetation. If management had waited a few more years, it actually could have been great 1950s nostalgia, but the décor was in terrible shape—and 1950s wasn't the concept."

Existing conditions posed many challenges. The 5,000-square-foot room dotted by six structural columns did not offer any inherently interesting architecture. It was long and relatively narrow. The entire far wall consisted of windows facing an unrenovated outdoor courtyard, which was not considered an appropriate view for an elegant restaurant. Further, "when a person walked into the space, he was lost, both in terms of where to sit and in terms of intimacy in the one big room." Part of the program involved breaking up the room into a series of spaces so that the operators could open up progressive areas of the restaurant as the need arose and so that the diners could experience a sense of intimacy. What this translated into architecturally, said Wos, was "providing the proper scale so that the right degree of intimacy was always kept, whether there were five people in the space or a hundred people in the space."

The series of six semiprivate dining rooms that Voorsanger & Mills came up with are multifunctional solutions (fig. 6-6). Each 21-foot-by-21-foot room seats twenty-seven people and

6-6. *Each twenty-one-seat dining bay is perfectly suited to a three-person service team.*
(©*Peter Aaron/ESTO*)

perfectly accommodates a three-person service team. When seated, the diners' experience is akin to being in a very small, very elegant restaurant because each "room" feels quite private; when standing, patrons have an unobstructed view through the "windows" of the low dividing walls, an orderly vista of dining bays and columns that appears infinite. Seated, the diners are secluded; standing, they are part of the life of the restaurant. In other words, sitting is in a private realm and standing is in a public realm. This was a conscious decision by the architects.

As mentioned earlier in the design description, the architects patterned Cardini's floor plan after the configuration of an Italian town, specifically the Strade Nuova in Genoa. The long entrance corridor that marks main street helps guests grasp the circulation flow of the restaurant and extends the public realm of the lobby. A transition between the outside lobby and the inside restaurant, this major circulation artery splits the kitchen at left from the dining area at right. "It meant that we couldn't get a logical, straight-line flow from back to front, but it turned out to be a wonderful solution regardless," explained Wos. "We built in a series of side street aisles behind and between the banquettes which became service corridors." The architects designed service carts in response to requests from the hotel staff. Waitpeople use the carts to bring plated food from back to front of the house. The gueridon-type carts, kept in the side streets, also function as service stations.

"The nature of the experience for guests," said Mills, "was that they walk down a public 'main street' made of fine materials such as marble and stone, with the banding and rustication that one would find in Italy. Then they arrive at the trattoria—their own private little twenty-seven-seat restaurant, which almost feels like a very exclusive mom and pop operation." In the dining bays, each of which has banquettes and free-standing fourtops, the architects chose softer materials than in the marble and stone entryway. Carpeting, fabric, and dramatic, vaulted mahogany ceilings not only add warmth to the dining areas but also impart a feeling of luxury.

For architect Konrad Wos, the creation of Cardini was similar to "the birth of a child." He traveled from New York to L.A. one to four times each month for design meetings and talked with the contractor constantly. "Because of the geographic distance, we had to organize our drawings so that we could communicate well by telephone," recalled Wos. The distance factor was not regarded as a problem, especially given the fact that ownership had resolved on bringing a New York attitude west.

The complexity of the architecture, however, meant that the contractor's role became absolutely crucial to the success of Cardini's design. "At Voorsanger & Mills, the contractor is as valuable a team player as any member of our staff," declared Wos. "Oftentimes a good contractor can suggest things which are not evident from the drawings themselves. Jim Amato had a big impact on the design. What kept our relationship from being confrontational was that we made changes as long as they didn't alter our philosophy or concept."

Relationships with other team members also reflected the architects' willingness to compromise but not to sacrifice design integrity. The largest battle lost was the proposed installation of a large equestrian statue in the back, octagonal dining room. The architects fought and won a battle for the Italian terrazzo that, painted in fat black and white bands, now covers walls and columns. "Andre Schaefer was a very important ally, but in the last three months he got nervous about the terrazzo," said Wos. "He felt it was too cold and wanted us to cover it with wallpaper. It took some persuasion to change his mind." The architects admitted that hard materials such as marble are cold but pointed out that they are naturally durable, far more so than warm materials such as wood. Their decision to use colder materials in the entry corridor and warmer materials in the dining bays was based in part on maintenance and durability considerations and in part on esthetic balance.

"Initially, it was a bit difficult for us to come to an attitude of mutual trust and understanding," noted Mills, "but it eventually became a great symbiotic relationship. Both Hilton and Reliance deserve a lot of credit for giving us the opportunity to produce this design without going through all the standard channels—which would have produced a standard product."

Cardini's design represents the culmination of Voorsanger & Mills's exploration of the post-modern design style. It was "the last project of that ilk, and the one that is most highly developed," explained Mills, noting that the firm has since moved on to a "sleeker architecture that relies less on applied color and more on the natural state of materials." Although the architects didn't believe that the public's attention span would support Cardini's current design forever, they predicted at least fifteen years of design viability. After that, the framework allows for relatively simple redecoration with paint and color; the architectural idea does not depend on a specific theme or type of menu.

"The biggest problem with hotel restaurants," concluded Wos, "is that often there is no individual team leader. And without that clear direction, it can be impossible to implement good design. I think that if Cardini is a success, it is due to Henry Lambert putting his personal stamp on it."

CARL HILLMANN, LIGHTING DESIGNER

The illumination program for Cardini, which garnered two prestigious lighting design awards, reflects a delicate balance of daylight, overall ambient light, and accent light. Carl Hillmann, president of New York–based CHA Design, Inc., believes that the most important maxim to remember about restaurant lighting is that accent lighting should be used to spotlight objects and indirect lighting should cast its glow on people. At Cardini, he worked with Voorsanger & Mills to achieve a balance of light that creates a warm, comfortable ambiance.

In Cardini, most fixtures, including fluorescents, are always kept dimmed. A preset dimming system varies the intensity according to time of day. The architects point out that the local lighting codes are extremely strict and that very few fixtures actually meet code requirements. Therefore, the lighting scheme utilizes standard, U.L.-approved downlights with focusing mechanisms, separated out from the "lampshade." These special shades are what people perceive as the lights, but they are in fact purely decorative. The light is actually provided by the code-approved downlights.

Hillmann, who cited Voorsanger & Mills's extensive knowledge about lighting, spent just two days working out the technical problems of the job. "The architects had the image; we helped think through the problems and figure out the detailing," he remarked. In the entry and circulation corridors, concealed fluorescent uplighting creates a brighter light level than in the dining pavilions in order to distinguish "inside" from "outside." Additionally, low-voltage downlighting glows through the decorative etched-glass panels mounted atop the columns at the corridor intersections, and track lighting accents the maitre d' stand and side wall niches in the entry corridor.

Lighting the dining bays was challenging, said Hillmann, because "we didn't know how to get the wood ceiling lit. These domed ceilings are made of mahogany and crowned with a cupola-like device. The goal was to get the wood to glow with light. Probably the single most important idea we gave the architects was to install some low-voltage downlights at the center of the ceiling and suspend etched-glass panels underneath them. The etched glass deflects light upward to cast a glow on the domed ceiling and also softens the light going downward to the tables below."

JAMES AMATO, CONTRACTOR

Everyone who worked with Jim Amato of Environmental Planning complimented his ability to build Cardini with a rare degree of craftsmanship. The job was complex, made even more so because "we had to live within an ongoing facility," said Amato. With a background of twenty-six years in the construction business, Amato doesn't specialize in restaurants, but he did admit to a liking for challenging projects. In Cardini, "the unusual shapes, the walls, the columns, and the materials all presented challenges. It was also a very trying project because we had limited access to the space."

Not only did Amato transcend the physical challenges of the job, but he transcended the psychological challenges as well. This was one of the rare designer-contractor relationships that stayed cordial throughout the entire design and installation process. "There was a feeling of openness and trust from the start," noted Amato, "and the attitude that this was not an adversarial relationship. Too often, projects start out with architect and contractor in adversarial positions and things just stay that way. At Cardini, the Hilton people and the architects were all first rate. Our attitude was, hey, we're all in this to get a good job, so let's work together."

One of the most difficult problems, said Amato, was presented by the custom-made lighting "shades." He worked closely with Konrad Wos who "played with the shapes until he developed the correct form, right there on the site." In addition, "interpreting the drawings was a constant challenge. Gene Woods, our on-site supervisor, was great. He slaved to ensure that the execution was just right. Sometimes he called New York four or five times a day. The phone bill went crazy." Other costs escalated as well. "Super-deluxe custom jobs like these are hard to figure," explained Amato, " but Lambert hung in there even though project costs went way over what he originally anticipated."

Amato said that what he enjoyed most

about Cardini was working with the architects. He summed up the sentiments of the entire design team when he remarked, "It was the relationship between people that really made this project."

Summary

Several themes emerge from an analysis of Cardini. First and foremost is the importance of a strong team leader for a complex foodservice project. Especially in the design of a hotel restaurant, which involves far more team members than most other types of establishments, a strong leader is essential for successful integration of food, service, and design. Second, the story of Cardini suggests that separate management of a first-class hotel restaurant leads to operational success. Third, special architecture can help transform an ordinary space, handicapped by the lack of an outside street entrance, into a destination restaurant. Fourth, hotel restaurant design can act as a marketing tool to sell hotel rooms and banquet business.

TWO-WEEK TRANSFORMATION

EXTRA! EXTRA!   New York, NY

Restaurant owners Don Lubin and Jeff Spiegel will never forget their first glimpse of designer Sam Lopata, who came flying through the doors of their restaurant decked out in leather pants with a billowing black cape streaming behind him. Lopata's dose of drama was like salve on their wounds, for the restaurateurs were desperately unhappy with the staid design of their six-month-old establishment. In retrospect, they speak of the flamboyant "Dr. Sam" as if he were a sort of irreverent guardian angel, one complete with a discernible French accent, a dashing, all-black wardrobe, and a ponytail. Most important, Lopata was able to successfully translate the owners' concept into a design that met their esthetic criteria, limited budget, and two-week construction timetable.

Project Background

The story behind the design of Extra! Extra! is as much about the complexities of the designer-client relationship as it is about problem solving. Lubin and Spiegel were old Peace Corps buddies who eventually became partners and restaurateurs. By the time they and a third partner, Tom Roline, decided to transform space that was formerly a delivery loading dock for the *Daily News* into a restaurant, they had two profitable operations under their belts. What made Extra! Extra! different was that it required a total change from industrial space to restaurant space—in essence, building a restaurant from scratch.

The owners' previous experience did not include such extensive design work, and they depended on their designer to tell them what the space should look like. They had retained an architect recommended by friends and had held many meetings to discuss the feeling they wanted to evoke in Extra! Extra!'s design. The architect seemed to understand, yet produced a somber, mahogany-clad room whose clubby ambiance was completely incongruous with the owners' wish for a breezy, informal atmosphere.

During the first few months of operation, the owners not only felt unhappy about Extra! Extra!'s design but also failed to meet their operational goals. Situated inside the Daily News building in Manhattan's busy midtown district, Extra! Extra! did a healthy lunch business but was dead at night. Lubin and Spiegel believed that the interior design had everything to do with the restaurant's bottom-line potential and agreed that a make-over was essential. This time around, they talked to experienced restaurant designers.

When they met Sam Lopata, it "was almost as if he could read our minds," said Lubin, and the die was cast. The owners' decision to cut their losses and redesign a brand new restaurant was essentially a marketing tactic based on the belief that only a bit of sizzle could really sell the steak.

Design Description

FRONT OF THE HOUSE

Thematically, Extra! Extra!'s design plays off the obvious newspaper theme in an inventive fashion, with life-sized plywood cutouts of cartoon characters, giant "ink splats" on the floor, and fragments of newspaper copy painted on the walls. Spatially, the 160-seat restaurant is divided by levels into three dining areas and an expanded bar that seats roughly twenty more patrons than prior to the redesign (fig. 6-7). The long, curvaceous, centrally located bar is the first image customers see when they enter the restaurant (fig. 6-8).

Most people smile when they walk into Extra! Extra! because cartoon characters greet them: Wimpy, wearing a chef's hat and gazing down at his beloved burger; Felix the cat in the maitre d' position, holding a menu; Dagwood, about to bite into his hero sandwich; and more. Walls behind the bar feature takes from the personals column, which, like the headlines and crossword puzzles decorating walls throughout

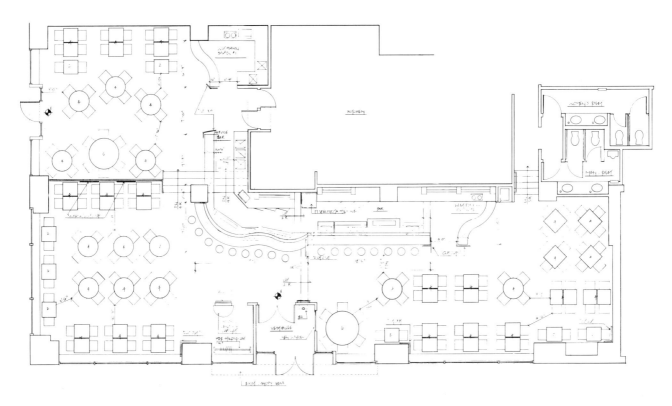

6-7. *The floor plan of Extra! Extra! shows three distinct dining areas pulled together by the serpentine bar (Sam Lopata, Inc., drawing).*

6-8. *The designers changed what was a sedate bar into a lively, open space that complements the new concept. (Joseph Coscia, Jr., photo)*

the restaurant, were taken straight from the *Daily News* archives (fig. 6-9).

The mood is fun and casual in this whimsical interior. Simple wooden chairs were painted red, white, and black to match the color scheme. Tile floors were left partially unfinished and randomly splashed with shiny black puddles that resemble printer's ink. The ceiling has an unfinished look as well, with suspended grids covering a bare concrete surface and exposed mechanical ductwork. Bare, low-wattage incandescent bulbs with sparkling filaments are draped over the ceiling grids. Their illumination is supplemented by ceiling-mounted can lights that shine on cardboard, cartoonlike faux lamps hanging over the windowed east wall. When filled with people, noise levels roar.

BACK OF THE HOUSE

Extra! Extra! has two kitchens, one on the basement floor and one on the street floor. The high rental cost of ground floor space forced the pre-

preparation and fabrication kitchen into the basement (fig. 6-10). All raw foods are received through the loading dock of the Daily News building and transferred to the basement kitchen by elevator. A single staircase is the only means of moving ingredients from storage or prepreparation to the final preparation kitchen upstairs. Because of this, all of the meats, fish, and poultry are carefully fabricated to minimize the weight of items carried up to the preparation kitchen. Fabricated meats and preprepared vegetables are held in walk-in refrigerators awaiting transport to the street floor kitchen. The consistent temperature of the walk-ins play an important role in maintaining the freshness of prepared products. In addition to the prepreparation of all cold food ingredients, pizza dough and toppings, baking, and dessert preparations are also completed in the subterranean kitchen.

The main kitchen incorporates a small work station for specialty preparations and a straight-line hot and cold foods section. The hot food section, staffed by three cooks and a floa-

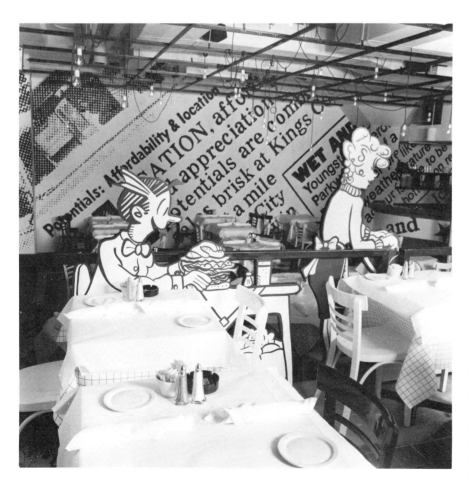

6-9. *The news theme—taken from the* Daily News *archives— is expressed by whimsical cutouts of cartoon characters and blown-up newspaper copy on the walls.*
(Joseph Coscia, Jr., photo)

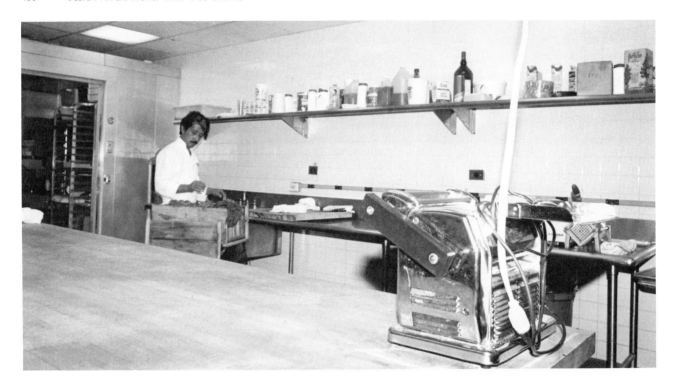

6-10. *Every type of food, from vegetables to pizza dough and pasta, is preprepared in the basement kitchen.*
(Joseph Durocher photo)

ter, is composed of a pizza station, fryer station, infrared and charbroiling station, and a sauté and sauce station (fig. 6-11). Immediately adjacent to the bank of ranges is a steam-jacketed kettle used to make stocks for a variety of soups and sauces.

Across the aisle from the bank of hot foods equipment is an assembly counter and holding equipment, including undercounter refrigeration and two hot bain maries. A key to the success of Extra Extra!'s kitchen design is the speed with which dishes can be prepared and served, especially during the busy lunch periods. To achieve this, the chef takes full advantage of the undercounter refrigeration to hold the mis en place (the portioned ingredients) for each dish. For holding batch-prepared hot foods, the two hot bain maries are invaluable.

The cold foods station, which is usually staffed by two cooks, incorporates a slicer and vegetable cutter, along with a large, iced bain marie and overhead refrigeration for holding preprepared desserts. The overhead refrigerator is also used to hold salads during the busy lunch time when servers are not able to pick them up quickly enough.

Across from the cold food station is a spacious dishwashing, pot-washing, and tableware storage area. These areas are immediately adjacent to the kitchen entry.

Type of Restaurant

Extra! Extra! is a casual, bistro type of restaurant. Its location inside the landmark Daily News building helped to dictate the newspaper theme and the eclectic, moderately priced menu of ethnically inspired sandwiches, salads, pizzas, and entrees.

The Market

Due to its location in midtown Manhattan, Extra! Extra! has a built-in neighborhood market for lunch. Not only could the owners count on business from the *Daily News* offices located in the same building, but also the immediate neighborhood is a sea of high-rise commercial towers. People working in those towers range from clerical help to corporate executives, all of whom are fair game for the restaurant's stylish fare, but the thrust is toward the middle of the market: Neither a cheap, fast food lunch nor an elegant gourmet lunch is served at Extra! Extra! Rather, diverse offerings, big portions, and an entertaining interior attract New York business-people for an animated meal.

The clientele reflects all manner of Manhattanites, including editors and journalists from the *Daily News* and other publishing companies nearby. The working population of New York is a melting pot of cultures, and so is the food at Extra! Extra! Both cuisine and design respond to the demanding tastes of a sophisticated clientele. Although the restaurant is not a white-tablecloth establishment, management makes sure that repeat guests are given special attention. Regulars have their favorite drinks made without asking and are even called up on the telephone on days when their favorite specials are being served. In the anonymous caverns of midtown Manhattan, such pampering means a lot to people and helps the restaurant to establish steady business.

Nighttime is a different story. The neighborhood dies in the evening, and when it first opened, so did the restaurant. The problem was that Manhattanites who live in midtown tend to go elsewhere for dinner. Still, potential customers were staying at nearby hotels and living in residential housing within walking distance—if only their mindsets could be changed. One of the main design goals was to give Extra! Extra! a face in the neighborhood and a clear identity as a local restaurant. The owners perceived design as a marketing tool that would help to "retrain the people who live here to think about going out to eat in their own neighborhood."

After the redesign, favorable publicity helped to boost the local dinner business a bit. The owners hoped to attract destination customers as well but had a seemingly insurmountable marketing challenge because New Yorkers do not commonly travel to midtown for dinner.

The owners felt that a turn and a half at lunch and a strong after-work bar business could carry a sparse dinner hour. In fact, the owners anticipated that the bigger, more convivial bar would boost the food/beverage sales mix of 70/30 up to 65/35. Again, a white-collar crowd of people who worked nearby would comprise the clientele.

Extra! Extra! management does not have to

6-11. *The compact yet fully equipped hot food line in the main floor kitchen supports a wide variety of menu items.*
(Joseph Durocher photo)

worry about lunchtime competition because far more people work in the immediate vicinity than there are restaurants to choose from. Chinese restaurants, Spanish restaurants, steakhouses, and bistros comprise the primary competition for lunch business. Secondary competition includes more expensive establishments, such as restaurants located at the Helmsley, Hyatt, and U.N. Plaza hotels, and less expensive eateries, such as delis and take-out gourmet shops. Extra! Extra!'s innovative ethnic menu and untraditional design scheme help to distinguish it from competing establishments located nearby.

Competition poses more challenges for bar and dinner business. During the after-work hours, nearby hotel bars compete for the happy hour crowd. At night, the real competition comes from established destination restaurants further uptown on the Upper East Side, or further downtown in the flatiron district, Greenwich Village, and other popular Manhattan locales.

The special qualities of Extra! Extra!'s location helped to forge the restaurant's singular identity: Its home in one of New York's most famous buildings gave a raison d'être for a theme related to that building.

As for the economic climate, midtown Manhattan's business base tends to remain stable. The working population is so large that even in recession years, when people watch their restaurant expenditures more closely, the daytime lunch market stays strong. Given New York's ever increasing taxi fares, predicting that neighborhood residents would prefer saving transportation money by remaining close to home for dinner seems reasonable.

Concept Development

The owners of Extra! Extra! claim that their concept remained constant from the restaurant's beginning planning stages: a moderately priced restaurant thematically related to the *Daily News*, with a light, open look that would be comfortable both for the business-person at lunch and the dinner customer in the evening. But the first design scheme just didn't reflect that concept.

Self-described intellectuals, Lubin and Spiegel spent a lot of time on concept development. After choosing a space they felt had great potential for lunch business and possible potential for dinner business, they began discussing the theme and the menu. In their minds, everything began to take shape around the name Extra! Extra!, with its straightforward newspaper reference. "We didn't know the specific design, but we knew the 'feel' that we wanted," said Lubin.

In the case of Extra! Extra!, the concept grew from the location and was expressed more by the interior design than by the menu. The owners weren't able to articulate their ideas in any more detail with Lopata than they were with the first designer, but Lopata appeared to understand their concept instantly. He used de-

sign elements in an obvious yet creative way to express the newspaper idea, and accurately interpreted the owners' desire for an enjoyable, amusing ambiance. As people move through the restaurant, they find the concept reflected in every aspect of the interior design.

By the time Lubin and Spiegel decided upon a redesign, they realized that the success of their concept depended upon a promotable design identity. The owners' choice of Sam Lopata, Inc., was based in part on Lubin and Spiegel's admiration of the firm's quirky and highly publicized restaurant designs for such New York establishments as Pig Heaven and Lox Around The Clock, which both evidenced a humorous, inventive design hand.

Lopata and project designer Denise Hall believed that the success of Extra! Extra!'s concept depended upon an identifiable restaurant image with street-side visibility and an instant impression when patrons walk through the door. Forbidden to change the building's exterior in any way, the designers nonetheless created a better street-side identity for the restaurant by removing the black venetian blinds that had covered the windows. They then hung cardboard cartoon lamps that are easily visible from the street. Without changing the building's facade, the designers imbued it with some thematic identity.

Prior to the redesign, people entering the restaurant were greeted with a view of an oversized service station. In response, Lopata and Hall changed the floor plan so that patrons' first interior view is of the playful bar area.

The Menu

From the time Extra! Extra! first opened, the menu was in a continual state of evolution. The front-of-the-house redesign, however, did not correspond with any significant changes in the menu.

Substantive changes were made to the menu with the hiring of a new chef, Richard Gaimaro, in early 1987. First, the printed menu (formerly in a tabloid format) appeared on a more formal menu card (fig. 6-12). Second, and most important, the menu items mirrored the diversity of the New York City marketplace. Gaimaro drew upon the ethnic backgrounds of

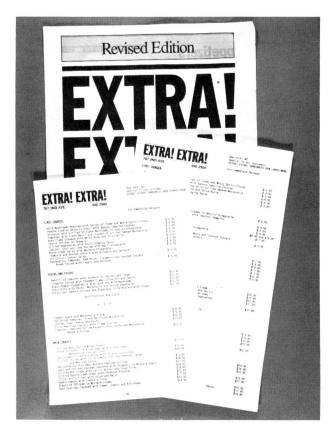

6-12. *Extra! Extra! menu. The tabloid used when Extra! Extra! opened was replaced with the ever-changing menu cards in the foreground.* (*Joseph Durocher photo*)

his cooks, the ready availability of specialty ingredients, and the demands of his customers for something new and different. The separate printed menus for lunch and dinner are supplemented with daily specials that incorporate fresh, seasonal foods. As Gael Greene put it in *New York* magazine, "It's a hodgepodge of goodies New Yorkers crave—pizza and pasta; sandwiches (including the Dagwood for two); something blackened, something grilled, Thai, Indian, Italian, and Mexican accents."

Much of the new direction for the menu came from Chef Gaimaro's willingness to work with his cooks to bring their native cuisines to Extra! Extra's! customers. The cooks, who have diverse ethnic backgrounds, are all given an opportunity to suggest menu items, develop them into workable recipes, and then see them added to the menu. The international mix of culinarians certainly supports the diversity of the menu.

Gaimaro reported that the kitchen works perfectly, save for an undersized pizza oven and

a single deep fryer. The same was true of his cooks, who like the openness of the space and layout of the equipment.

The Budget

The owners of Extra! Extra! spent a total of roughly $650,000 on FF&E for front and back of the house when the restaurant was first developed. At that time, they never intended to spend more money on a redesign, but, as they grew increasingly unhappy with the look of their restaurant, they agreed to budget money for a face lift.

Initially, Lubin and Spiegel believed that a cosmetic redo could change the look of the restaurant and keep costs to a minimum. Lopata convinced them, however, that physical changes were necessary in order to make a larger bar. This decision was not just to encourage a bigger bar scene but a decision that utilized the long, low, sinuous bar itself as a unifying element in the space.

Bar construction, therefore, made up the largest part of what became a $150,000 budget. "While Sam thought we had more work to do in the space than we had hoped, he actually listened to us, and we did agree on a number," said Lubin. "Our only worry was that he wouldn't adhere to that number." In fact, the job came in very close to the agreed-upon budget, plus met an incredibly tight time schedule and "went beyond" the owners' design expectations. They were ecstatic with the result and felt that the $150,000 budget was well spent.

Style of Service

When reopened, Extra! Extra! sported a sprightly service staff who offered quick and efficient plate service. Adjacent to the kitchen entry, Lopata had incorporated a service and buffet display station. Here, the service staff had backup supplies to reset tables and an assortment of antipasto-type appetizer items that could be plated and quickly carried to waiting guests. As volume grew, however, the display became difficult to service and control. The plating of all food was then moved to the kitchen and the area functioned solely as a support station for the wait staff (fig. 6-13).

6-13. *The service station, located to the left of the kitchen doors, is stocked with supplies for resetting tables and with hot beverages.* (*Joseph Durocher photo*)

The six to eight servers take orders from guests, yet the food runners tell the chef when to fire up each order and carry the finished orders to the dining room. This system keeps the table servers on the floor as much as possible.

Speed of Service

Fast service and quick turnover of the tables, especially during the bustling lunch hours, is one key to Extra! Extra!'s success. The restaurant is packed with customers by 12:15 P.M. and remains so until well after 2:00 P.M. High noise levels and relatively hard seats keep the customers moving through the restaurant. Not until the shoulder and evening hours, when the volume of business slacks off significantly, does the noise level drop enough to support a more leisurely dining experience.

Most of the dishes are prepared to order and require the coordination of items from multiple stations. The chef functions as the expeditor, using a loudspeaker to call out orders to all stations. This ensures maximum communication with the production staff when order-

ing and facilitates the assembly of individual dishes when the runners are ready to pick up their orders.

Per Customer Check Average

In 1987, the check average at Extra! Extra!, excluding drinks, was $13.00 for lunch and $14.00 for dinner. At lunch, the check average is just low enough to justify the noisy environment and relatively quick turnover. New Yorkers often want to sustain a high energy level right through the lunch break, and they're often in a hurry.

Still, in order to deliver a good price-value relationship, the restaurant offers large portions and culinary creativity. At dinner, the check average could be considered a relative bargain by local standards.

General Ambiance

The owners wanted Extra! Extra! to have a light and open feeling. The designers developed a bright and amusing interior, filled with sound and movement, whose motif relates to the obvious newspaper theme. To achieve an airy feeling, they developed the space as one big room and removed barriers that had been installed during the first design. Lopata and Hall also removed existing acoustic ceiling tiles because they deliberately wanted high noise levels to fill the room with upbeat energy.

Management Philosophy

Lubin and Spiegel's entrepreneurial, optimistic spirit drove the restaurant from start to finish. Their idea wasn't to create a classic, but a relatively short-term success that would last at least four years in one incarnation. A vital part of their management style is their willingness to take chances and trust the designer. Even though this philosophy failed the first time around, the owners still permitted Lopata to try wild ideas such as the giant ink splashes. Such willingness to abandon safe design avenues is unusual, especially in light of Extra! Extra!'s history.

The Design Team

The key players in Extra! Extra!'s design team were Don Lubin, Jeff Spiegel, Sam Lopata, and Denise Hall. The owners had a clear idea of the type of restaurant they wanted to create, and their philosophies and personalities set the tone of the redesign. Jeff Spiegel was very active until the two-week reconstruction period in dealing with technical consultants such as plumbers and electricians and staying closely involved with Lopata and Hall as they worked out design details. When the two-week reconstruction period began, however, Spiegel found his project supervision unnecessary. "I had expected to play a bigger role, but there was no need," he explained, "because Sam and Denise were on to every detail." Lubin added: "Don and I agreed that we wouldn't interfere with a designer who we believed would follow through on our vision."

Although Sam Lopata and Denise Hall were the architects of Extra! Extra!'s design, they credit the invaluable assistance of all the tradespeople and consultants who helped them build the restaurant in two weeks. These ac-

complishments included graphic execution of the cartoon cutouts by Serpentine Studio, bar construction by Wavedancer contractors, and lighting design by Ken Billington, Inc. "These are the people who turn our design ideas into reality," said Hall, "and we have a great deal of respect for them."

The following interviews point to the critical importance of a symbiotic owner-designer relationship. In this case, the owners were willing to place their faith in the second designer's creativity and expertise, even the second time around, but the designer had to listen very closely and accurately interpret the owners' vision.

DON LUBIN AND JEFF SPIEGEL, OWNERS

It's quite a journey from rural Peru, where Lubin and Spiegel worked together in the Peace Corps, to one of the busiest corners in New York City. Psychic distances notwithstanding, the two men sustained a well-honed sense of humor that helped to see them through very different kinds of challenges. Their quirky personalities were well matched to Lopata's irreverent design style. During a given lunch hour, Lubin and Spiegel could be found eating dessert before their main course.

Lubin and Spiegel got into the restaurant business "on a whim," succeeded with their initial efforts, and then decided to take a chance on Extra! Extra! Spiegel, typically dressed in a jacket and tie, has a more businesslike persona, and the bearded Lubin usually wears casual garb. The lively conversational banter between the two men indicates that each enjoys having the last word, but this appears to be the yin-yang competitiveness of two good friends who balance each other's strengths.

Regarding the owners' relationship with the architect of the first design scheme, Lubin pointed out that when they saw the plan, "we did confront the architect and tell him we had problems. Some modifications were made. But this was an articulate human being who had his own persuasive powers. He said he understood our goals." Why, then, did such a discrepancy develop between owners' goals and architect's design? "What he really did," opined Spiegel, "was independently decide what was best for us. So when he said, 'I'm taking care of you,' he was really thinking 'I know the market better than you. I'm not doing it your way, but you'll be very pleased afterwards.'" Ironically, the owners put in far more anguished hours the first time around discussing the design than they did for the make-over.

The owners stressed that the first design wasn't necessarily bad work, but it just wasn't what they wanted for Extra! Extra! The architect had taken his inspiration from Raymond Hood's 1930 Daily News building design and created a quiet, conservative interior with a mahogany bar and linen tablecloths. "The first time I walked through the space after it had been painted and wood trim had gone on, my heart started to beat triple pace," recalled Spiegel, who said he felt as if "my worst nightmare had been realized. We wanted light and this was dark. We wanted funny and this was serious. But we continued to move ahead, thinking that our cautions to the architect would yield an end result more sympathetic with our goals."

As the first design scheme neared completion, the owners made a last-ditch effort to salvage the interior by bringing in an experienced restaurant designer, but the architect strongly objected. So Lubin and Spiegel decided to be open-minded, "see what the restaurant was like with people in it," and then deal with the situation.

Their unhappiness prevailed. Lubin and Spiegel were quickly convinced that a cosmetic redesign was the only answer, but the owners had learned from their mistakes, and they did a lot of research before jumping into a new plan. "Because our first restaurant had been successful from day one, we thought at first that we didn't need help from anyone," remembered Lubin. "Then," he continued, "we found that we had this large restaurant that didn't look the way we wanted it to and wasn't performing the way we wanted it to. We believed we could do better, and realized we needed help."

First, during the beginning months of operation, Lubin and Spiegel got informal feedback on the restaurant from friends and acquaintances. One of the outsiders they talked to was Roger Martin, a marketing professional with an extensive background in food service. "We chatted with him for three and a half hours," said Lubin, "and he echoed our sentiments exactly. We needed an angle to help promote the restaurant. There had to be something

about the design that gave the place a marketing edge."

Next, they decided to look for experienced restaurant designers, especially ones who had designed small restaurants, "because we figured that this was a small job." Don Lubin led the search. "At this point," he said, "design was a big part of our lives. We investigated many firms and talked seriously to half a dozen people. Some were architects by training, but they all presented themselves as interior designers."

One day, when talking about all the designers they had interviewed, Sam Lopata's name came up. "We both really liked his work, but hadn't talked to him because we figured he would be too arrogant, too expensive, and probably wouldn't even meet with us," said Spiegel. Lopata was then known as New York's hottest restaurant designer. When Lubin gave it a go and called his office, however, Lopata answered the phone himself. The owners liked Lopata's style right from the beginning.

During their first meeting, Lopata told the owners that their design was "terrible." He told them that they needed more than a cosmetic fix-up. Nevertheless, the second he walked out, Lubin and Spiegel agreed to hire him. Lopata seemed to know exactly what they wanted. In addition, he was totally open. "There was a dramatic difference in our meeting with Sam," noted Spiegel, "because he was completely candid. He wasn't defensive, didn't try to suck us in, and didn't withhold any information. These were very endearing characteristics."

Throughout the two-month planning process and the two-week construction process, positive teamwork and good vibes sustained this challenging project. "We got enough feedback along the road to keep us feeling calm," said Lubin. The owners were thrilled with both Lopata and project designer Denise Hall, who was on site daily during the construction phase. They believed that the Lopata-designed interior created a marketing position for the restaurant to build upon, and they went from feeling uncomfortable about their restaurant to feeling terrific. "I like a lot of Sam Lopata's designs," grinned Lubin, "but I like this one most of all."

SAM LOPATA AND DENISE HALL, DESIGNERS

French-born Sam Lopata is a leading contender for the title of name restaurant designer. He received his architectural education at the École des Beaux Arts in Paris, where he also got involved in the restaurant business. After moving to the United States, Lopata began his career as club and restaurant designer in 1976. At that time, he was sharing an apartment with restaurateur Robert Pascal, working part-time as a waiter, and part-time as a window dresser. When Pascal opened a new, namesake restaurant on New York's Upper East Side, Lopata designed his first instant hit. All light wood, with banquettes covered in the newly introduced ultrasuede, the restaurant design launched Lopata as an innovator. In the early 1980s, he garnered attention for his dramatic discothèque designs, and later in the decade he became New York's most talked-about restaurant designer.

A long string of noteworthy, original restaurant interiors—combined with Lopata's dashing personal style—captured the imagination of press and public alike. Although his designs may have started trends, however, Lopata insists he wasn't out to be trendy. "I just make restaurants," he said. "It's people who make them trendy." Fame didn't change his modus operandi either: He kept "undesigned" offices with a small staff in downtown Manhattan and stayed personally involved with every job.

Partner Denise Hall balanced Lopata's theatrics with her stylish yet unassuming demeanor. Trained as an architect, Hall functioned as project designer and on-site supervisor for many of the firm's projects, including Extra! Extra! In the planning phase, she and Lopata constantly brainstormed ideas—no matter how outrageous—rejecting some and developing others. They always started from a functional point of view, according to Hall, and considered the food concept and kitchen layout before arriving at the design theme. Every job required complete sets of drawings as well, down to such details as the layout of ink splashes for Extra! Extra!

Interestingly, Lopata took on the redesign of Extra! Extra! despite the low budget and tight time frame. Why did he want the job? The answer lies with the fact that Lubin and Spiegel trusted the designer's expertise and gave him free creative rein. "These were great clients," stressed Hall. "Even when they didn't totally understand an idea, they let us go ahead with it. They were willing to take risks. At the end of the project I thanked them for allowing us to complete our design concept from start to finish."

"These guys had a problem," shrugged Lopata, "and we helped them to solve it. It was a challenge like any job is a challenge. I told them they had to change the space and we put together a budget. Then they told me there was a time restriction. I thought we could do the design in one month, but they said we only had two weeks. So the entire job revolved around the fact that we only had two weeks. I didn't believe we could do it, but I was willing to try."

The designers were able to accomplish such a quick transformation by an intensive two-month planning period, during which they lined up all of the details. "We had to plan a design which could be made off-site, then brought in and installed in two weeks," explained Hall. "Our most important goals were, first, to integrate three separate spaces into one big room and, second, to make the place bright and amusing to reflect the owners' personality. The newspaper theme was obvious."

Despite union problems that made them feel they were "running a race with our legs tied together," the job was accomplished in two weeks and three days. During that time, Lopata was on-site three times a week and Hall was there every day. They both stayed until four A.M. one morning to pour the ink splashes—actually swimming pool paint and binder. They totally violated the existing design and created a spunky, pop-art fantasy that gave the restaurant a whole new identity.

"Of course Don and Jeff like this the best of all my work," laughed Lopata. "It's their restaurant. I created the design just for them."

Summary

The case of Extra! Extra! illustrates the crucial importance of the right designer-client match. Given the same modus operandi on the part of the owners, two designers came up with radically different schemes. What can be extrapolated here is that personalities play a big role in the success of the owner-designer marriage. Further, Extra! Extra! is a marketing story. Like a new style of clothing, the restaurant was designed as an imagemaker. It is not expected to last forever.

FOCUS ON FOOD

CITY   Los Angeles, CA

The development of City, a West Los Angeles restaurant that opened to instant acclaim in 1985, was the product of years of effort during which trust, friendship, and a love of food grew to become an expression of the design team. This is a story about chefs, businesspeople, and architects who forged a family. It is a story that witnesses how the vision, determination, and just plain hard work of owners Susan Feniger and Mary Sue Milliken, both classically trained and accomplished chefs, resulted in culinary stardom and restaurant success. It chronicles the business acumen of City's third general partner Barbara McReynolds, who segued into the restaurant business after establishing L.A.'s hippest eyeglass store and gave the two young chefs ownership opportunity. In essence, the building of City was the dream come true of creative entrepreneurs—including architects Josh Dawson Schweitzer and David Kellen, who launched the reputation of their own firm with City's spare, soaring interior that allows food to become the restaurant's dramatic focus.

Project Background

The seed for City was planted in 1980, when Barbara McReynolds realized that the only way to get a good cup of espresso near her West Los Angeles L.A. Eyeworks headquarters was to open a gourmet cafe nearby. McReynolds is a meticulous businessperson. After months of research, she and her partners opened the thirty-five-seat City Cafe in May 1981 with a total $54,000 investment. McReynolds gleaned along the way all of the problems of putting an operation together: the licensing and legal pitfalls as well as the construction challenges. As her own general contractor and designer, she learned important lessons that would be carried forward to future restaurant projects.

City Cafe was a hit, even though the back of the house was nothing more than storage space and a hot plate. As business boomed, so did the need for an expanded and more varied menu. Eventually, McReynolds convinced Susan Feniger, who used to drop by for an espresso before taking off for her job in the kitchen of Wolfgang Puck's Ma Maison, to help out on a part-time basis. Soon Feniger was spending the first half of her day cooking up daily specials in City Cafe's tiny 12-foot-by-13-foot kitchen and then rushing off to her evening shift at Ma Maison. Her fame as an innovative chef grew quickly and so did the demands on her time.

The opportunity to run her own kitchen, albeit miniscule, persuaded Feniger to become a partner in the City Cafe. She brought her cooking compatriot and old friend Mary Sue Milliken—then working near Chicago as personal chef to W. Clement Stone—into the business, and the troika was formed. The three women made a perfect, symbiotic team: two talented culinarians to create gustatory excitement and the ever-watchful business partner to keep hold of the reins.

Word soon spread about the food at City Cafe, where the chefs were smoking their own meats, creating homemade vinegars and pâtés, and producing ambrosial pastries. The strength of the team was greater than the capacity of the space, however, and the partners decided to remodel and expand the cafe into a full-fledged restaurant. They shifted the focus to Mexican cuisine as well, and thus, after closing briefly for reconstruction, the City Cafe was reborn as the Border Grill in 1985. At this point the restaurateurs began working with Schweitzer Kellen, who designed the Border Grill.

Concurrent with their conversion of City Cafe into the Border Grill, McReynolds, Feniger, and Milliken were making plans for a second, larger restaurant. All of their combined skills, developed and sharpened by the City Cafe and Border Grill experience, went into the making of the new, 125-seat City Restaurant. It was a hands-on project for everyone. Feniger and Milliken scouted around L.A. on their motorbikes until they found the perfect location, a former carpet warehouse in a low-rent yet geographically convenient area. McReynolds wrote up a prospectus for a private limited partnership that quickly attracted investors. After site and finances were secured, work began on transforming the warehouse into a restaurant.

All three partners stayed closely involved with the details of the design plan developed by Schweitzer and Kellen. In turn, the architects worked assiduously to produce a room that stood on its own as good design, yet supported City's raison d'être as a showpiece for food. The result is a strong yet understated space in which practical design solutions were creatively developed to tie in with the architectural idea. In fact, creativity—in financing, design, construction, and cuisine—underscored the making of City from start to finish.

FRONT OF THE HOUSE

The carpet warehouse that became City Restaurant was built in 1939 and typified the deco industrial L.A. style so perfectly that the architects didn't want to fool around with changing the character of the building. Rather, Schweitzer and Kellen preserved the open, in-dustrial quality of the space both outside and inside.

City's bright, airy interior is a study in planes and volume. The room gives a clean, minimalist impression. There is no décor at all. The bare white and pale green backdrop acts as an unobtrusive stage set for the real business at hand—enjoying a meal. Bright red chairs and a rainbow of dishware center attention at the tables themselves, which is exactly what the owners and architects intended.

Spatially, City is organized into a progression of experiences that begins when guests walk past a street-side cafe area before entering the restaurant (fig. 6-14). Once inside, they pass through a 35-foot-long corridor that juts into the space on a diagonal—a modern-day front hall. To the left (north) are offices and the kitchen, and to the right (south) are the bar and dining area. Square window cutouts in the corridor wall allow patrons quick peeks into the restaurant interior, but not until they arrive at the maitre d' station does the 13-foot-high corridor open up to reveal the soaring, 23-foot-high dining room.

In the dining area, an arched ceiling, supported by pale green wooden trusswork and dot-

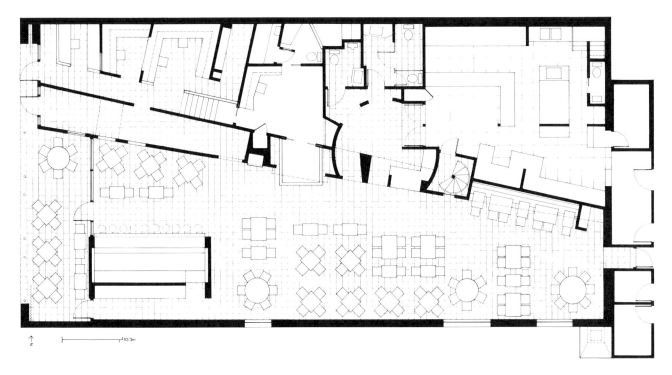

6-14. *The diagonal wall that cuts through City separates the public spaces from the private spaces (Schweitzer/Kellen drawing).*

ted with round ventilation ducts, rises overhead (fig. 6-15). Everything is crisp and hard-edged: the green vinyl "slate" flooring, the white sheetrock walls, and the custom-designed wooden chairs painted Chinese red. Seating is a mix of deuces and fourtops, with a single, short row of banquettes recessed into an alcove along the outside kitchen wall. On the opposite side of the room, at the south wall, the architects punched out three large windows to let in light and give diners a view of the parking lot that is pure L.A.

In the front right corner of the restaurant, butted up to the street-side cafe, sits a big, chunky bar fashioned from a charcoal-colored

6-15. *The exposed truss ceiling creates a feeling of spaciousness.*
(Joseph Durocher photo)

terrazzo block, with 1950s-style bar stools (fig. 6-16). Over the corner of the bar hovers the omnipresent video monitor. However, at City the only show in the house is a closed-circuit view of the hot foods production line.

Hidden behind the bar is a service station that holds all the materials needed to reset tables, along with a complete hot beverage station. A second, dry wait station with limited storage is tucked away in the rear of the dining room. In addition, colorful service carts, specially designed for the restaurant, are openly displayed throughout the space (fig. 6-17).

About midway through the dining room, an open rotunda circulation area connects the dining room to the restrooms, the kitchen, and the espresso-dessert station. Here, "private" and "public" spaces merge. Guests have the chance to peer into the kitchen as they take a trip to the restroom. The espresso-dessert station (Fig. 6-18), with its glass-fronted display case on view to the dining area, helps to merchandise beauti-

fully decorated cakes and pastries. This station also helps to speed after-dinner treats to the guests because servers don't have to go into the kitchen to pick up desserts.

BACK OF THE HOUSE

City's back of the house is, to say the least, compact. The most spacious sections are the dirty dish drop-off and service pickup areas, situated immediately inside the doors of the kitchen. The chefs recognized the importance of adequate circulation in these areas and therefore allowed them more square footage than any other part of the kitchen.

To the left of the dirty dish drop-off and service pickup spaces are the hot foods pickup and production areas (fig. 6-19). Here, the unorthodox choice of equipment was influenced by the chefs' international travels and love of "high-heat cooking." Equipment includes a clay tandoori oven—installed as a special treat—that

6-16. *In an otherwise wide-open room, the blocky architecture of the bar anchors its own separate area.*
(Joseph Durocher photo)

6-17. *Custom-designed, multicolored service carts supplement two built-in service stations.*
(Joseph Durocher photo)

cooks breads and meats at 600° F. A wood-fired charbroiler gives high heat and a smoky taste to grilled meats, fish, and poultry. Two gas-fired woks are well suited to menu items drawn from Milliken's journeys in Thailand.

Ranges and deep fryers round out the hot foods section. To hold the myriad sauces, a bain marie sits in the center of the plating area. A double-deck overshelf holds clean plates on the top level and food-laden dishes on the bottom level under heat strips.

Adjacent to the hot foods section is the cold preparation station, which also functions as the fabrication area during nonservice hours. Toward the back of the kitchen is the roasting and baking area, a space that is roughly 10 feet by 6 feet. Storage areas and preprep stations, where cooks prepare vegetables and smoked meats, are located at the rear of the kitchen.

6-18. *A dessert and hot beverage station located outside the kitchen entryway helps to speed service.*
(Joseph Durocher photo)

6-19. *Every inch of space is well utilized in the compact kitchen.* *(Joseph Durocher photo)*

Type of Restaurant

City is a rather eccentric type of restaurant. Situated in a free-standing building in an urban area, it is a gathering place that draws diners as compared to drinkers. Food reigns supreme here, but in true gathering place tradition, it is also a hip place to be. Unlike many serious food restaurants, the environment at City is quite informal. City feels indigenous to the state of California. As more Americans everywhere turn into food lovers, however, and increasing numbers of chefs become restaurant owners, it foreshadows a new American type of restaurant.

The Market

The owners of City thought of their potential customer market as so broad as to be virtually unlimited. They had developed a loyal clientele at City Cafe, where two-hour waiting lines were not uncommon, and believed that the diversity of "City cuisine" matched the diverse population and lifestyles of Angelenos. The owners' most important concern was to appeal to a mar-

ket that cared passionately about food. Their intent was to attract a wide cross-section of diners of different ages and cultures, from the conservative Beverly Hills attorney to the punk downtown artist.

What makes this egalitarian approach work is a very deliberate service philosophy, whose most important tenet is to treat all customers equally. The pleasant young servers in their baggy green-striped Italian workers' jackets and black pants give no special treatment to movie stars and millionaires. Instead, every customer is treated with the same courtesy and good humor.

Based on a 1987 visit, the owners succeeded in their goal of attracting a wide spectrum of clients. A small sampling of the people who strolled down the entry corridor during one lunch period included: a lanky middle-aged man wearing a black suede jacket with fringes, two young women in cotton shorts and halter tops; a party of businessmen in suits and ties; a pair of hip, muscled young men who each sported a long ponytail, and a perfectly coiffed blonde woman in a white linen suit.

City has no direct competition. Immediately surrounding the site is a residential area with a large Hasidic Jewish population whose dietary laws forbid them to eat at nonkosher establishments. Except for lunch clients from the few businesses sprinkled nearby, most of City's customers are destination diners.

Indirect competition comes from the myriad fine dining restaurants where cuisine is also king throughout the Los Angeles area. However, the unpretentious attitude at City encourages a more casual crowd than in many other trendy restaurants.

The site is in an underdeveloped section of town, so there was no predetermination as to what kind of restaurant belonged in the space (fig. 6-20). Basically, City's owners took a chance and broke into virgin territory. The restaurant's location close to several major L.A. arteries makes it easily accessible from many business and residential areas, such as Hollywood, Beverly Hills, and the bustling Melrose Avenue area of downtown. Moreover, it is in a low-rent district, and the partners negotiated a fifteen-year lease. Therefore, they do not have to factor high rents into the price of their food, as would have been necessary in established destination neighborhoods.

Albeit unconventional, City's site was just what the partners were looking for. When Feniger and Milliken first spotted the old warehouse, with its vintage looks and handy parking lot, they immediately tracked down the owner —even though the building was not for sale. Eventually, the restaurateurs secured their lease. The economic conditions in Los Angeles in 1985 were very positive for City restaurant. Nearby business areas were thriving and disposable incomes were up. The economic climate seemed good for City's midpriced, creative dining experience, and the fifteen-year lease mentioned earlier guaranteed long-term rent stability.

Feniger, Milliken, and McReynolds appear to have found their market. In 1987, an average weekday brought in 180 customers for lunch and 225 for dinner. Busy weekend nights pushed the totals to 300 per night. The slowest

6-20. *As patrons walk from the parking lot to the restaurant, they pass the outdoor seating area.*
(Joseph Durocher photo)

period was from 3 to 6 P.M. when a light menu was served. To expand their sales and market penetration even further, City's owners plan to offer carry-out food and open a catering business.

Concept Development

City's concept stems from the artistry of the chefs. This restaurant evolved from the back of the house to the front; its design was carefully crafted to maximize the quality of food and service. In addition, the owners felt that the people in the restaurant are very important, and they wanted a design that helped to showcase the clientele, not intimidate them. Their concept was philosophical: a place that welcomes all sorts of people and provides a fabulous meal. A theme of openness, in terms of architecture, cuisine, and service, was central to the concept development.

City's concept hinged on the owners' willingness to take risks. They were culinary pioneers, even by California standards. They had the only restaurant in a sleepy residential neighborhood. Nevertheless, as McReynolds expressed it, "we already had an established reputation on many levels, so we believed we could pull it off."

The Menu

City's menu is as diverse as the populace of southern California. The chefs drew from their classical training and strengthened it with experiences on the Continent, in the States, and in Thailand, Mexico, and India. Entrees range from such items as tandoori roast chicken and onion naan with turmeric, cilantro, and cracked-wheat pilaf; to lamb kidney with fried spinach; to braised duck legs with Thai red curry, lime, and scallions.

Despite its exotic menu, City does not necessarily offer the most expensive cuts of veal or rare fungi. Rather, the chefs select the best and freshest from the market and prepare it in their own inimitable style. Typified by high-heat cooking and clear, direct flavors, their style became known as *City cuisine*, which also became the title of a cookbook.

City's purveyors play an important role in the menu-planning process. For example, if they receive a shipment of Australian mussels or some other specialty item, they immediately call the chefs at City who can add it to the specials that evening. Feniger and Milliken do not entrust their food buying to a purchasing agent but often are up at dawn to shop the markets themselves.

The menu is expansive, with different items and daily specials offered at lunch, on the afternoon menu, and at dinner. The dessert menu contains twenty-five decadent delicacies ranging from almond mocha torte to red yam flan.

The menu itself is printed as needed with an on-site Macintosh computer and bound in a plastic binder. Stylized menu art provided by local artists add to its contemporary yet frivolous feeling.

The Budget

From start to finish, the building of City depended on a tightly controlled budget. Barbara McReynolds developed the prospectus for a limited partnership that provided the $660,000 initial investment for the restaurant. (Greater profits than expected enabled the owners to pay off investors in twelve rather than the projected twenty-four months.) However, an additional $214,000 cost overrun—in part due to a lengthened construction period—was paid for through a bank loan. This loan remained City's only capital debt after its first year of operation.

City's budget breakdown reflects careful allocations of funds. Leasehold improvements, including structural modifications, cost $427,515. Some $12,888 was spent on furniture and fixtures for the dining room. The computerized cash-control system, which was used for ordering, plating, and accounting, required a $59,620 investment. Machinery and equipment, including back of the house, came in at $84,105. In total, the preopening construction expenses for the 5,500-square-foot restaurant ran $106 per square foot, or $584,128, in 1985. The remaining funds were expended on smallwares, opening inventory, and other preopening expenses.

Creating a restaurant like City on the budget outlined above was not easy. That it was successfully accomplished is due to the frugal and creative measures taken by the team at every turn. Feniger and Milliken saved thousands of dollars by buying used equipment, but they had to persevere and keep sifting through grimy piles even when snakes began to slither out of a greasy old deep fryer. The chefs built their tandoori oven themselves from a $500 clay pot. In lieu of purchasing costly wine buckets, the City logo was sandblasted onto marble planter pots found at a local discount store. The standard gueridon was priced at $900 but for a few dollars more, the architects designed customized service carts that exactly suit the needs of the dining room and complement the architecture. At every turn, the three partners worked to cut corners without cutting quality or the ultimate experience for their customers. In fact, elements such as the wine buckets and the service stations became emblems of the offbeat City style.

Revenues during the City's first year were $3 million, which was 33 percent ahead of the owners' projections. Bottom-line profits were recorded at 21 percent, compared with a national average of 12 percent. These impressive figures can be attributed to the watchful eye of Barbara McReynolds, who maintains a close tab on all operating costs, including the kind of small expenditures that are often overlooked.

Style of Service

Well-garnished platters are finished in the kitchen under the supervision of the chef-owners and hand-carried to the waiting customers. Desert hues of blue, green, yellow, and orange plates are color-coordinated to individual entrees. The color coordination goes against all traditional guidelines, but it works. The vivid contrast of rare tandoori skirt steak presented on an aquamarine plate and the subtle juxtaposition of Thai melon salad with a coral plate, for example, create artful canvases.

Most important is the service philosophy of equal treatment for all diners. In a town where special attention is given to the few, anyone can come to City and be treated well. The owners have worked hard to develop a staff who really believe in their idea of egalitarian service.

Speed of Service

City is a place for dining, and the special preparations from the kitchen sometimes take quite a bit of time. Therefore, the speed of service is relatively slow. City is not a hushed, subdued environment, however, but a noisy restaurant that hums with lively conversation. The wait staff doesn't hover, but they are always nearby if people need drink refills as they wait for their food.

Per Person Check Average

In 1987 the per person check average, including beverage, was $21.00 for lunch and $35.00 for dinner. An extensive wine list and select cognac and armagnac list contribute to the 30/70 beverage to food sales mix. To maintain profitability from wines but still offer oenophiles the opportunity to bring in their own preferred wines, a $12 corkage fee is charged.

Although not inexpensive, City's prices are considered very reasonable for gourmet cuisine. The owners maintain menu prices by careful menu planning and purchasing procedures, along with attentive portion control.

General Ambiance

Schweitzer and Kellen maintained the funky appeal of the building and created an open, airy dining environment where all tables are equal. Their entire orientation was architectural: City's austere ambiance has virtually no décor (fig. 6-21). Color, centered on the tables and chairs, is a significant design element in the bare-boned room. Schweitzer and Kellen manipulated space to suit the functions of the restaurant and never allowed the architecture to become overpowering.

Management Philosophy

The management philosophy of City is based on a sense of personal pride and dedication. City is not owned by a group of unseen investors but by entrepreneurs who are totally involved with all aspects of the operation. As Feniger ex-

6-21. *Cut through the diagonal wall are (from left to right) an access door to the kitchen and restrooms, the dessert display case, a spiral staircase leading to mezzanine level offices, and recessed banquette seating.*
(Joseph Durocher photo)

pressed it, "we wanted to open our own favorite restaurant; the one that we would choose to eat in." Many aspiring restaurateurs share this goal; few achieve it.

Feniger, Milliken, and McReynolds's success is based in part on their intense involvement with City, an involvement that has no boundaries. They have participated in every aspect of planning, design, construction, installation, and ongoing restaurant management.

The partners are committed not just to a profit-making enterprise but to maintaining a positive, fun, productive environment. They developed a close-knit kitchen and service staff team, think of them as family, and spend a lot of time visiting with their guests in the dining room to maintain personal contacts.

The Design Team

City was not a complex project that required dozens of layers of approvals and a battery of design consultants. Basically, the core team consisted of the owners and the architects, who welcomed input and counsel from a lot of good friends and customers. Dynamics between team members were lively and good-humored. The team was obviously bonded by friendship as well as by business.

SUSAN FENIGER, MARY SUE MILLIKEN, AND BARBARA McREYNOLDS, OWNERS

In 1987 Susan Feniger and Mary Sue Milliken were among America's most celebrated young chefs. Getting there involved not only hard work but also forging new territory for women. Both Feniger and Milliken grew up in the Midwest, and both began working in food service when they were teenagers. Throughout their years of higher education, each continued to work in the industry. After graduating from college with a liberal arts degree, Feniger attended the Culinary Institute of America in Hyde Park, New York. Milliken received her formal culinary training at Washburn Academy Trade School in Chicago and gained acclaim in both national and international culinary competitions while still in school.

Upon graduation, Milliken approached Jovan Treboyevic, owner and operator of Chi-

cago's renowned Le Perroquet, for a job. Treboyevic had never allowed women to work in his kitchen, and he reportedly offered Milliken a job as a hatcheck girl because he feared that a pretty young woman would wreak havoc in his all-male kitchen. She refused but persisted in her efforts to get in the back door until Treboyevic finally relented and offered her an entry-level job peeling vegetables. Two years later, the first woman to work in Le Perroquet's kitchen had become the sous chef.

Milliken's exemplary performance opened Le Perroquet's back of the house to equal opportunity. Before too long, another woman was hired—Susan Feniger. The two women began their friendship here and developed the bond of kindred spirits. Each left Le Perroquet with the dream of someday running her own restaurant kitchen.

Feniger and Milliken went their separate ways to pursue their careers. Coincidentally they both traveled to France to work and met again in Paris. Here, they vowed on a handshake to work together in the States someday.

The rest, as they say, is history. Feniger and Milliken have been the subject of TV specials, garnered many awards, and received a spate of favorable press coverage. Success has not changed their personal styles; they continue to ride to work on motorbikes and, despite hectic agendas and the frantic pace of a busy kitchen, have not lost their exuberance or sense of humor.

As noted earlier, Barbara McReynolds was the business partner of the team. Her training as an accountant and attorney made her perfectly suited for this role. McReynolds had not intended to become a restaurateur; rather, she is the quintessential businessperson who recognized a need in the market and tried to fill it.

Despite her relentlessly efficient ways, McReynolds evidences a warm and caring regard for her two younger partners. Moreover, she has kept the business on target. When City's contractors failed to live up to their contract, McReynolds became the GC herself. "I learned the hard way that it's really important to ask the right questions of potential contractors," she stressed. "You should find out how many and what type of restaurants they've worked on before, if they are bonded, if the supervisor is going to be on-site during working hours, and so on. The biggest concern is to hook yourself up with someone who is honest." After McReynolds took over, the three partners ramrodded the remaining construction schedule. Their subcontractors soon discovered that these women knew their business, and the work got back on track.

Since City was completed, McReynolds has kept a keen eye on daily restaurant activities. Her office is located on a mezzanine balcony, with a command post that overlooks the dining area and allows her a bird's-eye view of everything going on in the space.

As for Feniger and Milliken, they are pleased with the way City's interior design supports their food concept. "This was a trust situation with the architects," emphasized Feniger, who had known Josh Schweitzer since they were both in fifth grade. "It was our dream, and we needed someone to articulate it without being on an ego trip." The owners talked about their business goals, their spiritual beliefs, their culinary philosophy, and everything in between, and the architects translated the talk into a singular restaurant design.

Given the fame of City cuisine, why not have a display kitchen? "Too trendy and not private enough," said Milliken. "It would destroy the teamwork in the kitchen, where we operate like a family." Still, recognizing that the public loves to peek in at the back of the house, the chefs approved the installation of a video monitor at the bar that shows viewers what is cooking in the kitchen. They strongly recommend that the chef(s) be involved in the planning process for any restaurant, in order to achieve the most efficient kitchen design.

The owners carefully considered every design detail. They searched for uniforms, for example, that would reflect both the idea of a city and the clean architectural esthetic, and found that the loose-fitting, striped jacket worn by city workers in Italy perfectly fit both criteria. City's staff now wears these brightly colored jackets, purchased direct from Italy for the restaurant. Servers wear green and black striped jackets, busboys wear red and black striped jackets, and runners wear gold and black striped jackets.

Although no one on the team set out to create a trendy restaurant, City was in fact a trend setter. How long can the restaurant last? At least as long as the fifteen-year lease, said McReynolds. Further, said the chefs, they intend to keep the menu ever-changing. "It's true that people get tired of trends, but we're always trying out new ideas, always evolving," remarked Feniger. The owners believe that the restaurant interior's clean architectural backdrop is a timeless stage set. Perhaps most significant is the owners' intent to stay closely involved with City even as they pursue new ventures.

JOSH SCHWEITZER AND DAVID KELLEN, ARCHITECTS

Both Josh Schweitzer and David Kellen worked for the noted Los Angeles architect Frank Gehry before launching their own firm in 1984. They have been involved with all sorts of residential and commercial projects but, starting with their design for City, have developed a specialty in restaurants.

"It was the close teamwork at City that made the project a real success," emphasized Schweitzer. "It wasn't us and them. We interacted together constantly, and it strengthened the end result. The kind of ongoing dialogue that we had with the owners during the design process of City is the very best way to create a restaurant."

The architects did not evolve City's design from a specific theme but rather from the owners' ideas and requirements for their restaurant. "The first thing we did was develop a program that identified all the things the owners were trying to acheive. Then we began experimenting with models and drawings," said Schweitzer.

"But even when we're dealing with functional issues, we work in an abstract sense as well," explained Kellen. How the circulation flow can facilitate interaction between public and private spaces and the ways in which architecture can alter people's perception are the kinds of abstract problems the architects grappled with. The result was that City's deceptively simple interior includes some complex architectural problem solving. In essence, Schweitzer and Kellen preserved the airy, industrial quality of the space and inserted architectural objects such as the diagonal circulation corridor to define functional areas.

The initial planning and concept development took four months. "Once the design permits were in hand, everything progressed quickly," said Schweitzer, "and we devoted all our time to getting the job done. The biggest constraint was the extremely limited budget." One area the architects wanted to do more with was lighting, but they did the best with what they had by specifying indirect incandescents that cast a soft glow to the dining areas and low-voltage track lights that spotlight diners as they walk down the entry runway.

Every detail of the design was important to City's owners. "The owners deserve a lot of credit for sticking with a cohesive idea of the restaurant and not compromising that idea despite the limited budget," said Schweitzer. Therefore, when no one was satisfied with commercial seating choices on the market, Schweitzer designed a special chair for the restaurant. The architects also designed special serving carts because nothing on the market really fit in with City's esthetics. No aspect was overlooked, but nothing was overdone, either. City's interior is understated and un-self-conscious.

It is also deliberately noisy. The owners and architects wanted "a high energy, party atmosphere," said Schweitzer. "There was an inherent energy to what we had got going here, and we wanted to sustain an energetic, festive pace." Added Kellen: "We wanted everything about the space to wake people up a bit, to switch on the senses. We didn't want a cozy, homelike dining room." Painful reverberation is kept to a minimum, however, because of the way sound rises up and then bounces back at an angle from the curved surfaces.

What makes City special is a superb integration of food, service, and design that perfectly reflects the owners' vision. At no time did the architects forget that, as Josh Schweitzer expressed it, "the chefs are the stars."

Summary

City represents a new breed of restaurant that speaks volumes about the California lifestyle, entrepreneurial opportunity, and a new age of chef-owners. What makes it different from other casual gathering places is its focus on food —clear, tangy, unusual combinations of ingredients and cooking techniques. It shows that a hip place to be doesn't have to be elitist. It illustrates the power of a simple architectural backdrop designed to support operational efficiency. And it indicates what can be accomplished by the design team when good friends and colleagues share a common goal.

CREATION OF A CLASSIC

AURORA   New York, NY

Restaurant aficionados buzzed with anticipation in late 1985 as they waited for the legendary Joe Baum—who birthed such operations as The Four Seasons and Windows on the World—to open his own restaurant for the first time. Working with the equally illustrious graphic designer Milton Glaser, Baum was reputedly sparing no expense in the creation of Aurora.

Aurora turned out to be both more and less than people expected. It is a small, luxurious restaurant that is not so much cutting edge as comfortable. The design is less striking than it is subtle. What makes Aurora such a special achievement is that food, service, and design come together in perfect harmony. It was instantly accepted by the elite world of New York's power diners.

Many talented parties contributed to the making of Aurora, but they all deferred to Joe Baum's relentless quest for perfection as the driving force behind design decisions. The restaurant's smooth and seemingly effortless flow was achieved through painstaking planning of every detail.

Project Background

Although Aurora may indeed represent Baum's vision of an ideal deluxe establishment, he did not begin the project with that goal in mind. First came the location. The former Cowboy restaurant was incongruously situated in one of Manhattan's toniest business districts, on the ground floor of a high-rise office building. Baum and his associates, Michael Whiteman and Dennis Sweeney, recognized the beauty of the locale's built-in luncheon market and saw potential to attract dinner customers as well. They originally planned to capture wasted space from a spacious outdoor plaza (the building facade is set back several feet behind this plaza) and build a modestly priced, relatively large restaurant.

After the lease was signed, however, new zoning regulations prohibited such expansion.

The owners had to rethink the potential of the location and the 3,000 square feet of front-of-the-house space.

Thus, the idea of an elegant restaurant was born, one in which every element was custom-tailored but that nevertheless had "evocative and familiar recalls" to create real comfort. Baum talked to his longtime friend Milton Glaser about design. The room was to be fashionable but not trendy. In a city full of gourmet restaurants, it was to stand out as something special. Baum envisioned the salon of a great, imaginary European hotel, a place humming quietly with smart conversation and filled with important people surreptitiously glancing at other important people across the room.

Crucial to the success of this restaurant was that it had to be as comfortable for the businessperson closing an important deal at lunch as for the couple pledging their affection over a romantic dinner. "What this meant in design terms," said Glaser, "was that we had to establish a form that could happily accommodate both of these markets simultaneously. Therefore, we attempted to establish a dialogue between masculine and feminine, sensate and intellectual, hard and soft." Glaser stressed that the idea for Aurora did not come out of an interior design intention but out of "an attempt to satisfy a number of very specific requirements in order to attract our audience." His notes on the project span three-and-a-half years, and his office spent a year and a half actively working on the restaurant design. Countless plans were created in the process.

Baum named his restaurant Aurora for the Roman goddess of the dawn, the "mother of stars and winds." Glaser, inspired by the celestial idea, used star charts of the southern hemisphere as the basis for a circular motif that became the restaurant's graphic symbol. Architect Philip George, an experienced restaurant and kitchen designer, joined the team as associate designer in 1984 and was responsible for the bar design and seating plan. Baum, Whiteman, Sweeney, Glaser and his project designer Tim Higgins, and George formed the core design team. They worked assiduously to create, in Baum's words, "a restaurant where the most sophisticated food audience in the city, and perhaps in the world, could come and feel rewarded by the experience." So rewarded, in fact, that they would return again and again.

Design Description

FRONT OF THE HOUSE

Aurora is situated on a midtown city block flanked by undistinguished office buildings. Located on the ground floor of one of these towers, the restaurant has a long, elegant canopy that extends out over the sidewalk and leads to a refined entryway portal (fig. 6-22). Windows and glass entry doors are covered over with a soft blue-green grid, adding unexpected color to the monochromatic streetscape. The window treatment blocks the view of the restaurant's interior, which is unusual for restaurants built in the mid-1980s in New York. This sequestering of the restaurant experience creates an air of mystery and promises patrons an exclusive experience inside.

After walking through a small vestibule lit by table lamps, customers enter the restaurant (fig. 6-23). The entry area is just a small space inside the front door, bordered by cherrywood armoires that serve as coat closets and a small maitre d' station. The point of arrival brings people front and center with the focal point of the space: an exquisitely crafted pink granite and cherrywood bar, curving around in a modified horseshoe shape and surrounded by a circle of widely spaced, curved banquettes (fig. 6-24). Over this area hang multitudes of tiered globe chandeliers, glowing in complementary hues of gold and pink and salmon. Resting on an altar behind the bar is an abstract bubble sculpture of Aurora herself. Dining areas are located to either side of the bar.

The atmosphere is refined, with widely spaced tables and cushy glove-leather upholstery covering chairs and banquettes. A "reconciliation of opposites," as Glaser put it, resulted in a room that is at once corporate yet romantic, masculine yet feminine. A clubby ambiance, for example, is created by a wall treatment of cherrywood wainscoting and swiveling office armchairs that are a variation of a famous Charles Eames chair (fig. 6-25). This businesslike aspect of Aurora's personality is softened by sweeping curvaceous forms and glowing pink lighting. Throughout the room—on carpeting, dishes,

6-22. *The formal exterior of Aurora signals an exclusive dining experience.* (*Joseph Durocher photo*)

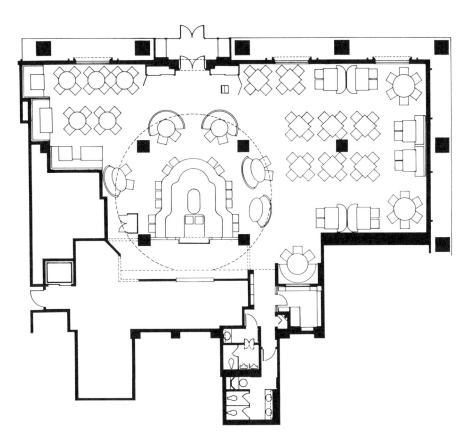

6-23. *The bar placement, directly in front of the entry, plays an important role in Aurora's floor plan (Milton Glaser, Inc., drawing).*

6-24. *Aurora's elaborate bar design is the restaurant's visual focal point. (Joseph Durocher photo)*

6-25. *Finely crafted gueridons and leather-upholstered swivel chairs further the clubby ambiance.*
(Joseph Durocher photo)

menu, lighting, and even on the frosted-glass panel that caps the maitre d' station—Glaser's circular motif adds lighthearted play to an otherwise staid interior.

Aurora looks every inch the white-tablecloth restaurant. Oftentimes, the most elegant look is the simplest, and so it is at Aurora. Neither candles nor flowers adorn the tables. Instead, white linen is punctuated with heavily weighted flatware, crystal wineglasses, and a three-part silver condiment dish topped by a small rose quartz bubble.

In a space where most restaurateurs would have seated at least 150, Baum chose to seat only 125. This evokes a feeling of real luxury in the space. Noise levels in Aurora hover around sixty-five decibels when full, a perfect sound level for conversation. There is a muted buzz in the room but no carry-over noise from table to table. Seating is so comfortable that lunchtime diners can be seen lingering until four in the afternoon.

BACK OF THE HOUSE

We would like to think that the kitchen of one of the best restaurants in New York City was designed expressly for the menu. However, that is not the case. Because Aurora is located in a former restaurant space, the owners simply modified the existing kitchen to suit the needs of Executive Chef Gerard Pangaud.

Aurora has two floors of kitchen space, on the basement floor and the street floor. Nineteen culinarians staff the two kitchens. Twelve cooks perform the preparation and baking of foods in the basement kitchen; seven additional cooks work in the service kitchen, two in the cold foods area and five in the hot foods area.

The basement level is accessible from the street by elevator for deliveries of food. Storage areas along a hallway are adjacent to the receiving area, where all foods are carefully checked by the chef or manager. In addition, offices are located on the basement level, and management can monitor deliveries and keep an eye on activities.

The equipment in the basement kitchen of Aurora is left over from the preceding restaurant. The walk-in freezer (formerly used to hold frozen meats and poultry) is underutilized by Aurora's staff, who rely heavily on fresh food products. Existing smoke ovens used in the Cowboy restaurant are irrelevant for Aurora's menu. Management recognizes these underutilized areas of the kitchen and plans to convert the freezer to a walk-in refrigerator and remove the smoke ovens. In place of the smoke ovens, a bakery section would be installed. However, two years after opening, these modifications had not yet been completed.

In the fabrication area, primal cuts (large cuts of meat) are broken down into smaller, portion-size pieces. In some cases, the primal cuts are merely trimmed, with the final portioning taking place in the service finishing kitchen upstairs. The basement kitchen itself serves as a fabrication and prepreparation area for the service kitchen. Cooks begin vegetable preparation downstairs, as well as the baking and decorating of desserts and pastries. Moreover, the functions of the prepreparation kitchen do not stop during service time. Via telephone, the chef working in the service kitchen can call orders for additional food down to the basement kitchen. Additional products are then prepared and transported upstairs via elevator (and all too often the stairs because the elevator broke down). Although having two kitchens is helpful for the overall effectiveness of the restaurant, the problems associated with vertical transportation sometimes pose severe restrictions.

Aurora's street-level service kitchen includes the hot foods a la carte section, cold food assembly section, and warewashing and service stations. Except for the pressure steamer, all of the equipment on the hot food line is left over from the previous occupants.

The hot foods section is compact yet efficient. The bain marie is surprisingly small because the sauce for each dish is prepared expressly for that dish; therefore, the bain marie is needed only for holding stocks that are used in sauce making and a few other cooking ingredients. Several layers of shelving over the ranges and the serving window provide storage for

dishes, sauce pans, and sauté pans. The ease of access to pans for preparation and plates for service helps to create a very functional workplace for the five chefs in the hot foods area.

The pickup station at Aurora is at a hole cut through the wall between the hot foods area and the service pickup area (fig. 6-26). This relatively confined opening limits the carry-over of kitchen noise from the back of the house to the dining room, which is particularly important because there are no doors between the service pickup area and the front of the house. The treatment also creates a level of intimacy between kitchen and dining room that is uncommon to gourmet restaurants. Because the intimacy is visual rather than auditory, it is much less intense than in a restaurant with an open display kitchen. Only one table affords a full view into the kitchen, and even here guests are insulated from kitchen clatter.

6-26. A limited passthrough window between the preparation area and the service pickup area helps keep kitchen noise out of the dining room. (Joseph Durocher photo)

The Type of Restaurant

Aurora is a gourmet restaurant that caters to an elite, sophisticated crowd. It differs from other establishments of the same type in that the centrally located bar serves as an important visual and social focus. More than a drinking spot, the sixteen-seat bar serves lunch and is very popular with single diners and others who want a more casual meal. It also contributes to the air of conviviality about Aurora, an atmosphere that reflects Baum's vision of a grand salon. It does not detract from Aurora's overall ambiance of wealth and ease. In this restaurant, every seat is a power seat.

The Market

Aurora depends on well-heeled professionals who work nearby to frequent the restaurant for lunch. It has become a regular lunch place for successful businesspeople who include some of New York's (and the world's) most prestigious movers and shakers.

Attracting a full house for dinner means becoming an evening destination spot for gourmet dining. Repeat diners are important to success for both meal periods; in 1987 management recognized at least one person at each table during lunch and one person at forty percent of the tables during dinner.

Baum characterizes Aurora's clientele as "aware people, people involved with theatre, fashion, real estate, publishing . . . people at the top of their profession." He is very much aware of the restaurant's need for repeat business. "The audience I depend on," explained Baum, "keeps coming back to experience the restaurant again and again. This allows us permanency. It allows us to build our market."

Aurora's market tends to include people over thirty. "We have no specific age group that comes here, because age groups of appreciation are changing today," remarked Baum. "I'm continually amazed at the number of young people in their early thirties who frequent the restaurant."

Aurora opened in late 1985 with no promotion or advertising. The idea was to "let the clientele find its own level," according to Baum. By 1987, Aurora had an established market and full occupancy at lunch and dinner. Baum hopes to broaden the customer base even further, however, in order to ensure future profitability.

Aurora belongs in such a rarefied stratum of restaurants that few others nearby can compete on the same level of food, service, and design. One exception is The Four Seasons, Manhattan's classic modern restaurant designed by Philip Johnson (and created, ironically, by Joseph Baum when he was with Restaurant Associates).

At night, because Aurora depends on people traveling to a business neighborhood, secondary competition poses a serious problem. People need a very good reason to go to Aurora instead of to a more established destination spot.

Location is crucial to Aurora's success. As mentioned earlier, Baum did not originally intend to build such a luxe establishment. When he changed his plans, he thought carefully about how to match location with market, menu, and design. The restaurant's choice business address came first, and every other aspect of restaurant development came afterwards.

Aurora's upper-crust clientele are less affected by changing economic conditions than other market segments. Even in hard times, New York City remains home to wealthy professionals and society's elite. The only negative economic indicator was the 1986 tax law, which limited meal deductions to an 80 percent write-off. As of 1987, it remained to be seen if the tax situation would affect Aurora's bottom line. However, Baum's intention to broaden the customer base was caused in part by the implications of tax reform.

Concept Development

Although he is quick to credit his associates, Joseph Baum was the key decision maker in Aurora's concept development. The process was painstaking. Accurately pinpointing the market was crucial to concept development. Baum's approach involved asking many general and specific questions, which led to defining the type of restaurant and the specific experiences it should engender.

As Baum conceived Aurora, it was to be an

"important restaurant," one that "had a sense of theater as well as a certain comfort." He thought of the clientele as an "audience." A clublike atmosphere with very personalized service would ensure that the audience returned for repeat performances.

Food, service, and design were given equal weight in Aurora's concept. No one element overshadowed another. The idea was that all elements would all come together to provide a superb dining experience, one in which nothing distracts diners from the meal and the conversation going on at their table.

The Menu

Baum convinced Gerard Pangaud, a two-star Michelin chef, to leave France for Aurora's kitchen. Pangaud spent a good six months of cooking and talking with the owners during menu development, said Baum's associate Michael Whiteman. The chef also provided input for the selection of new kitchen equipment for the first floor preparation stations.

Chef Pangaud's Gallic orientation is evident in Aurora's menu, which changes daily according to the season and availability of

6-27. *Aurora's elegant menu was designed by Milton Glaser, Inc.*
(Joseph Durocher photo)

ingredients (fig. 6-27). Shortly after opening, Aurora received three stars from the *New York Times* restaurant critic Bryan Miller, who said that the food "can soar high as Mr. Glaser's bubbles on a windy day." Dishes such as sea scallops with a sauce of champagne vinegar and herbs, and fricadelles of veal and prosciutto with wild mushrooms are beautifully presented on the restaurant's signature china.

The Budget

Baum declined to reveal specific cost figures, but reportedly he spent more than a million dollars to create Aurora. Money was not unlimited, however, and certain concessions had to be made due to cost constraints. The ceiling treatment in dining areas, for example, consists of concealed spline acoustic tiles. This solution was not the most elegant, but it was the most practical. The placement of existing HVAC systems in the ceiling meant that other, more esthetic treatments would have been prohibitively expensive.

In 1987, Baum expected the restaurant to gross $5 million. Clearly, Aurora was a financial success, which is fascinating in light of the decision to go with only thirty-one tables, most of them fourtops. Not only did Baum sacrifice precious square footage, but he sacrificed seats by using so few deuces. (Deuces are not considered ideal for business conversations because of their small size). As a result, although the restaurant enjoys full occupancy, the average table occupancy is only 60 percent. Baum knew the financial consequences of having so few deuces but felt that creating the right atmosphere was most important. With Aurora, the restaurateur could afford to invest in the long-term bottom line.

Style of Service

Aurora offers classic a la carte service, executed with a multilevel, European service breakdown of maitre d', area captain, waitperson, and busperson. Yet the service is nearly invisible. Food is artfully plated in the kitchen, carried to the dining room, and carefully placed before the guests. None of the ostentatious fanfare often associated with luxe restaurants is apparent at Aurora.

Speed of Service

The service at Aurora is leisurely yet paced to match the demands of the group. At times the staff seems almost telepathic. When diners take a few extra minutes to read the menu or converse after being seated, they are never rushed into ordering.

Aurora's service philosophy requires that reservations be taken carefully to avoid any backup of guests waiting for a table. Because many guests are regulars, the maitre d' has an idea of how long turning a given table will take, but fast turnover is not a goal. The turnover of tables is carefully controlled to allow guests to linger comfortably over their meal.

Per Customer Check Average

In 1987, Aurora's customers spent an average of $45 for lunch and $74 for dinner, including beverage and not including tax and tip. Obviously, customers expect the finest level of food, service, and design in order to justify such a high check average. The restaurant needs to sustain a reliable and extraordinarily high level of performance both to keep repeat clientele and attract new business.

General Ambiance

The atmosphere at Aurora recedes into the background as diners experience their meal. The room is rich but subdued. Scallop-shaped wall sconces glow soft pink on gleaming cherrywood walls. Custom-designed carpeting, decorated with the celestial bubbles, furthers the quietude. Patrons are enfolded in a warm cocoon of sinuous shapes and warm surfaces. The bar area, enlivened by the squadron of chandeliers, is a bit more ebullient.

Management Philosophy

Although his company consults on a variety of projects, Baum also maintains an owner-operator relationship with Aurora. He believes that the restaurant's ongoing success depends upon constant refinement and improvement. The service staff is impeccably trained and tested regularly. In addition, Baum feels that "one of the eternal pleasures of a good restaurant is the

relationship between host and diner." Aurora's management staff, therefore, keeps close tabs on the clientele. They are not intrusive, but they know all of the regular customers by name and the location of their favorite tables. The maitre d' keeps a guest history book that is referred to before each meal period.

"Since the day we opened, we've made a practice to seat people back at the same table they sat in before," said General Manager Raymond Wellington, who remarked that this treatment helped to establish a clublike atmosphere. In addition, if a regular client hasn't booked a table by 11 A.M., the maitre d' calls the office just to check if the client wants to dine at Aurora that day.

As to the intended life span of the restaurant: "I'm looking to stay a long time," said Baum. "I believe this place will last because of the people who like it here and who keep coming back."

The Design Team

Headed by Baum, the design team for Aurora consisted of a host of illustrious professionals. As noted earlier, the core team included Baum's partners Michael Whiteman and Dennis Sweeney; Milton Glaser, design principal, and Tim Higgins, project designer, from Milton Glaser, Inc.; and Associate Project Designer Philip George from The Office of Philip George. This group met at least two or three times a week during the design process, which took about a year and a half. Each and every design detail for the restaurant was discussed extensively until a solution was agreed upon. Additional consultants included Fisher & Marantz, lighting; Barbara Kafka, tabletop; and H. Friedman & Sons, kitchen. The general contractor was Herbert Construction. As interviews with core team members illustrate, the building of Aurora demanded intense personal involvement from all of the key players. Baum, however, remained the team leader and philosophical guru throughout the project.

JOSEPH H. BAUM, OWNER

Hailed as America's most innovative restaurant consultant, Joe Baum's illustrious career spanned seventeen years with Restaurant Associates, where he served as president from 1963 until 1970. Subsequent to leaving Restaurant Associates, he formed his own company, the Joseph H. Baum Co. Over the years, Baum was responsible for the creation of some of New York's most acclaimed restaurants, from The Forum of the Twelve Caesars to the Market Center (as well as Windows on the World) at the World Trade Towers. Tailored and articulate, Baum speaks with soft tones and elegant gestures. His presence clearly commands respect. In Aurora, Baum seems to float on air through the room, and his darting eyes miss nothing going on around him.

Baum believed that building a repeat clientele in New York in the mid-1980s was a daunting task. Because restaurants were commonly regarded as theater, people went out to try the new show in town that week. The interior needed to be fashionable, but the trendy restaurant wouldn't last long. Instead, Baum tried to create "a comfortable place that had the expressed values of a good restaurant. And its design was certainly part of that."

Baum and Glaser had known each other for fifteen years, and the two men enjoyed a comfortable repartee that heightened the creative process of designing Aurora. "Milton has the artist's ability to visualize results while evolving original solutions," said Baum. "It was hard for me to visualize exactly what he had in mind, but I found in the end that there was no reason for my concern."

Restaurateurs often err by choosing a designer on the basis of style, according to Baum. Instead, he counsels that consideration of the designer's philosophy, beliefs, and capabilities engenders a better designer-owner marriage.

What Baum wanted for Aurora was an environment in which nothing was more important than the individual diner. Yet he envisioned a room that had "quality in every detail, every piece of material. We wanted customers to know that someone cared enough to really think out their seat, because the height, depth and padding were all just right. But it shouldn't seem like a big deal. It should just feel right. We lose when a customer turns over a plate to see who designed it."

In order to achieve the appropriate feel for Aurora, every design detail was thoroughly discussed, dissected, and analyzed. Baum laughingly said that he would have built a full-scale model if that were possible. His quest for perfection left nothing to chance. After considering hundreds of ashtray choices, for instance, Baum approved a nearly invisible glass ashtray. In a smoke-sensitive time, he didn't want to make a big deal about ashtrays. However, he did want to "create the opportunity for anticipatory service." Matchbooks—but not ashtrays—are kept out on the tables. The essence of Aurora is that, when a customer reaches for a cigarette or a match, a server instantly appears with an ashtray.

What would Baum have done differently? He would have liked a larger vestibule area to control drafts and a different ceiling in the dining room. "But I know this is the right design," he reflected, "because I can't imagine it any other way."

MILTON GLASER, DESIGNER

Anyone who has seen a copy of *New York* magazine, the "I Love New York" graphics, or a redesigned Grand Union supermarket knows Milton Glaser's signature. A prolific designer whose work since the 1950s has epitomized good design, Glaser enjoys all sorts of challenges. In 1987, his firm was entrenched on several floors of a Manhattan townhouse where an interdisciplinary staff worked on projects that ranged from book covers to subway station renovations.

A lover of food and restaurants, Glaser had consulted on other foodservice projects, but not until Aurora did he become totally involved with a restaurant design. "With Joe," he remarked, "you're always at ground zero, because you start by raising the most fundamental questions. What is a plate? What is a glass? What is a chair? Joe would not allow any aspect of this restaurant to go unobserved, and I mean anything." Dining tables, for example, were specified not at the standard industry height of 30 inches, but at 28¼ inches, because that is the most comfortable height for dining.

The idea of a comfort level that goes beyond the ordinary is an important tenet of Aurora's design. Although the interior was to be special, it was not intended to be showy. "One of the things that Joe and I like best about this restaurant is the fact that the room disappears," noted Glaser. "When you are here eating, there is nothing in the room to distract you from your dining companion. The result of the experience is a consciousness of how easy it is to be with another person. That has become extraordinarily rare in today's restaurant interiors."

One aspect of the design plan that concerned Glaser was the unusual bar placement. "We were very apprehensive that the bar scene would intrude into the dining room and diminish the experience of the people eating there. But in fact it turned out to be just the opposite. The more people eating at the bar, the more vitality you have in the room." Glaser also worried about diners having enough privacy in the curved banquettes that encircle the bar area, but the high, faux-marble banquette backs afford ample protection from the bar and the nearby entry door. "People are very happy sitting there for dinner," said Glaser, "with absolutely no sense of being victimized."

As to the design style engendered by Glaser's ubiquitous bubble motif, "this particular restaurant has been characterized as being everything from postmodern to baroque," chuckled Glaser. "It has been criticized as too austere and criticized as too frivolous." Part of Glaser's point is that the complexities of Aurora's design defy stylistic labels. "It's a restaurant that at first seems very simple and comprehensible. But the more times you visit, the more complex Aurora becomes. The design keeps growing in meaning."

PHILIP GEORGE, ASSOCIATE DESIGNER

A specialist in restaurant and kitchen design, architect Philip George has consulted on many notable projects, including New York's Le Bernadin and Kansas City's Crown Center complex. He was retained as associate designer for Aurora to help the team iron out technical problems, particularly in the bar and seating areas. Because Baum, Glaser, and George had worked together before, "We spoke in a sort of shorthand," said George, "and our relationship was characterized by a continual dialogue."

The first thing George did when he came on board was to modify and help resolve the basic floor plan. The concept of placing the bar in the midst of the dining room became an important challenge. "It's really a European concept," explained George. "Our key question was, How do you design a restaurant where the bar is, in effect, the focus of the dining room?" George cited the use of luxury materials, including pink granite and cherrywood paneling, as part of the solution. He also pointed out that the intricately crafted back bar is an architectural treatment, not a "liquor element." Further, the bar stools have arms and, like all the seats in the restaurant, leather upholstery. "We wanted a swoosh when you sat," said George.

In essence, Aurora's bar area became the restaurant's most significant design statement, one that does not in the least resemble the typical American drinking counter. The undulating shape and interesting textural contrasts help to create a special identity. "The intent was to give the bar a sexy feel," remarked George, "by using sensuous curves and rich materials. Heavy, bull-nosed edges establish a feeling of permanency." All liquor bottles are kept out of sight of the customer, furthering the impression that this is indeed a different kind of bar (fig. 6-28).

TIM HIGGINS, PROJECT DESIGNER

Architect Tim Higgins, who worked for Milton Glaser, Inc., was involved with the on-site supervision of Aurora's design while the restaurant was being built. One of his biggest challenges concerned the existing HVAC ducting located in the room's ceiling. "We tried to get the highest possible ceiling, but the ducts we had to tie into were located lower than we wanted," said Higgins. What the architect was trying to balance was acoustic control, esthetics, and easy access to ductwork. The solution, a concealed-spline, acoustic panel ceiling with concealed tabs for access panels, was the most practical choice, according to Higgins. "We talked about more interesting choices like fabric-wrapped panels, but it proved too expensive and too complex to weave them into the existing framework," Higgins explained. Although the acoustic ceiling does not reflect the same level of style as Aurora's other design elements, it fades into the background so unobtrusively that

6-28. *The layout of Aurora's bar works well for bartenders and provides patrons with a good view of sparkling glassware.*
(Joseph Durocher photo)

it is almost invisible, and it effectively mutes noise.

As noted earlier, the place where no expense was spared is the bar area, where a plaster ceiling was hung to support the multitude of glowing bubble chandeliers. In order to accomplish this, "we had to reroute a lot of HVAC," said Higgins, who added that "the ceiling over the bar is one of the most important forms in the restaurant. No matter where customers sit, they are aware of this ceiling. It gives the whole bar area focus and helps to solidify its location."

At Aurora, many of the design elements grew from creative problem solving. For example, the team had to deal with existing glass walls that allowed a view into the restaurant from the street. "We didn't want a wall of windows looking into the room," recalled Higgins. "It would not have been appropriate for this type of restaurant. There was also no advantage

in allowing diners to see outside. Our goal was to control the interior in such a way that light would filter through the room. Patrons would get a sense of the outside, but not see out into the street—and people walking by would not be able to see in at all." This goal was accomplished by the development of a "double sandwich wall, back painted with lattice screens on the interior wall." The sea green latticework filters light just as the designers intended and lends a distinctive presence to the restaurant's exterior. Although these window "lattice strings" appear to be one color, they were actually specified in a subtle gradation of colors. The effect is much like the varied light hues in the bar chandeliers.

Another design element that illustrates clever problem solving is the cherrywood armoires that serve as coat closets (fig. 6-29). Space is extremely tight in Aurora's entry area, and yet both a gracious entry and a place to put

6-29. *Beginning in the entry area, sinuous curves add a feminine dimension to the restaurant design.*
(Joseph Durocher photo)

coats are essential. A tiny vestibule was carved out to allow an appropriate sense of progression and arrival. Then armoires were located inside on each side of the door that opens into the restaurant. The armoires hug the walls in "as unobtrusive a way as possible," said Higgins. "Their placement was crucial because we didn't want anything to destroy the integrity of the open room." Albeit a functional solution, the armoires appear to belong in the space. They contribute a residential touch that furthers the image of a private club.

Higgins pointed out that altogether Milton Glaser, Inc., worked five years with Baum on developing Aurora. Hundreds of drawings, countless plans, and several models later, he felt "great satisfaction and a sense of accomplishment. It was a good team."

MICHAEL WHITEMAN, CO-OWNER

Michael Whiteman and Joseph Baum began their collaboration about eighteen years ago, when Whiteman joined Baum to work on the food service at New York's World Trade Center. Previously Whiteman was editor of *Nation's Restaurant News*. The Joseph Baum Company, said Whiteman, "believes in an evolutionary design process, which means that the design isn't totally finished until the restaurant is completely built. We see the process as an opera, a piece of choreography."

When orchestrating the room, the team worked to get a sense of movement in the interior, both "architectural movement and people movement" that would catch patrons' eyes as they scanned the space. The spatial plan was deliberately a bit asymmetrical because "in our experience, people don't respond to geometry and perfect symmetry, but to things that are off-center," Whiteman noted. Although the layout is easy to grasp, it is not perfectly ordered. The bar, for example, is located not at the exact center of the room, but further to the right. This means that the seating sections on either side are quite uneven: five tables on one side and twenty-two on the other.

Because Aurora is a gourmet restaurant, was it designed around the chef's art? Yes and no, according to Whiteman. "We knew that food would be the ultimate reason people came here, but the restaurant wasn't designed around the chef or the specific menu. Rather, it was designed around a certain quality of food. And we believe that food, service, and design all have equal weight in terms of keeping our repeat business," he stressed.

Although the owners expected to attract gourmands, they did not want an ultra-serious restaurant. That's another reason why the focal-point bar became so important to the total scheme. In Whiteman's words, "It was a welcoming gesture and an architectural signal that Aurora was not stiff and formal, even though we took food very seriously."

The success of Aurora's design is also due to the fact that this brand new restaurant didn't really feel like a new restaurant. "It has familiar recalls," commented Whiteman, "but used differently. Paneled walls in cherrywood instead of dark mahogany. Light, fawn-colored leather on seating instead of cracked red leather. Chairs that are an extension of the office environment. And it is stripped of clichés: no brick, no beveled glass, no polished brass, and no blackened anything. Aurora was really conceived as an old-fashioned type of restaurant expressed in new ways."

Summary

The design of Aurora involved a meticulous orchestration of details that together support a seamless gourmet dining experience. It reflects the strong guidance of one man, Joseph Baum, who brought together a formidable design team. The team took a calculated risk by locating an elaborately designed bar area front and center in the restaurant. However, the story of Aurora is less about breaking new ground than it is about careful planning. Baum left nothing to chance. Aurora's design is perfectly suited to its market, its menu, and its style of service.

CAFETERIA PIZAZZ

THE GREENERY   St. Vincent Medical Center, Toledo, OH

During the mid-1980s, noncommercial foodservice design took an evolutionary leap. The old-fashioned institutional cafeteria, with its straight-line servery and noisy, unattractive dining room, gave way to restaurant concept spaces. The new cafeterias boast scatter-system serveries where customers shop for their meals from eye-catching food displays. Dining rooms resemble contemporary cafes more than plasticized cafeterias. The changes relate to keeping patrons happy with their in-house dining facilities. Design, as in commercial restaurants, is used as a marketing tool to attract clientele and keep them coming back.

Emblematic of this new breed of foodservice environment is The Greenery, a 408-seat cafeteria at St. Vincent Medical Center in Toledo, Ohio. Opened in September 1986, The Greenery reflects a dramatic transformation from an inadequate facility into a sparkling new space that affects the image of the entire hospital. Developed under the guidance of St. Vincent's foodservice administrator Peter Zawacki, and designed by Rhode Island–based Morris Nathanson Design, Inc., it has all the trappings of a full-fledged restaurant.

Project Background

Situated in downtown Toledo, St. Vincent was founded by the Grey Nun order in 1855. As the city grew, so did the hospital. In 1986, still owned and operated by the Grey Nuns, St. Vincent housed 624 beds, employed over 3,000 health care professionals, and had over 600 physicians on its medical staff. With a complete range of patient care, it was said to be the major medical center for northwest Ohio and southeast Michigan.

Back in the late 1970s, St. Vincent had begun a long-term, hospital-wide image-building campaign. The opening of other major hospitals in the same market area had greatly increased the competition for patients. In 1983, the advent of DRGs (diagnostic-related groups)

further intensified competition because they mandated shorter patient stays and affected the foodservice budget. Hospital administrators felt that St. Vincent had to upgrade its facilities to create a physical image that matched its service image.

The existing cafeteria, which sat 235 diners, had been built in 1958 and upgraded in 1964. Twenty-five of the seats were allocated as doctors' dining. The large, square room was extremely crowded and noisy during meal periods. Former Administrator of Hospital Support Services Tim Hyma remembered the cafeteria as a "zoo." The carpet, said Foodservice Administrator Zawacki, looked like "baby's first picnic. It seemed to show everything that had been eaten here for the past five years." People sometimes queued up for twenty-five minutes to get through the straight-line servery. The experience was so frustrating that many of the three thousand employees brought their own lunches and consumed food all over the hospital, causing housekeeping and sanitation problems. Visitors were virtually crowded out of the cafeteria during the peak lunch hours. In addition, the physicians were very unhappy with the cafeteria setup and wanted their own private dining room.

Obviously, as Zawacki expressed it, "Major surgery was in order." His goals were far-reaching. Not content to go with a hospital architect, he wanted to bring in an experienced restaurant designer to create an authentic restaurant identity. Further, he wanted to bring an East Coast look to Toledo, so that the cafeteria wouldn't become a visual clone of other local restaurants.

Zawacki contacted Morris Nathanson, whom he had worked with many years previously in Rhode Island. Nathanson's firm was well known for restaurant design work, and Zawacki was "hoping against hope" that they could be persuaded to do a hospital cafeteria.

In fact, Nathanson was not initially interested in designing hospital cafeterias, but his attitude changed after his own son was hospitalized. At that time, Nathanson had the uncomfortable experience of trying to find a place to relax during his hospital visits. The hospital cafeteria, which should have provided respite, was crowded and frenetic.

Nathanson's personal experience helped to convince him to accept Zawacki's invitation to design the St. Vincent cafeteria. "Morris projected his feeling of wanting to get his hands on that other hospital by agreeing to fix up this facility," said Zawacki.

Redesign took place over the summer of 1986, and it went way beyond cosmetic problem solving. The space was literally stripped down to bare concrete and turned into an entirely new dining area, doctors' dining room, and servery, which collectively comprised The Greenery. Rather than phasing in the project one area at a time, the cafeteria was completely shut down for reconstruction and redesign. Diners were re-routed via a connecting tunnel to the School of Nursing Auditorium, where the foodservice staff set up a temporary cafeteria.

The Greenery opened with great fanfare in September 1986. According to Zawacki, the former black hole became a destination spot for off-street customers as well as hospital employees and visitors. He cited a 60 percent increase in customer count and 45 percent increase in sales to prove his point.

Design Description

FRONT OF THE HOUSE

Patrons approach The Greenery by walking down an entrance corridor decorated with diamond-patterned mosaic floor tile, wood molding, and strips of pale blue pipe rail (fig. 6-30). These upscale design treatments foreshadow the experience to come and heighten customers' expectations. An illuminated menu board, framed in oak, advertises the specials of the day.

When customers reach the servery, they are treated to a high-tech shopping experience (fig. 6-31). Faced with black-and-white checkered tile, the sawtooth-shaped serving line allows diners to queue up to individual food stations. Red neon signs and stepped ceiling soffits identify the different stations: hot entrees, soups, sandwiches, grill, low-calorie prepared plates, and desserts. A free-standing beverage station, salad bar, and condiment and flatware station are located in the middle of the servery. Brass-edged sneeze guards and a shimmering, polished-brass ceiling overhead lend sparkle to the space. Fresh-baked breads and colorful floral arrangements displayed in baskets help to merchandise the fare and soften the hard-edged materials. Incandescent lighting shows food to its best advantage.

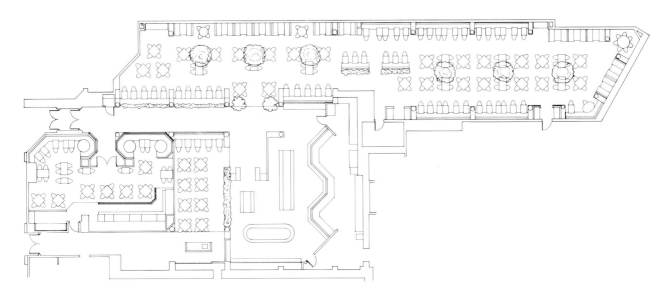

6-30. *The new floor plan of The Greenery, with its separate doctors' dining room and scatter-system servery, fits the needs of both the doctors and the hospital staff (Morris Nathanson Design Inc., drawing).*

6-31. *A variety of high-tech and textural design treatments in The Greenery servery carry it light years away from the old-fashioned institutional space it replaced.*
(Warren Jagger photo)

Leaving the servery, patrons enter a more subdued environment. A skylit dining promenade with natural wood and brass accents, colorful artwork, and leafy ficus trees is punctuated by columns and divided by low, plant-filled partitions into discrete dining areas (fig. 6-32). The environment is extremely bright and cheerful, with light pouring in from overhead skylights. This area had previously been an outdoor courtyard, and the designers elected to keep the brick wall that had been the exterior surface of an existing building. The cream-colored brick, embellished with an eclectic selection of contemporary prints, adds texture to the space.

Lighting in The Greenery is uncommonly sophisticated for a hospital cafeteria and contributes both environmentally and decoratively to the overall design. Squat structural columns, capped with painted stripes of pale blue and dusty rose above a thick band of brass, support art deco–styled light sconces. Their graceful globes cast soft pillows of light on walls and ceiling. Overhead can lights provide direct illumination on tabletops.

Every design element in The Greenery is part of the picture, including the tabletop. For example, Zawacki chose dishware rimmed with a grey band and a coral flower pattern. Grey napkins and china mugs were custom-designed with The Greenery's coral and green logo (fig. 6-33). White laminate tables edged with oak provide an easy-to-maintain yet pleasing backdrop.

The doctors' dining room and servery, located to the right of the entry corridor, is a totally autonomous area. Here, oak paneling and English hunt prints create a more corporate atmosphere (fig. 6-34). A small, straight-line servery crafted of oak offers a selection of hot entrees and sandwiches. Acoustic ceilings and plush carpeting absorb noise. Telephone jacks located near tables enable the foodservice staff to plug in telephones for the physicians when they are paged.

6-32. *The Greenery dining room benefits from a mix of natural and incandescent lighting, white-painted brick, a variety of artwork, and well-maintained ficus trees.*
(Warren Jagger photo)

6-33. *The logo of The Greenery is used throughout the operation to create an image typical of commercial establishments.*

6-34. *English hunt prints and wood-paneled walls create a clubby atmosphere in the doctors' dining room.*
(Warren Jagger photo)

BACK OF THE HOUSE

Two years prior to the cafeteria renovation, in 1984, Zawacki directed a kitchen renovation. It was not a complete redesign. Old equipment in good working order was reconditioned and kept. The dishroom was relocated from a basement site to the main floor. The patient tray line was shortened. Some new equipment was specified to augment and modernize existing equipment.

The progression of spaces in the kitchen of the St. Vincent Medical Center is very logical. Incoming foods move easily from the loading dock area into refrigerated storage spaces on the kitchen level and, via elevator, into dry storage areas in the basement.

The design of the kitchen supports a complex food delivery system that incorporates cafeteria, banquet, buffet, and patient tray service from one kitchen. With a daily volume that at times exceeds six thousand meals, efficiency is paramount. An ingredient room, where a full-time person is charged with measuring out ingredients for all recipes, affords excellent control over ingredients issued to the kitchen, minimizes waste, and keeps the chefs cooking rather than weighing and measuring.

Separate rooms are employed for the cold food, dessert, and baking areas. These specialized areas surround an expansive hot foods area that incorporates both long-term preparation equipment and quick cooking equipment. Although much of the fried, grilled, and broiled foods served in the cafeteria are prepared on the serving line, a full bank of equipment for frying and broiling, along with multifunction tilting braising pans, was incorporated into the back-of-the-house design. Specialized equipment for slow-roasting meats and a convection microwave oven for cooking a single roast at the last minute were added to support all of the service areas. To hold backup food for the cafeteria and patient-feeding area, a variety of holding equipment including bain maries and warming cabinets were installed. The bain marie table is also useful for plating small banquets.

Type of Restaurant

A hospital cafeteria, The Greenery is located inside a wing of the medical center. The cafeteria has no outside entrance. It is managed by St. Vincent's foodservice department and is used for special hospital events as well as for breakfast, lunch, and dinner. The doctors' dining room is used exclusively by physicians, but the public is welcome in the main dining room.

The Market

The Greenery's customer base is composed of three distinct groups: hospital employees, visitors, and physicians. All were disgruntled with the previous facility. Because employees have short, half-hour lunch breaks, they need to get through the line quickly. Equally important is their need for a psychic break from their high-stress jobs.

The three thousand employees form the biggest customer group, but "we didn't want to slight our other publics," stressed Tim Hyma. Visitors, friends, and families of patients as well as off-street customers, are encouraged to eat at The Greenery. Moreover, hospital administration responded to the doctors' complaints by giving them what they asked for: their own separate dining room. The physicians felt a need for total privacy away from concerned family members of patients. They also wanted a place to conduct business.

The competitive marketplace for The Greenery consists of both nearby restaurants and nearby hospitals. Few directly competitive restaurants are located in the immediate geographic area. Most hospital employees are a captive audience who don't leave the hospital for lunch, but lunches from home are significant indirect competition. Brown-baggers were far more prevalent before the redesign than after, according to Zawacki.

On the other hand, the hospital environment is extremely competitive: nine hospitals are located in the Toledo metropolitan area, three in outlying suburbs, and six a bit further out in areas St. Vincent considers its secondary market. Competition is so intense that some projections foresee hospitals shutting down in the early 1990s.

What hospital competition means for The Greenery is that it has to be an effective marketing tool for the hospital. Raves about the cafeteria from former patients and visitors may influence people to choose St. Vincent when they require a hospital visit. In addition, a new cafeteria helps keep hospital employees happy and shows them that the administration cares about their well-being. It is a fringe benefit that helps to attract new employees and to decrease high worker turnover. After the redesign, in fact, the hospital's recruitment manager stopped meeting potential staff in his office. He took them to lunch at The Greenery instead.

St. Vincent is situated in downtown Toledo and has grown with the community as it changed from a swamp to a city. Most recently, waterfront revitalization and a new convention center marked a change for the better in the area surrounding St. Vincent. Headquarters of international corporations were beginning to crop up nearby as well. Toledo is slowly evolving into a service-oriented community that is trying to attract light and high-tech industry. It has even been cited as an "all-American city" by the press and as a good place to bring up children. Close to Detroit, it had suffered from a sluggish economy in the mid-1980s, but seemed to be picking up in recent years. Still, the hospital faces an uphill battle to maintain its market share.

Concept Development

Although hospital administration had been talking for years about cafeteria renovation, "it wasn't until Pete [Zawacki] came on board in 1981 that it all came together," commented Hyma. Zawacki spearheaded the idea of an exciting "restaurant," one that would add a lot of perceived value to the standard hospital cafeteria.

As noted earlier, The Greenery was part of a grander scheme that included a total hospital renovation intended to revamp the facility's image. In the cafeteria, however, the design team wanted to create an atmosphere "unlike any other place in the hospital," said Zawacki. It was not intended to invoke any particular design style, but it was to provide a cheerful contrast to the employees' high-pressure working environment. In fact, said Hyma, when people sit down at their tables, they should have the impression that they had gone out to eat.

The Menu

The Greenery offers a wide selection of hot entrees, sandwiches, and grilled items, with daily specials for each meal period. Breakfast specials include a popular item called 2+2+2, which consists of two eggs prepared to order, two slices of bacon or sausage links, two slices of toast, hash browns, and beverage. For lunch and dinner, hot entrees feature everything from Cajun catfish to vegetable lasagna to Hungarian goulash. Sandwiches such as rib eye steak or grilled swordfish on a roll and hot, homemade soups are also offered daily. A comprehensive dessert station displays every sort of tempting treat.

In keeping with an increasingly calorie- and health-conscious clientele, a diet chicken or fish item is always offered, and a lot of attention is given in general to having plenty of low-cholesterol, low-fat, and low-sodium items. The spacious salad bar, which replaced a much smaller unit, has a healthful choice of fresh greens, vegetables, and salads.

In the doctors' dining room, a much smaller servery offers such dishes as broiled salmon fillets and chicken fricassee, a hand-carved roast for platters and sandwiches, and a salad bar.

The Budget

In a project such as this, in which the foodservice renovation is tied in with a much larger capital improvement, pinpointing exact budget items is difficult. Although hospital administration would not reveal the design costs, they obviously invested a great deal in the design of The Greenery. "We did go over our initial budget, but that was at the hospital's request, because they wanted the highest quality materials and furnishings," said Morris Nathanson project designer Peter Niemitz.

Still, "our biggest constraint was finance," admitted Hyma, "and we had to make a lot of compromises between what we wanted to do and what we could afford to do." One area that jacked up the design budget was the doctors' dining room, but, said Hyma, "the board was very supportive in developing something special for the doctors."

In the case of St. Vincent, money spent on redesign not only had positive image-building consequences but also had positive financial ramifications. Due to the earlier kitchen renovation, Zawacki was able to reduce his FTE (full-time equivalent employees) count by twenty people. Catering activities expanded and added new revenues to the foodservice department's bottom line. The cafeteria had been a moneyloser to the tune of approximately $50,000 per year. After redesign, it broke even. Zawacki predicted that, helped along by its spiffy and functional new front of the house, The Greenery would become a profit center in the future. He estimated that the hospital would recoup its design investment in three to four years from opening day.

Style of Service

In the public dining room, customers pick up their trays when they enter the servery and then queue up to food stations where they are served hot entrees, deli sandwiches, and grilled items. Patrons serve themselves salad, beverages, and desserts, and they can also pick up prepared sandwiches and platters from refrigerated display counters. One of the most popular areas is the grill station, a new feature at St. Vincent. Here, the grill chef works in full view of the customers in the same fashion as a chef in an open display kitchen.

In the doctors' dining room, physicians queue up to a straight-line servery. They are served their main course and help themselves to salad. There is partial wait service for beverages and desserts.

Speed of Service

The time it takes customers to move through the servery was a critical issue in the redesign. The goal was to enable people to get their food as quickly as possible, so they could spend their lunch break dining instead of waiting in line. Another benefit of speed of service is that patrons reach the dining room with their hot food still hot. In the old straight-line system, it took so long to get through the servery at peak times that the hot dishes were cool by the time people sat down to eat.

In the new servery, the scatter system of separate food stations allows people to move at random through the space instead of having to line up at a single queue. If customers want a burger and fries, they go straight to the grill. If they desire hot entrees, they go straight to the hot food station. They can also bypass the line altogether and fill up at the salad bar.

According to Hyma, the speed of service vastly improved with the advent of The Greenery. Even in the peak lunch hour, waiting time was cut from twenty-five minutes to less than ten minutes. Service is slowest at the crowded grill line, and Zawacki plans to expand that section to cut waiting time.

Per Customer Check Average

Inherent to the concept is a modest pricing structure, because keeping The Greenery's prices within reasonable bounds for hospital employees is important. To accomplish this and to foster goodwill with the three thousand potential diners, a 10 percent discount is given to St. Vincent employees. Overall check average in March 1987 was $1.10 for breakfast, $2.25 for lunch, $2.20 for dinner, and $1.85 for a late-night snack.

General Ambiance

The Greenery has three different personalities. In the main servery, slick, energized design stimulates the senses and seems to heighten the appetite. In the main dining room, a cheerful, low-key atmosphere encourages a convivial, comfortable dining experience. In the physicians' dining room, a clubby milieu provides a restful, soothing backdrop.

Entering the main dining room, customers are instantly enveloped in color and light. All lighting in The Greenery is on a computerized dimming system that can be programmed for different areas of the space. Music also contributes to the ambiance. Zawacki can set the foreground music system to play anything from classical to rock to soft jazz, depending on the occasion (the room is often used for catering functions) and the time of day.

Management Philosophy

As the hospital's foodservice administrator, Peter Zawacki's philosophy set the tenor of The Greenery. In essence, he wanted the cafeteria to become a destination restaurant. Zawacki's intent was to carry through the design in every detail, from coffee mugs to staff uniforms. He believed in The Greenery's potential to attract off-street business as well as hospital employees, visitors, and physicians.

Zawacki stayed closely involved with the operation of the cafeteria. He was often out on the floor talking with customers and getting feedback on The Greenery's food, service, and design.

An important part of management philosophy at St. Vincent involved giving the foodservice employees new opportunities concurrent with the redesign. Not only Zawacki but also his staff felt intimately involved with the project. During the design process, "everything changed," said Zawacki. "People were allowed some upward mobility. If you were a first cook, for example, you had the chance to become a grill person out on the servery line. And everyone was into the spirit of the renovation, picking their new uniforms, anticipating the light at the end of the tunnel."

The result is that foodservice employees exhibit a newly developed "pride of ownership" in The Greenery that is evidenced by an enthusiastic attitude and high productivity. Each employee who staffs a servery food station, for instance, also has to take care of the daily maintenance chores for that station. Rather than resent the extra work involved in polishing the brass-trimmed sneeze guards and tray areas, staffers take pride in keeping their areas shining and immaculate.

The Design Team

Core members of the design team were Peter Zawacki, Tim Hyma (who served as hospital liaison throughout the project), and project designers Peter Niemitz, Blase Gallo, and Morris Nathanson of Morris Nathanson Design, Inc. The hospital's in-house architect was Darriel Brown.

The complexities of going through a hospi-

tal board for decision-making approval presented daunting challenges to the design team. As Zawacki expressed it, "This design was not easily accepted by the decision makers." Hyma was the constant go-between and "because of Tim's support," said Zawacki, "I had the desire to fight the battle."

PETER A. ZAWACKI, FOODSERVICE ADMINISTRATOR

Peter Zawacki's career in food service included a stint in Saudi Arabia before he settled in Toledo. There, in addition to serving as foodservice administrator for the Dietetic Services Department at St. Vincent, he maintained a foodservice consulting company. To Zawacki, The Greenery represented a whole new way of thinking about hospital foodservice design, and he was totally involved with every step of the project.

Regarding the decision to retain an East Coast firm, Zawacki admitted that the long-distance situation could have been problematic. "Of course I had to ask myself, Will it really work to have a Rhode Island–based firm design a hospital restaurant in Toledo? But in fact the information flow and the design installation flow progressed smoothly," he said, adding that "the design brought something completely different to the area. People walked in and said 'wow.'"

Early on in the project, the group decided to give the cafeteria a name. "This was a very important decision," stressed Zawacki. "We didn't want it to be an anonymous dining facility. Calling it The Greenery was a marketing decision that helped to sell the idea of a real restaurant, a pleasurable eating place." As opening day approached, printed notices inscribed "Meet me at The Greenery" were distributed to the staff. Zawacki, Hyma, and the rest of the design team began to drop the name in all of their memos and conversations to employees, doctors, and administrators. By the time it was completed, The Greenery had become a familiar name to future patrons.

What were the maintenance requirements in the main servery and dining room, where in 1987 approximately two thousand diners ate every day? "We asked the designers to specify long-lasting materials that were easy to take care of," commented Zawacki. Ceramic tile, carpeting, and laminate tabletops are all easy to maintain. Wooden chairs were structurally reinforced, and their vinyl-padded seats can be wiped clean in an instant. As noted earlier, the foodservice staff at each food station are responsible for polishing the brass sneeze guards and tray rails in their area. Plants and trees are on a maintenance contract with an outside company. This is a design that Zawacki hopes will last another thirty years before the next renovation is needed.

Zawacki believes that the profusion of artwork, which portrays themes relating to opera, fashion, travel, sports, and nature, is an important design component at The Greenery. It sparks the room with color and helps to define different seating areas. For example, "People like to hold small meetings in one area that's been dubbed the Matisse corner," Zawacki noted.

Doctors and employees alike responded enthusiastically to the new design, according to Zawacki. The hospital's recruitment manager stopped meeting potential staff in his office and took them to The Greenery instead. Rather than dreading lunch, as they used to, The Greenery customers look forward to it. "People even say how wonderful the food is," Zawacki chuckled, "even though most of the old menu items are still on the line. We use the same purveyors, the same products. But our new design makes people believe they are getting a better value. It enhances our entire operation."

TIM HYMA, HOSPITAL LIAISON

After many years as an administrator at St. Vincent Medical Center, Tim Hyma left in 1987 to form his own consulting company. Throughout the entire foodservice redesign at "St. V's," however, Hyma was the link between the hospital board and all the members of the design team. "One of our biggest challenges," he said, "was to keep the team working despite the politics. There were many involved parties—the in-house architect in charge of construction, the contingent of physicians who were very concerned with their dining room, the board members who had financial concerns, and others." Hyma met weekly with Zawacki, and about

once every six weeks with project designer Niemitz when he traveled to Toledo. "I made sure that everyone knew what everyone else was doing and what the time frame was," he recalled. "One of my responsibilities was keeping everything under control."

One way the team kept the project on time was to delay beginning demolition and reconstruction until all the new equipment had been ordered and delivered. "That way we didn't have any scares waiting for deliveries," said Hyma.

Reconstruction took place over the summer of 1986, when the cafeteria shut down and people were rerouted to a temporary facility. "We teased the people through this difficult period," noted Hyma. "The construction area was closed off to public view. We played a kind of peekaboo. People would see the neon delivered. They would see the artwork come in. But nobody knew what the whole design would look like when it was completed. They became increasingly curious, so that when we finally had the grand opening in mid-September 1986, everybody was more than anxious to see the finished space."

PETER NIEMITZ, PROJECT DESIGNER

In his capacity as project designer for Morris Nathanson Design, Inc., Peter Niemitz worked on countless foodservice interiors. The Greenery, he maintained, was not very different. "We really approached the project from a restaurant point of view," he stressed. "Merchandising elements such as food displays in the servery were very important to us. We wanted a space that exuded freshness and good eating habits, without getting too cute."

The designers answered many of the hospital's philosophical and operational concerns as well. "As Peter [Zawacki] explained it to us, there was tremendous anxiety in the hospital environment, not just among patients' visitors but among the staff too," explained Niemitz. "We aimed for a design that would help take the pressure off in a way that wasn't monotonous. We also tried to create variety in the space without having separate rooms. The hospital needed The Greenery to serve as a place for meetings and receptions, so we thought of the room in terms of areas that could be segregated for different events."

The biggest spatial challenge, said Niemitz, was posed by the long, awkward courtyard area that was enclosed to become The Greenery's main dining room. "We really weren't sure what to do with all the miles of wall space." However, the designers so effectively broke up the space with columns, banquette planters, and low partitions that it appears to offer several distinct seating areas.

To unify the spacious floor plan, a limited number of elements were used consistently throughout The Greenery. The effect is an underlying order that induces a feeling of comfort. For example, the bull-nosed oak chair rail was specified at the exact same height as the bull-nosed oak trim detail on countertops and low partitions. The area has just one type of decorative lighting fixture and one type of recessed lighting fixture. "To help make a strong state-ment in this very large space," commented the designer, "we kept elements consistent. We also overscaled everything just a bit."

As to design style, "Our goal was to make the space interesting," said Niemitz. "We used relatively classic detailing and furnishings to create a contemporary restaurant."

Summary

In the case of The Greenery, good design totally changed the image—and the profit picture—of a noncommercial cafeteria. Design was the key merchandising tool that repositioned an archaic facility into a well-received "restaurant." It turned a dining area formerly perceived as depressing and inconvenient into a real benefit for employees. The efficiency of a scatter-system servery and the psychological value of an exuberant cafe setting contributed a great deal to the success of this renovation.

THE QUINTESSENTIAL GATHERING PLACE

AMERICA   New York, NY

During the 1980s, Michael Weinstein became the hottest name on the New York restaurant scene. In a city where restaurants open and close at an alarming pace, Weinstein's establishments seemed almost impervious to the whims of fashion. He had a knack for going into run-down, uncharted neighborhoods just before they became important Manhattan destinations. His philosophy created a whole new genre of restaurants: big, wide-open-to-the-street gathering places that offered an entertaining see-and-be-seen milieu and an expansive, moderately priced menu.

The former investment banker took about ten years to become one of Manhattan's premier restaurateurs. By 1987, Weinstein had founded the Ark Restaurants Corporation with his partner Ernie Bogen. A public corporation, Ark owned approximately seventeen restaurants and was expanding its services into consulting and operations management. According to Weinstein, nine of the seventeen Ark-owned establishments returned their investment within the first year of operation.

Ark's most profitable restaurant was America, a mammoth, 350-seat gathering place that opened at the end of 1984. Designed by McClintock, Grammenopoulos, Soloway (MGS) Architects, it is a big, bold, architecturally exuberant space that evokes a patriotic theme in subtle ways. Dismissed by food critics, labeled New York's noisiest restaurant, and regarded as a trendy grand cafe, America nevertheless remained hugely successful while many other similar establishments went belly up. This restaurant has staying power. Its design works. America in 1987 was a New York institution. It remained, as Michael Weinstein expressed it, "a product that was very much in demand."

Project Background

In the spring of 1982, Weinstein fell in love with a grand old industrial building in Manhattan's flatiron district, on East Eighteenth Street. At that time, the neighborhood consisted primarily of light manufacturing and photographers' studios, but Weinstein believed it was an up-and-coming area. He made a bid for the space that was rejected as too low. Weinstein waited it out. A year and a half later, in October 1983, the landlord collapsed down to Weinstein's bid, and the restaurateur signed a twenty-year lease for the 9,600-square-foot space.

Weinstein perceived a "lunch business of sorts" for the restaurant, but felt that to work at night, it had to be a "larger than life event." He had been considering the idea of regional American cuisine for a long time. These two ideas were the basic tenets that became America.

Three architectural firms competed for the job by submitting drawings of their concepts for the space. The winner was New York–based MGS Architects, who had designed another of Weinstein's restaurants, Ernies. By the time America was completed, however, it bore little resemblance to the architects' early plans. The design process, which took over a year, was an evolutionary process in which no design decision was finalized until owners and designers were satisfied that it was the very best possible solution. MGS principals and project designers Elizabeth (Libby) McClintock and Anthony Grammenopoulos were given the conceptual ideas and asked to translate those ideas into good design solutions.

Weinstein is a very involved owner with strong opinions regarding what he wants from architecture and design. For example, he insisted on the radical idea of locating the bar in the back of the restaurant underneath an existing skylight. He had a definite sense of the immensity of the space and "knew exactly how the restaurant should look standing back at the bar gazing forward into the room." When bar construction was in jeopardy because no one could locate a structural steel system that would meet the load capacity required by the city, Weinstein still wouldn't give up on his idea. "I sent

Libby and Anthony back one last time to tell the structural engineers that we were going to build this bar, and they had better figure out a way to do it." Sure enough, the engineers found a way.

During the last four months of America's construction, Weinstein moved his office to the site. He was there twenty hours a day. At that point, he said, he "took over the job, because the idea had taken definite form in my head and it had become important for me to be there all the time." America's design was very much a reflection of Michael Weinstein's sensibilities.

Design Description
FRONT OF THE HOUSE

A single, sandblasted star perched on a brass pole announces the restaurant's exterior presence (fig. 6-35). The glass-lined facade is set behind existing cast-iron mullions, with a large, curved-glass curtain that spills out toward the sidewalk. Passers-by have an unobstructed view into the restaurant, but they have to walk up four steps to enter. The vestibule has a blue ceiling pierced by low-voltage, star-shaped downlights laid out in the configuration of the night sky as it was on July 4, 1776.

America's cavernous interior reflects its architectural origins in the original brick pillars, cast-iron columns, and an intricately crafted skylight that crowns the bilevel pink terrazzo bar at the rear of the restaurant. Basically, America is one huge, high-ceilinged room with a bar at the back (fig. 6-36). A central walkway, theatrically lit with starlight projections, leads to the bar. Suspended from the ceiling above this promenade is an abstract American flag crafted of neon. Dining sections of tightly packed tables are located on either side of the walkway. Black-and-white checked seating platforms hug the side walls, contrast with the wooden floor throughout the rest of the space, and provide the only deuce tables in the restaurant (fig. 6-37).

Sweeping pastel murals fill the restaurant's walls. New York City is portrayed on the west

6-35. *America's open-to-the-street facade allows passers-by a clear view of the action inside.*
(Joseph Durocher photo)

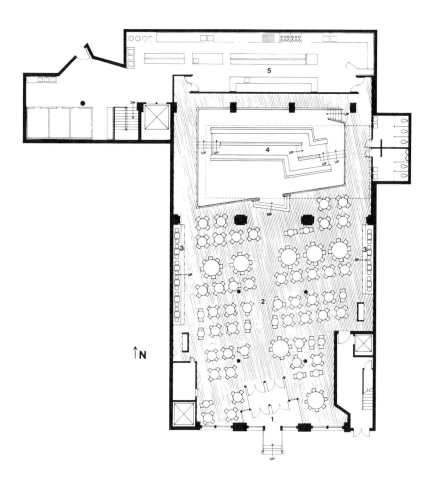

6-36. *America's floor plan illustrates an interesting gathering place layout: (1) the angled entry with its oversize doors; (2) the central promenade flanked by tables; (3) the raised seating platforms for deuces; (4) the raised bar strikingly positioned in the back of the restaurant; and (5) the long, narrow kitchen. (MGS Architects drawing)*

6-37. *Raised seating platforms along two of America's walls provide superb see-and-be-seen visibility. (Regina S. Baraban photo)*

wall, the industrial revolution takes up the north wall, and the great American heartland sweeps across the east wall. Fragments of abstract Navajo sand paintings that look like black bolts of lightning break up the dreamy American scenes. To the left of the entry, an over-scaled Navajo fragment defines the coatcheck room. A sophisticated system of black theatrical spotlights is strung across the buff-toned ceiling.

Design applications convey a range of American imagery without prototypical theme nostalgia. Round oak tables and slat-backed schoolhouse chairs look solid and old-fashioned. Oversized white china is reminiscent of the roadhouse diner, but the linen-covered tables give the feel of a restaurant.

The room is wide open, much like a gigantic artist's loft (fig. 6-38). Its most dramatic image is the huge pink bar studded with green stars that sits like a monumental altar at the back of the restaurant. Three hundred people can mill around its terrazzo platform and watch the world go by in the restaurant below them.

BACK OF THE HOUSE

The kitchen space at America is over 120 feet long, 20 feet wide in the serving area, and 20 feet tall. Despite its long, narrow shape, its various areas seem to have a well-coordinated sense of oneness and order. Such coordination must exist because on the busiest days upwards of 1,500 diners are served from this kitchen. In 1987, America averaged three hundred lunch customers and 700 dinner customers daily.

In addition to the 2,000 square feet of kitchen, the back of the house includes a large receiving entryway that opens up onto Nineteenth Street, plus basement storage, employee support, and office space that can be accessed by a service elevator or staircase. In addition to the storage space in the original design, storage space was built atop the walk-in refrigerators in the kitchen, thus making full use of the high ceilings. This innovative storage area is emblematic of how the restaurant's kitchen design continued to evolve as employees found new

6-38. *The central promenade culminates in America's huge terrazzo bar, which can hold up to 300 people.*
(Joseph Durocher photo)

and better ways of improving production, speeding service, adding new menu items, and reacting to the changing tastes of America's customers.

Immediately adjacent to the receiving corridor are walk-in refrigeration units and the elevator that accesses the basement storage spaces. Continuing into the kitchen, amorphously shaped fabrication, bakeshop, and prepreparation areas meld together (fig. 6-39). The corners and angles of the old building set some boundaries to the spaces, but the cooks in this area work and interact as though no barriers or divisions intrude between them.

Next, the cold food and sandwich stations are connected in a straight line with the hot food section (fig. 6-40). Across from both of these areas are the service support stations that hold breads, condiments, hot beverages, and a service bar that is open during peak hours. At the far end of the kitchen is the dish- and pot-washing area where bustubs of dirty dishes are dropped off and clean tableware and trays are stored.

Servers can enter the pickup area from either of two doors nestled behind the raised bar in the back of the dining room. During peak service periods, the kitchen is packed with service and production personnel. An expeditor station maintains a sense of order and serves as an intermediary between production and service personnel.

Type of Restaurant

America is a type of restaurant pioneered by Weinstein in the early 1980s. Characterized by a dramatic architectural space treated as one big room, it became known as a grand cafe. Essentially a gathering place restaurant with a large bar left open to the dining area, it has an extensive menu that offers big portions for reasonable prices. Noise drives the animated atmosphere.

6-39. *The preparation area of America's kitchen is central to serving an average of a thousand people daily.*
(Joseph Durocher photo)

6-40. *The cold food area, completely stocked before each meal period, functions much like an assembly line.*
(Joseph Durocher photo)

The Market

Initially, Weinstein projected a glamorous urban clientele for America. When a younger, less sophisticated crowd plus a big tourist clientele became the mainstay of the restaurant, he wasn't disappointed. "Very few of our restaurants have been targeted to a specific market," he explained. "At America, for example, we didn't really have a plan in our head as to who we were trying to attract and then design the restaurant for those people. One of the reasons why our menus are so broad and our prices are so varied is that we want anyone who comes in the restaurant to be comfortable. We're delighted with anybody who walks in." In fact, said Weinstein, the market for America is "the public at large."

When America opened, just a few other restaurants were in the immediate vicinity. Then the area exploded and became one of the city's new restaurant rows. Several chic gathering places sprang up. A few years later, many had closed. As other restaurants came and went, America prevailed. Obviously, it had created a special niche in a volatile market. "I can't tell you why," said Weinstein, "but we really take a lot of care to match the product to the design and make it long-lasting." Competition has not affected America as much as it has other restaurants, perhaps because (after a brief shakeout period) it has maintained a consistent level of food, service, and design.

When America was first built, its neighbors on East Eighteenth Street were primarily small businesses. As the area changed, more and more professional studios took the place of small industrial concerns. In addition, between 1985 and 1987 several other restaurants opened nearby. The location is within walking distance from some downtown residential areas, but most of America's nighttime business is destination customers.

An important note regarding America's location involves the building itself. The soaring, dramatic space with its vintage brick columns, high ceilings, and skylight plays a critical role in attracting the market. "The restaurant space needs to be 'larger than life' to lure New Yorkers to out-of-the-way destinations," commented Weinstein. "We want more than just location from our buildings; we want something architecturally interesting."

Regional economic conditions were good when America opened. Moderate menu pricing was aimed toward such a wide market base that minor fluctuations in the economy did not seriously affect sales predictions. Further, the site was located in an economically depressed area on the verge of positive change. As the neighborhood became more affluent, America could expect an increase in lunch business.

Concept Development

When Weinstein signed the lease for America in 1983, he felt that the time was right for a restaurant concept based on a patriotic theme and a regional American menu. His contemporaries (Weinstein was forty at the time) had grown out of their laid-back ways and entered the age of consumerism. Reagan was president. The Bicentennial of the Constitution was coming up. "No one had tried this concept before," he said, "and it just seemed to me that it was the right idea at the right time." After finding the location for the restaurant, Weinstein developed the conceptual idea, then the design applications, and finally the menu.

The Menu

An extensive menu is a hallmark of Ark restaurants, and Executive Chef Bill Lalor would have nothing less for America. America's food menu incorporates more than 160 different items in fifteen categories. "Not a pretentious cuisine, but the kind of food we ate while we were growing up," noted Weinstein.

Although some of the sauces and stewed items are batch prepared, the vast majority of dishes are prepared to order. To accomplish this feat, the preparation phase of production has to be carefully executed. Both fabrication and preparation areas play an important role in America's kitchen. Meats, vegetables, and sauces are all prepared and held in holding areas awaiting the service hour. Backup ingredients are kept in the walk-in refrigerators.

Within seven months, the kitchen crew and service staff were able to satisfy the large numbers of diners who frequented the restaurant.

Such was not the case during the first month of operation, when some 2,700 meals were reported "comped [free of charge], because the staff wasn't getting the food to the customers on time." Part of the problem came from opening-month jitters and part from the sometimes overwhelming size of the menu. Nevertheless, the broad-based menu was important in order to attract a wide spectrum of customers.

Still, that same breadth posed problems. Just how many fluffernutter sandwiches should you plan to serve? How many sacks of potatoes should you peel for mashed potatoes? How many lugs of tomatoes should you order for the dozens of dishes they would be used in? These problems were not resolved until management was able to develop a track record that could be used to forecast the sales of individual items.

Lalor conducted extensive research over a period of six months into regional American cuisine. An important part of the research was to capture the diversity of names used for common menu items. Items such as sliders (small grilled hamburgers with grilled onions served much like White Castle burgers), a New York specialty; Sheboygan double brats (garlic sausage with sauerkraut on an onion roll) from Wisconsin; and the classic Philadelphia cheese steak on a hoagie roll add to the regional diversity of the menu and to its broad-based appeal. Some food critics panned Lalor's cuisine, but Michael Weinstein pointed out that when you cook for upwards of a thousand people a day, the quality of food is different from that of a small gourmet restaurant.

The Budget

Weinstein declined to confirm budget figures, but America reportedly cost approximately $1.25 million to build. The architects estimated a front-of-the-house fitting-out cost of $140 per square foot. "We don't really budget," explained Weinstein. "We do try to make economical decisions, but we also don't want to lower the design quality. We want to contain costs to an acceptable level, but still allow creativity to flourish between ourselves and our designers. If a great idea comes up halfway through construction, we would like to be able to switch gears and incorporate it into the design." Ark

Management served as their own general contractor for America, which helped to keep costs in line.

Style of Service

Plate service is offered for all foods served at America. The oversized, heavy white dishware is plated in the kitchen and carried to tables without the assistance of trays. To serve tables of four or more, the wait staff has to work in pairs or make several trips to and from the kitchen.

Speed of Service

As noted earlier, some 2,700 meals were served free of charge during America's first month because of slow service. Improving the speed of service became one of management's top priorities. By the restaurant's eighth month of operation, the speed of service had improved significantly.

Still, the distance from the kitchen to some of the tables in the front of the space is a major cause of slow service. There is no service station in the front of the restaurant. If a guest sitting at one of the front tables drops a fork, the server has to travel 140 feet to bring a replacement (or else steal it from another table). One modification that helped but did not cure the situation involved increasing the size and improving the layout of the existing service stations. When America first opened, the service stations were only one-third the size of the stations that were in use in 1987.

Per Customer Check Average

The key to America's check average is value. In 1987, patrons paid approximately $12 for lunch and $17 for dinner, including beverage but not tax and tip. The restaurant is extremely competitive from a menu-pricing point of view. Combine price with generous portions and striking architectural design, and eating out at America appears to offer customers a very good deal.

General Ambiance

The driving energy of America is emblematic of big, gathering place restaurants. The atmosphere reflects a new generation of entertainment spaces where people eat, talk, and watch each other. Extremely high noise levels (by some accounts, America is New York's noisiest restaurant) ignite the scene.

Management Philosophy

Weinstein's management style is based on "hard work, honesty, and common sense." From the beginning of his career as a restaurateur, he believed in hiring "nice people" and giving them an opportunity to move up in the organization. Staff is allowed to move from restaurant to restaurant; a good employee who is unhappy at one of Weinstein's restaurants can opt for the same position in another.

As Ark grew, management became increasingly specialized, with each partner overseeing different aspects of the business. In general, Weinstein was involved with restaurant conception and design; Ernie Bogen was involved with finance and cost controls; Bill Lalor concentrated on establishing food and kitchen design specifications and supervising ongoing kitchen management, and a fourth partner, Vinnie Pascal, was in charge of employee training.

Ark runs a very tight ship and is known for its lean management style. The company operates out of unassuming offices on West Twenty-ninth Street in Manhattan with a very small staff. Significant purchasing power and a central, computerized purchasing system keep their food costs low. However, much of Ark's computerized accounting is done by individual managers at the unit level rather than in the main office. "We want our managers to learn how to run a business," said Weinstein.

Although Weinstein has had to spread himself thinner as the company expanded, he nevertheless keeps close tabs on all of Ark's restaurants and employees. He believes that "in big restaurants like America, you bring a lot of talented staff together, but they need time to work out their coordination problems. Lack of coordination is what really kills you." At America, as mentioned earlier, management worked closely with the staff several months after opening in order to improve the service. "It's not like a Broadway show where you can prepare by rehearsing, because you're not delivering a song,

you're delivering a plate of food. We're always trying to continually improve."

The Design Team

Michael Weinstein was unquestionably the team leader for America. Other Ark team members included Executive Chef Bill Lalor, who was in charge of kitchen design, and Vinnie Pascal, who was America's general manager. The front-of-the-house designers were Elizabeth McClintock and Anthony Grammenopoulos from MGS Architects. As noted earlier, Ark was the general contractor.

MICHAEL WEINSTEIN, OWNER

With a college degree in business, Michael Weinstein's first career was as an investment banker. After leaving finance in 1973, he opened his first restaurant, The Museum Cafe, in 1975. Located in Manhattan's Upper West Side, an area that was just starting to blossom into the affluent home of some of the world's most conspicuous consumers, the restaurant took off like wildfire. The Museum Cafe was a neighborhood bistro with a far-reaching menu and a casual ambiance that was equally comfortable for tuxedos or blue jeans. It very much reflected Weinstein's own laid-back personal style. Twelve years later, in 1987, The Museum Cafe was returning its original investment roughly every five weeks, said Weinstein.

The restaurateur expanded his operations on the Upper West Side and into other parts of Manhattan and eventually burgeoned into a multimillion-dollar company, Ark Restaurants Corp. The Ark establishments were marketed as individual, not chain restaurants. Each had its own name and its own identity. However, many shared certain conceptual elements such as expansive menus and dramatic architecture.

One Ark success followed another until in 1986 an ill-fated move to the New Jersey suburbs with four of their restaurant concepts set the company back a bit. By 1987, Ark was looking strong, not only with their own restaurants but also as a restaurant consulting and management company.

Meanwhile, success hadn't changed Weinstein's style. Wearing sweat pants and a T-shirt, he still traveled to his restaurants on his ten-speed bike. Restless and inquisitive beneath his casual facade, he appeared to be driven with entrepreneurial energy. Few details in any of his restaurants appeared to escape his scrutiny. He relied on both instinct and experience to help him build "the very best restaurant in the neighborhood."

America, said Weinstein, was an extraordinary success. In its first week of business, the restaurant served nine thousand people. Three years later, volume had settled down to an average of a thousand meal covers daily. It remained Ark's most profitable restaurant.

What made it work so well? "It's partly instinctive," he mused, "and hard to explain. But one thing that goes into all of our restaurants (to my partners' dismay) is that I don't push the space in a direction. It tells me where to go. I am always looking for the point at which the idea is so strong that it calls out to me. It sounds very amorphous and impractical, but that's what goes on. At some point, the restaurant demands certain things from me and at that point I get very, very busy. I was very active laying out the space for America and then became inactive until the last four months. Then, all of a sudden, the idea had taken enough form in my head that it became important for me to be there all the time."

Weinstein insisted upon certain design elements. As noted earlier, he would brook no opposition to placing the bar in the back. Round tables were a must, because "they helped to focus diners on the conversation at their own tables instead of listening to what was going on around them." Anticipating the eating habits of young, upwardly mobile restaurantgoers who travel in groups, he specified very few deuce tables. He knew that he wanted murals. Inspired by a wall in the Museum of Modern Art in Paris that depicted great inventors from around the world, he first proposed the idea of using American heroes. That didn't quite work, and the architects did a lot of research before coming up with the final look of the murals.

"In general," noted Weinstein, "we believe in breaking some rules, but keeping the space understandable. We may go to the edge with an idea, such as putting the bar in the back, but we never go beyond the outer limit of acceptability." As to the value of good design, "it gives you an opportunity to set yourself apart from the competition and to get people in the door more quickly," said the restaurateur. "But," he cautioned, "the problem today is that too many restaurant owners are building places at prices which they can't support."

Asked what he would do differently if he could design America all over again, Weinstein answered that he would have chosen different subcontractors because some of the workmanship could have been better. He hastened to add that he was "very proud of the way the staff has kept up the restaurant. And it's like the Brooklyn Bridge; we're constantly painting it. We keep a painter on retainer who comes in every week to touch up the murals. Maintenance is a daily, ongoing activity." Indeed, America maintains its dramatic design impact and sparkling appearance despite the huge numbers of people who frequent the restaurant. Three years after it opened it was still a favorite destination for New Yorkers to entertain their out-of-town guests and maintained a substantial repeat customer base.

One interesting change since America first opened is the deliberately reduced beverage/food sales mix. Management discouraged the initially huge bar business and got the ratio down from 40/60 to 30/70. "We found the bar scene to be too interruptive," explained Weinstein. "We don't run bars, we run restaurants."

As for owner-designer dynamics, "Teamwork was difficult," admitted Weinstein, "because I am very strong-willed. And we come into an empty space with very definite feelings about what we are going to do. But Libby and Anthony brought something to the project which is actually quite rare: inspired ideas. They were able to react to what we thought the restaurant should be with creative solutions."

According to Weinstein, the designers had difficulty adhering to exact dates and schedules, but that problem wasn't necessarily a negative. "We all had the same goal, and that was to build the best possible restaurant. If Libby and Anthony didn't feel quite comfortable with a solution, then they wouldn't give up on it. They kept going until they were satisfied with the result. It's true that this held up the restaurant opening and became very costly. But the result was worth it. America made money from the first half hour it opened."

ELIZABETH McCLINTOCK AND ANTHONY GRAMMENOPOULOS, DESIGNERS

McClintock and Grammenopoulos, both architects, began their collaboration in 1980. Three years later they teamed up with architect Bill Soloway to form MGS. Based in downtown New York, the firm has designed all types of projects, including a substantial number of restaurants.

MGS had previously designed Ernies, one of Weinstein's restaurants on Manhattan's Upper West Side, so they were familiar with ownership's basic requirements for a see-and-be-seen grand cafe. The design of America began with "the idea of a large space where patrons could clearly see each other and lighting that helped to put people on display," said McClintock. Beyond that, added Grammenopoulos, "our goal was to take the given theme of America and refresh it, make it something exciting."

An area the architects felt was crucial to the success of the design was the entryway. "It was important to get the feeling of transition between the street outside and the enormous space inside," explained Grammenopoulos. The solution was a spacious, angled entry area comprised of two large, cherrywood grids set parallel to each other and linked by transparent glazing—actually glass panes normally used for squash courts that the architects imported from Great Britain. A dropped ceiling punctuated with star downlights furthers the effectiveness of the entry as a transition zone.

The architects never lost sight of the type of restaurant; design treatments were chosen to enhance the grand cafe ambiance. The illumination scheme was an important aspect of the milieu. "We did quite a lot of small beam spotlighting," explained McClintock, "because when a narrow beam shines on people as they move through space, it causes a flicker. The effect gave a lot of sparkle to the room. We lit the bar a bit more softly, and we also washed the walls so that the columns showed up in silhouette against them. But the people dining on the side platforms were brightly spotlit because they were sitting in the key see-and-be-seen position." McClintock added that the selection of pivoting secretarial chairs for the sideline seating enabled diners there to pivot out and look over the crowd and then swing back to talk to their companions.

America's murals—the most expressive symbol of thematic identity in the restaurant—evolved over time. Weinstein's original idea to depict American heroes just didn't work. After extensive research and much experimentation, the architects "left the figurative behind and developed the idea of combining ancient native American history with the current American landscape," remembered Grammenopoulos. Bold black-and-white fragments of Navajo sand paintings juxtaposed with pastel-colored pastures, trains, and cityscapes were executed by Slaj. The murals were applied directly to the walls in a combination of hand and spray painting. "The imagery," said Grammenopoulos, "used the Navajo as the universal theme, with the mysterious new culture running through it."

In fact, the restaurant design in general is imbued with a certain mystery because MGS manipulated space in a way that kept people's perceptions just a little off-balance. A subtle but very effective design psychology is at work in the space, based on the belief that people are stimulated by the unknown. As seen in the floor plan in figure 6-36, oblique angles are everywhere; the porch, aisle, neon flag, and bar are all slightly cocked around, so that, as McClintock expressed it, "spatial comprehension was delayed." The design makes the room appear even bigger than it really is because "you never actually see where the ceiling leaves the wall," said McClintock, who added that "we did everything we could to complicate people's perception of the space [without causing confusion], because that made it mysterious. It's a cerebral idea that involves very technical planning, but it works. When people don't quite get every detail of the picture in one shot, then they stay intrigued. We really believe that these psychological techniques keep people happy with America's design."

BILL LALOR, EXECUTIVE CHEF

Bill Lalor, who is responsible for menu development and kitchen design for all of Ark's restaurants, said that "as a rule of thumb, we like to underdesign our kitchens. The less room our employees have to play, the more efficient they become." Lalor feels that tight spaces are overall the best to work in and that a "cramped kitchen" is the best kitchen. He modified his comments to emphasize that adequate storage space is an absolute necessity.

When questioned about the overall space allocations for America's kitchen, Lalor lamented, "Kitchens are designed into what's left over after the architects have taken the desirable space. America's kitchen needed 10 extra feet of width and 10 less feet of length."

At America, as in the other Ark restaurants, the kitchen was designed around Executive Chef Lalor's requirements rather than around the specific menu. Lalor believes that menu trends change quickly and specialized kitchens stylized to a particular menu can quickly become obsolete.

When selecting equipment, Lalor opts for pieces that are very flexible. He also looks for equipment that can be used for any type of cuisine. When choosing any piece of equipment, one important rule keeps running through La-

lor's mind: "Keep it simple." Following that philosophy, Lalor specified simple, $250 candy burners in America's kitchen rather than steam-jacketed kettles that would have cost ten times as much. "We can do everything we could do in a steam-jacketed kettle and more on these burners," boasted Lalor, "and it cost us a lot less." However, Lalor also said that "Overall quality of the equipment is most important. It sometimes makes sense to spend an extra $500 on a better piece of equipment because it will run more efficiently; you will spend less money on maintenance and you will suffer less from downtime."

Summary

The success of America stems from Michael Weinstein's unique combination of instinct, tenacity, and shrewd business acumen. That the restaurateur waited a year and a half to sign a lease rather than raise his bid exemplifies a conservative fiscal philosophy. Yet the story of America is also about taking risks: placing the bar in the back of the restaurant, moving into an unestablished neighborhood, and allowing the designers to keep working out problems until solutions were perfected. Weinstein is an owner who knows exactly what he wants. In this case, the architects were able to interpret the owner's ideas creatively without changing them. What distinguishes America's design is a timeless quality perfectly matched to the type of restaurant and a slightly out-of-kilter spatial plan that lends an air of mystery to the space.

WILD WEST WUNDERKIND

THE RATTLESNAKE CLUB   Denver, CO

When *Esquire* reviewed the Rattlesnake Club as one of America's best new restaurants, they said that "it may well be indicative of the direction of American restaurants for the next five years." That's heady stuff, but anyone lucky enough to dine at this unusual Denver restaurant, a place at once glamourous and rustic, ultra-contemporary and respectful of tradition, would be hard pressed to disagree. Owned by noted Santa Monica restaurateur Michael McCarty and chef Jimmy Schmidt, who gained culinary fame at Detroit's London Chop House, the Rattlesnake Club opened in December of 1985. The owners and the designers—Boulder's Communication Arts—took three years to build the restaurant.

Only time will tell if the Rattlesnake Club in fact previews new directions for American restaurants. It certainly differs from most establishments. Located in Denver's historic Tivoli Center, a former brewery built circa 1859, it includes three separate foodservice areas: a bar and grill with a casual Southwestern menu; fine dining with an elegant, gourmet menu; and a separate banquet facility.

Project Background

Several years ago, the developer of Denver's Tivoli Center began talking to Communication Arts, a full-service design firm specializing in large retail complexes, about building a restaurant in a 13,000-square-foot former brewery. Communication Arts' Henry Beer, who became the principal-in-charge-of-design for the project, brought restaurateur Michael McCarty and the developer together to discuss the restaurant concept, and McCarty became increasingly involved with the project. Later, Jimmy Schmidt was retained as a kitchen design consultant. Eventually, the developer withdrew from the project and McCarty and Schmidt became co-owners.

This synopsis is a condensed version covering many years of a complex process. The first phase, said Beer, "involved putting together the most complicated lease agreement ever conceived of by man," and the second phase encompassed the real estate developer's search for operational experts to run the restaurant. Then, to complicate matters further, the financing package was not completely assembled before construction began, so there were many costly delays. "The knitting of this place together on a rather erratic start-and-stop basis was very complex," explained Beer, who added that "because the developer did not have the programmatic data together, the job became very expensive."

Kitchen design was equally challenging. When Jimmy Schmidt arrived on the scene as a consultant, he threw out an existing kitchen design and started all over. "The kitchen as planned was much too undersized for this large of a space," he commented, "and for my style of food, it was necessary for the kitchen to be very powerful."

Schmidt was not originally interested in taking on the position of chef for the restaurant. However, after "designing my own kitchen," he was hooked. He and McCarty became a team. On a basic level, their idea was to provide superb food and service in a rich, contemporary environment that had architectural significance.

McCarty suggested a separate grillroom for more informal dining and was responsible for the selection of a $500,000 modern art collection. Schmidt, who was on site daily, developed operational systems and was involved with such details as selection of the china and silver. They both met regularly with the Communication Arts designers.

First came the concept, said Schmidt, then the kitchen, and finally, about a week before opening, the menu. The name "was originally a joke, but we couldn't get rid of it. We kept making lists of names and Rattlesnake Club was always the last one to get crossed off the list."

From a design standpoint, said Beer, the project was a nightmare. The story of Rattlesnake is very much a tale of sensitive, adaptive reuse of a valued historic structure. The existing building presented myriad technical problems. In addition, no fewer than seven different governmental bodies—including health agencies, the national park service, the state historical preservation office, the city of Denver—were forces to be reckoned with. "Talk about serving many masters!" chuckled Beer. "It was really very challenging to come away with something that looked like it didn't suffer from compromises."

Design Description

FRONT OF THE HOUSE

The designers carved three levels—in essence, three restaurants—out of what was an enormous, wide-open volume of space (figs. 6-41, 6-42, and 6-43). Twenty-foot arched windows, cast-iron columns, and massive copper fermenting kettles were fabulous original details, but the gigantic room was initially unfriendly, Beer said. The completed restaurant seems quite friendly. On the ground level are the bar, lounge, and grill, a casual yet not inelegant area with a refined Southwestern atmosphere and an open kitchen. Here, observed by diners on a platformed seating area, a chef cooks up a fun assortment of Southwestern fare (fig. 6-44). Theatrical track lighting spotlights the chef's activities and casts a warm glow on copper hoods over the grill.

Altogether, the grill area seats fifty-five diners. Food is also served at the copper-accented bar. In back of the bar is a huge leaded window that affords a view of the lounge directly behind it. Here, in a pretty room accented with a baby grand piano and arched windows overlooking the city, patrons are offered drinks only.

When guests enter the Rattlesnake Club, they proceed straight to a maitre d' station. Then, they either continue directly ahead to the bar or the grill, or enter a copper-lined, glass elevator that goes up to the more formal dining areas above. A stairway also connects the floors. As soon as patrons enter the elevator, the downstairs maitre d' signals the upstairs maitre d' that they are on their way. When they arrive upstairs, customers are greeted by name and escorted to their table.

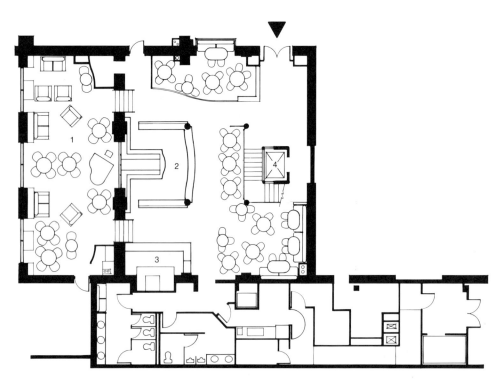

6-41. *The ground floor plan of the Rattlesnake Club shows:* (1) *the cocktail lounge;* (2) *the bar;* (3) *the grill; and* (4) *the elevator that carries guests to the upper-level dining floors (Courtesy of Communication Arts Incorporated).*

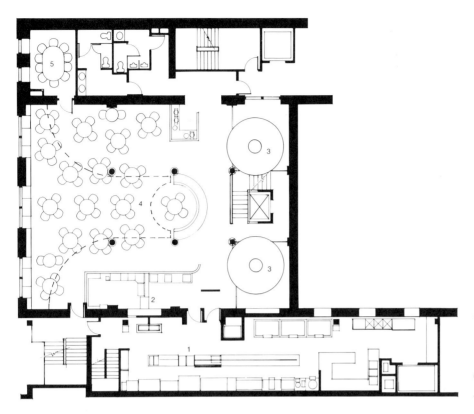

6-42. *The first floor of the restaurant houses:* (1) *the main cooking kitchen;* (2) *a service area where hot or alcoholic drinks can be ordered;* (3) *the bases of the copper brewing kettles;* (4) *the main dining room; and* (5) *a private dining room (Courtesy of Communications Arts Incorporated).*

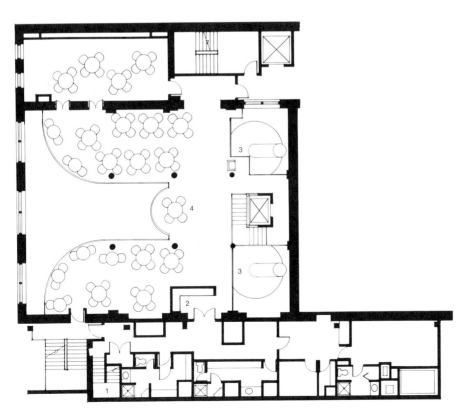

6-43. *The mezzanine floor of the restaurant includes:* (1) *access stairs from the cooking kitchen;* (2) *a service area for backup supplies;* (3) *the tops of the brewing kettles; and* (4) *the balcony seating areas (Courtesy of Communications Arts Incorporated).*

6-44. *The downstairs grill area sizzles with the sights and sounds of an open display kitchen.*
(Regina S. Baraban photo)

The two dining levels upstairs are a main floor and a mezzanine balcony that together seat 192 diners (fig. 6-45). In addition, a separate banquet room on the mezzanine level can seat 120.

Despite the spatial complexity of this plan, a symmetrical layout makes the upstairs public dining spaces easy for guests to navigate, and an underlying order lends a certain grace. Obviously an important space, it nonetheless is not at all pretentious. Suffused with a coppery glow, surrounded with unfinished walls whose rough surfaces are the backdrop for such modern masters as David Hockney, Jasper Johns, and Frank Stella, the restaurant is at once formal yet friendly (fig. 6-46). It resonates with messages from the past yet has the attitude of plunging headlong into the future. Structural corbeled columns, cathedral windows, and the big, round copper brewing tubs recall the building's architectural history, but at the round, white, linen-covered tabletops, Chef Schmidt's innovative cuisine—beautifully presented on tux-edo-patterned plates designed by Gwathmey Siegel—makes an evolutionary statement.

The environment is clean and uncluttered, although not austere. Color is centered on the artwork, flower arrangements at the center of each table, and the food itself.

BACK OF THE HOUSE

The back of the house at the Rattlesnake Club was spread out over four floors. "It was a very weird space, but we made it work," said chef-owner Schmidt, who redesigned the kitchen when he came on board. The original plans had called for a much smaller preparation area with far less equipment. In terms of cooking power alone, Schmidt increased cooking capacity from 1 million to 4.5 million BTUs. With that change, he had to modify all of the related utility-support systems.

In addition to modifying the kitchen equipment for higher output, Schmidt also had to change it to adapt to the location's high altitude.

6-45. *Diners have many seating choices in the main restaurant, including intimate dining on the newly constructed mezzanine level. (Regina S. Baraban photo)*

6-46. *Colorful artwork from modern masters creates a fascinating contrast against the architectural backdrop. (Regina S. Baraban photo)*

Higher than normal gas pressure had to be carefully regulated to yield the highest possible heat, because severe temperatures are necessary to produce the chef's unique style of cuisine.

Schmidt believes that flexibility is one of the keys to successful kitchen design. Therefore, much of the equipment was installed on casters so it can be easily moved around. Quick-disconnect gas couplings even make possible moving such equipment as ranges and broilers. "It's no big deal to find equipment that fits your menu," commented the chef, "but it is really important that everything be portable and easily cleanable." After the Rattlesnake Club opened, Schmidt was able to observe the idiosyncrasies of the operation as well as the likes and dislikes of the customers. The built-in flexibility of the equipment enabled him to respond appropriately by making changes in the line and by switching the position of equipment to get an improved work flow.

The ground floor back-of-the-house area incorporates beverage support equipment and resupply for the grill menu. The food served in the grill is preprepared in the main kitchen and mezzanine preprep area and then cooked to order in the display cooking area adjacent to the bar.

On the ground floor mezzanine, a substantial vegetable preppreparation and meat fabrication area was constructed. On this level a meat-aging box is accessed through a refrigerated, walk-in, meat-cutting room. To assure the quality of vegetables and produce, refrigerated space was provided for their prepreparation. Also on this floor, the $80,000 inventory of wine is secured in temperature-controlled storage.

The main kitchen is located above the fabrication and storage mezzanine on the main restaurant floor. A complete hot beverage and service support station sits at the entrance to the kitchen. Servers also access the service bar through this space.

Inside the kitchen, the hot and cold food sections are set in a single straight line. The cold food station is immediately in front of the entrance to the kitchen, with the hot foods section set to its left. Across from the hot foods section are step-in refrigerators that hold backup foods. Adjacent to the hot foods area is the dishwashing and pot-washing area. The chef is positioned in a central spot where he can see everything going on in the cooking lines.

To support the banquet room, a separate kitchen was installed. Here, each plate is prepared with the same care as for the restaurant clientele. Although he does not mass-produce banquet-style food in the traditional sense, Schmidt boasted in 1987 that his record to date was the preparation of 120 dinners in eight minutes.

A dedicated elevator links the various kitchen levels and is used to transport both raw and prepared foods. In addition, a dumbwaiter connects the ground floor back-of-the-house area and the restaurant mezzanine service support area with the main kitchen. It is utilized solely for dirty dishes. Clean tableware is returned to the service floors during setup times via the elevator.

Type of Restaurant

As noted earlier, the Rattlesnake Club is really three different types of areas under one roof: a bar and grill for casual dining, a gourmet restaurant for elegant dining, and a banquet room for group functions. All share the special aura of the landmark Tivoli brewery, and all are bound together by Chef Schmidt's original cuisine, whether informal or highly intricate. The owners invented a new type of restaurant that is essentially a highly organized, complex foodservice system geared to a high-end market.

The Market

Denver, as far as American cities go, has a relatively small market base. In 1986, total restaurant sales were roughly $660 million. When they planned the Rattlesnake Club, McCarty and Schmidt perceived the opportunity to fill a gap in Denver's restaurant scene, one aimed toward an affluent clientele. "Denver," said Schmidt, "has a very proud upscale market. Most people know what they like, and they're interested in quality." In contrast to the city's many "dark, booth-filled" restaurants, the Rattlesnake Club owners hoped to build a loyal clientele with both terrific food and a dynamic contemporary environment.

Potential clientele for all three foodservice

areas in the restaurant consisted of middle- to upper-income professionals in the Denver metropolitan area. "About half of our customers during the week are conducting business," commented Schmidt. In addition to building a customer base from the local community, the owners picked up a lot of vacationers en route to Vail or other Rocky Mountain vacation spots. By 1987, Schmidt estimated that at least sixty percent of Rattlesnake's business was from repeat customers. Although there is no dress code, people come very well dressed to the main dining room.

At the time Rattlesnake opened, it had no direct competition. The Tivoli Center was situated downtown off the beaten track; no other restaurants of Rattlesnake's stature were either inside the Center or located nearby. Indirect competition consisted of other fine dining establishments in the Denver metropolitan area that, unlike the Rattlesnake Club, offered traditional cuisine and design.

The location away from Denver's central business district was not an asset, despite the chance that a new convention center would be constructed nearby. The owners had to bank on the Rattlesnake's drawing power to lure customers to an out-of-the-way destination. The restaurant is more upscale than the retail stores in the complex, so the owners didn't expect to draw shoppers. Moreover, the restaurant has no outside entrance, and patrons have to walk through the enclosed mall to get there.

What was most important to McCarty and Schmidt, however, was the architectural location of the restaurant. "Its nice, but not essential to be in a high density spot," explained Schmidt. "For us, geography is not the critical part of the location. It's the architectural site that's important. High ceilings, a special view—it has to be capable of becoming a gorgeous piece of architecture."

The building itself helps to draw people to the restaurant. Few people drop by for a meal; rather, they select the Rattlesnake Club as a destination spot. As the restaurant gained fame for the quality of its architectural setting and its outstanding cuisine, patrons were not deterred by its off-the-beaten-path location. In fact, the locale may have gained a bit of status due to the Rattlesnake Club.

Denver was in an economic slump in the mideighties, with no dramatic turnaround in sight. "Rattlesnake is a big restaurant for this market, especially in today's economy," admitted Schmidt in 1987. Still, the owners found their market niche and anticipated gross sales of over $4 million in 1987, when other Denver restaurants were seriously hurting. "Sales have been lower than we'd like but higher than we expected, given the sluggish economy," noted Schmidt, who added that Rattlesnake was designed to gross $6 million.

Concept Development

The Rattlesnake Club in Denver is a prototype in terms of concept and stringent management control systems for future operations planned by McCarty and Schmidt. They envision urban locations across the country as homes for additional Rattlesnake Clubs, "all individual units designed as if each were the gem, the one restaurant you'd choose to own—except that we'll own a number of them," explained Schmidt. Like the Denver Rattlesnake, these are to be "grand, open rooms, where people can have privacy at their individual tables but still be part of the action." Both front and back of the house are characterized by a sense of "clarity and direction."

In 1987, plans for a Detroit-based Rattlesnake Club were progressing, and the owners were considering sites in other cities. Each site would be special from an architectural point of view, and each restaurant would incorporate the tight, computerized control systems that Schmidt developed for the Denver Rattlesnake Club. The custom-tailored design and the regionally inspired menu would differ from restaurant to restaurant.

The Menu

The Rattlesnake Club's ground floor grillroom offers creative Southwest cuisine that includes such items as a rattleburger with swami sauce and fire chips and crawfish empanadas with tomato-mint salsa. Altogether, thirty-eight items, including a broad assortment of starters, salads, and pizzas, as well as the varied and very sophisticated list of *chowls*, or main plates, are offered.

Most of the items are the same on the "high noon" and "sundown" menus, and the prices at dinner are typically twenty-five to fifty cents higher per item than at lunch.

The menu in the main restaurant upstairs is classified by Chef Schmidt as "modern American food; a blend of the best fresh ingredients from across the country. There's some local Southwestern influence, but it's not limited to that." Indeed, the restaurant's air freight bills to deliver exotic foodstuffs from all over the country to the Rattlesnake Club's kitchen are reportedly $5,000 monthly. Every dish is cooked to order. Most are prepared with high heat, which means that the eighteen rangetop burners, two fryers, and 16-foot-long grill in the main kitchen production line are well used.

Every day, Schmidt changes from 20 to 40 percent of the main restaurant's menu, which is printed daily on-site. Only twenty-seven items appear on the average menu for each meal period, but because the selections differ from meal to meal and from day to day, the offerings are actually quite varied.

Schmidt's method of menu planning and menu layout is classical. For the evening of June 23, 1987, for example, he broke his offerings down into the following categories: cold appetizers, hot appetizers, soups, pasta, salads, desserts, and main courses. The main courses, printed on an entire page of the menu, were divided into fish and seafood, poultry, lamb, beef, veal, and pork. Combined with the classical menu presentation, however, were unconventional mixtures of foods and flavors. The chef is a serious culinarian who incorporates items such as ahi tuna, roast duck, and lamb tenderloin into his entrees and then embellishes them with novel combinations such as passion fruit, peppercorns, and chives (with the tuna), achiots, tamarillos, and greens (with the duck), and artichokes, roast shallots, and thyme (with the lamb). In each of his creations, Schmidt seeks to offer refined dishes built with many layers of flavors.

Food and design have a very clear relationship at the Rattlesnake Club. Both evidence a balance between old and new and between classic and contemporary.

The Budget

The FF&E budget for the Rattlesnake Club, including the kitchen, came to approximately $1.25 million. Such an extensive renovation always spells high costs, and an extra $500,000 was spent on art. "Ten percent of our total FF&E budget always goes towards art, so that we can get substantial pieces in the restaurant," Schmidt explained. "We think that is much more important than putting big design dollars into carpeting, chair coverings, and accessories." The owners, however, spent what was necessary to achieve the effects they wanted. They went back and had the walls and ceiling of the grillroom repainted from rust red to light taupe because they believed that the room was too dark. In addition to art, they see value in spending money on "the detail work, places like entrance ways and floor finishes. We don't blow the budget on some wild piece of furniture that costs a fortune."

Style of Service

The Rattlesnake Club is the quintessential a la carte restaurant. Every dish and every table is handled in a special way. Schmidt's forte is the back of the house, and McCarty's forte is developing the style of service. Each table is taken care of by a team that includes the table server, a runner or runners, and a busperson. The staff is young, personable, and professional. The servers, who spend most of their time in the dining room, take the orders and relay them to the kitchen via a computerized cash-control and ordering system. The runners, who spend most of their time in the kitchen, closely follow the progress of food being prepared for a given table.

Dishes are plated in the kitchen and hand-carried by runners to the waiting guests. Everyone at the table is served at the same time. Each runner can handle up to three plates, and the number of runners per table depends upon the size of the table. For example, three or four runners might be needed for servicing a single table of twelve. No trays or tray stands are used because McCarty is adamant in his belief that food shouldn't sit. The buspersons are responsible for clearing and resetting the tables.

Interestingly, if anything is wrong with an order for a given table, all of the orders are taken back to the kitchen and recreated. Clearly, the Rattlesnake's style of service requires a great deal of coordination by the production staff in order to ensure that guests receive their meals at the height of perfection.

Speed of Service

The Rattlesnake Club is a serious restaurant, and the service staff are trained and retrained to understand that idea. The speed of service is leisurely yet attentive. The computerized ordering system enables the service staff to stay on the floor and attend to the needs of the guests. Although every dish is cooked to order, extensive time lags between courses do not occur because of the highly organized system of service.

A finely tuned sense of pacing is the key to Rattlesnake's speed of service. The well-trained staff is able to match speed of service with the demands of the guests.

Per Customer Check Average

Downstairs, a check average of $11 for lunch and $17 for dinner (food only) makes the grill a popular choice for customers who want a less expensive meal in a more casual atmosphere. Upstairs, the more formal dining experience carries with it higher check averages: $20 for lunch and $45 for dinner in 1987. The higher dinner prices reflect a different choice of entrees that involve more intricate combinations of ingredients than the simpler luncheon menu.

General Ambiance

Although the Rattlesnake is a huge space, the designers created the feeling of many intimate seating areas. They also specified a number of sound-absorbing materials and treatments to mute noise in the main dining room. The room has a lot of life, but the hum of conversation never turns into a roar. In the grill, harder materials allow more noise, which creates an energized, less formal atmosphere.

Management Philosophy

McCarty and Schmidt hope that the Rattlesnake Club will endure for twenty years, and they see Denver as the prototype for a string of future restaurants. Schmidt stayed on-site in Denver for the first few years after the restaurant opened, but part of his management plan involves developing staff and chefs to become partners in future sites as their skills grow. Management believes in promoting from within. "What we're aiming for is a built-in growth cycle," Schmidt commented. "You can start your own restaurant and end up with 10 or 20 percent of the business because you need financing. Or, you can come work with us and do the same thing, but with a huge support staff and tons of data behind you. We're sending roughly 40 percent of our Denver staff to start up the Detroit Rattlesnake Club, for instance, and we're breeding some brilliant chefs to be able to run these monster restaurants."

The Design Team

Rattlesnake owners Michael McCarty and Jimmy Schmidt originally met in 1980, when they worked together with the American Institute of Wine and Food. McCarty went on to become a well-known restaurateur with his swank Santa Monica establishment, Michaels. Schmidt went on to gain kudos for his food as chef of Detroit's London Chop House. Together, they brought extensive operational expertise and some very definite design input to the building of the Rattlesnake Club. Along with the owners, the core design team consisted of three individuals from Boulder-based Communication Arts: Principal-in-charge Henry Beer, principal Richard Foy, and project designer Roberta Cation. Additional consultants included electrical engineer John McGovern and contractor Deneuve Design. The banquet room was designed separately by a different firm.

MICHAEL McCARTY, CO-OWNER

Michael McCarty, a classically trained chef, burst onto the California culinary scene with the opening of Michael's in Santa Monica, California, in 1979. Michael's became an outpost of chic design and cuisine in the early 1980s and has continued its position as a trend-setter ever since.

According to McCarty, the biggest challenge faced by the Rattlesnake Club design team was bringing the Old Tivoli Brewery structure up to the code requirements of the local health regulations. He explained that the only violations to the integrity of the vintage building were openings cut through the old walls to access the 6,000-square-foot, back-of-the-house facilities, which were placed in a new addition adjacent to the historic brewery. Because the building was designated as a historic landmark, McCarty and Schmidt were able to apply for tax savings that came under the historic preservation law in effect when the restaurant opened in December 1985.

Although true to its original architectural shell, it is the combination of restoration and new ideas in Rattlesnake's interior that creates its singular charm. McCarty pointed out that "we initially considered taking the interior walls of the 12,000-square-foot front of the house back to their original scored plaster finish. Instead, we decided to keep the existing rough surface, which looked to me like the wonderfully textured walls I had recently seen in Italy. All we did was spray Rattlesnake's old walls with a silicon seal to keep them from structural decay." The decision to maintain the existing walls, according to McCarty, saved $200,000 in construction costs.

Due to the complex nature of this adaptive re-use project, it was impossible to finalize a set of plans. "The design work was ongoing," noted McCarty. "Our early plans were approved by government agencies, but Deneuve Design, the general contractors on the project, never did have a final set of plans to work from. It was the kind of project which required everyone on the design team to make a real commitment, and in the end became a showcase because of everyone's input."

The role of art in the Rattlesnake's interior can be attributed to McCarty and his artist wife Kim, who are avid, serious art collectors. They acquired a collection of modern masters for the restaurant (as they did for their own home and

for Michael's). "Art adds color, quality and sophistication to the space," enthused McCarty. The art pieces at the Rattlesnake Club are in a constant state of evolution; from time-to-time new pieces are added and others are rotated to the McCartys' other collections. Each future Rattlesnake Club will have its own special art collection selected by Kim and Michael McCarty.

McCarty said that he drew a lot from both front- and back-of-the-house experiences at Michael's when making decisions for the Rattlesnake Club. He worked with Schmidt to design an "efficiency-oriented" back of the house. He also believes that both the cuisine and the style of service play an important role in setting the Rattlesnake Club apart from its competition. His goal was "To create a contemporary restaurant that would be seen as a pioneer and predecessor of a new standard of service and food against which other restaurants would be measured." He developed a service format that called for a young, friendly staff who "would not brow-beat the customers," and for their uniforms selected pink "Polo" shirts designed by Ralph Lauren.

As for interior design, McCarty's philosophy was "to make sure that it endures, that it lasts. I think the definition of the Rattlesnake Club is that it is not trendy."

JIMMY SCHMIDT, CHEF AND CO-OWNER

One of America's heralded young chefs, Schmidt had earned his reputation during eight years of cooking in Detroit before moving to Denver to open the Rattlesnake Club in 1985. He and McCarty enjoyed a complementary partnership in which they "blended ideas together," said Schmidt. "We may sometimes have different views, but our major concern is for the whole design to work out the best way, not whether our personal idea gets in. We listen to each other."

Keeping the different design consultants coordinated for an efficient work flow was more difficult, recalled Schmidt. "People tend not to listen, even when meeting notes are passed out. But, the big thing is to get everybody in the same room at the same time, distribute minutes, spend the time on follow-up—you can't do enough of that," he advised. Further, "when you're designing something other than a standard building, you get into a lot of problems with workmen and the trades because they don't understand what you want. So you have to be extremely accurate with all your detail work."

Schmidt was the consummate kitchen designer: He drew his own plans and then had them professionally redrawn on a computer; he prepared all of the specification sheets and all of the information that went to the electrical and mechanical engineers. "That's the only way to get it done right," he believes, "because it's hard to find designers who really understand the kitchen. They don't know how it works."

Unlike some owners, McCarty and Schmidt had very pronounced ideas about front-of-the-house design. "We go for subtle tones with color accents in the artwork, flowers, and food, uncluttered rooms that are comfortable, and lighting that makes people look good," said Schmidt, who added that "We also like very symmetrical floor plans. Patrons should be able to look across the room and see all the way through it."

Schmidt pointed out that the ordered environment of the Rattlesnake Club's main dining room extends to such details as the chair upholstery. There are two subtly different upholstery colors: granite and sandstone. Each is positioned in the exact same place at every table: the granite chairs are always closest to the kitchen. Interestingly, the different colors are also used by the service staff as a system of identification for each table. This ensures that the proper plate is delivered to each given guest.

Schmidt and McCarty's attention to design detail covers such areas as the illumination scheme. They kept the ambient light level in Rattlesnake lower than the light level at the tables. Following their direction, every table in the restaurant has a direct spotlight shining on it. The beam is very carefully angled so that when light hits the table, the patternless white linen reflects a flattering glow on people's faces. "Anytime you put light on a person this way, you have to know what you're doing," Schmidt emphasized. "But these kinds of details are absolutely critical to the success of a design. We even worry about the size of the shadow that the flowers cast on the tabletop."

HENRY BEER, PRINCIPAL-IN-CHARGE

Communication Arts, a diversified design firm based in Boulder, tends to get involved with special projects like the Rattlesnake Club: "not your rank and file type of restaurant," noted principal Henry Beer. About half of the firm's thirty-five employees specialize in the design of large-scale specialty retail projects such as the Rouse Bayside development that opened in downtown Miami in 1987. Regarding the design of the Rattlesnake Club, Beer outlined many daunting challenges. "The size," he said, "was terrifying. How do you create intimate dining in a 13,000-square-foot room? How do you make an expensively priced place comfortable enough to bring people back two or three times a week? How do you make a cold space feel friendly?"

The designers developed a program that addressed these questions. Occasionally, a solution presented itself unexpectedly. At one point, when the walls had been partially prepared for plastering, "we looked around and realized it would be great if we left the unfinished walls as a sort of rusticated old envelope for the new design," remembered Beer. "This helped to create the friendly quality we wanted to engender in the restaurant. And it changed the tone of the design in a way that liberated us to do other things a bit more formally than we had originally intended" (fig. 6-47).

Some solutions were clear right from the beginning. "One of our first and foremost goals was to make sure that the acoustic characteristics in the room were absolutely right," commented Beer. "Irrespective of what the room looked like, we knew we had to have acoustic control." The sound level aimed at was "live enough so that people's conversations at one table masked people's conversations at an adjacent table, but without reverberation or an uncomfortable overall noise." The designers carefully considered the selection of every material, from the absorption qualities of the chair upholstery and carpet to the wall and ceiling treatments. They used acoustical tile underneath the mezzanine to form a lowered ceiling in the downstairs floor of the main dining room, and they specified an innovative and highly effective treatment for the top floor ceiling. This involved using a low-cost acoustic material, typ-

6-47. *Rough-textured, unfinished wall surfaces humanize the cavernous architecture of the restaurant.*
(Regina S. Baraban)

ically found in inexpensive apartment buildings, in a new way. The effect is a stuccolike texture that has great sound-absorbing properties. "It was a low-cost solution that gave an expensive look and did a super job of sucking up sound," noted Beer.

In the selection of finishes, surfaces, and materials, "we attempted to make choices that were both durable and timeless. We thought in terms of materials that would look better as they got worn as opposed to looking sleazier as they got worn. The goal was to achieve the patina

that comes from use rather than from neglect." Instead of a lot of brass and chrome, the designers chose copper as an accent material. Not only does it sparkle, but also "copper is the perfect metaphorical kitchen material," philosophized Beer.

In a room that reveals its architectural history, why not reveal its working parts? Never, said Beer. Not for a minute would he even consider exposed ductwork on the ceiling of the Rattlesnake Club. "I don't think exposed ducts are pretty or expressive of anything interesting. I believe that the HVAC should work and not be seen. Great rooms never have exposed ductwork, and we wanted to do a great room."

The quest to design a great room was greatly aided by owners McCarty and Schmidt, according to Beer. "Michael's art collection was a knock-out. It added the richness and complexity that the restaurant needed; that most architects put into the base building architecture. We were very lucky to be the beneficiaries of Michael's astute sense of what was needed for visual impact." As for Jimmy Schmidt, "He's an extraordinary person. As artistic as he is, Jimmy is also highly organized. If this were 1942 and he was twenty-seven, as he is today, he'd be a U-boat commander. After several kitchen design consultants flailed around, Jimmy just sat down and put this kitchen together like a top. It takes that kind of presence of mind in the background to make a project like the Rattlesnake work."

Summary

The Rattlesnake Club was an incredibly complex project that involved the creation of an intricate foodservice system. As a renovation of a historic space, it shows the potential of blending old with new: old architectural framework with modern art and innovative cooking with classical service, for example. It also exemplifies a prototype of sorts for future Rattlesnake Clubs in other locations—a new type of restaurant on the American scene. Moreover, it reveals the leadership of experienced owners whose combined expertise yielded synergistic results.

CONCLUSION

The life-span of a restaurant design often depends upon passing trends. Staying solvent for fifteen years equates to forever in these volatile times, when sophisticated consumers seem to be constantly searching for the best new places and styles change with the seasons. Indeed, as restaurants open and close at a dizzying pace—with today's hot hangout fast becoming tomorrow's outdated memory—some experts suggest reassessing the money spent on extravagant design. Further, as design costs escalate due to diverse causes ranging from the relative value of the American dollar to the complex requirements of local building codes, the restaurant owner is increasingly pushed to cut corners on design.

In the back of the house, chefs fight for adequate space to produce their ever more complex bill of fare. At the same time, designers and operators insist upon allocating more and more precious square footage to the revenue-producing dining room.

Still, the future of restaurant design holds promise of exciting things to come. In the past, one or two trends dominated the industry. Now, a multitude of very different, very successful places portend multiple directions. Restaurants have also regained stature as important public spaces. Not just a place to eat, the restaurant is an environment that provides an evening's entertainment, a spot for intimate conversation, and an escape from the daily grind.

Here we examine some of the ways in which past and present trends may shape the near future of restaurant design.

HOW FOODSERVICE TRENDS INFLUENCE DESIGN

Perhaps the single most important food trend, in terms of its influence on restaurant design, is the public's increasing interest in good, real, healthy food. Back in the late 1960s and early 1970s, when earthtones and fern-filled interiors defined the California look, the back-to-nature attitude was most apparent on college campuses. As those baby-boomers graduated, that attitude spread. Real materials began to take the place of molded plastic, and profusions of hanging plants brought the outdoors in. Self-service salad bars were integrated into front-of-the-house design.

Changing eating habits also influenced kitchen design. By the 1960s, frozen foods had taken hold in restaurant kitchens and brought about changes in work stations and equipment. For example, more freezer space had to be allocated, and vegetable preparation space could be diminished. Large, walk-in refrigerators to hold unshelled peas or crates of broccoli became less common. Fabrication areas shrank or were eliminated; where wholesale cuts of meat had been broken down and cut into individual steaks and roasts, now portion-controlled, individually wrapped, frozen cuts went directly from receiving to the freezer.

Starting in the 1970s, restaurateurs began responding to the public proclivity for fresh food. The installation of salad bars spread to every sort of restaurant. Wholesale cuts of meat were vacuum packed, which significantly extended their shelf life, and delivered in refrigerated form to operators. By the 1980s, fabrication areas for meat and fish came back into vogue, as increasing numbers of a la carte restaurants catered to the health-conscious American consumer. Fresh, natural ingredients were essential to the production of every type of fare.

Concurrent with the interest in fresh food was the advent of American cuisine. This new wave of grass roots food, pioneered in California by Alice Waters at Chez Panisse, featured on-premises gardens and locally grown meat and fowl. Soon chefs were scouring the width and breadth of the country to find all manner of American-grown exotica. Some operators even installed hydroponic gardens in their restaurants to bring fresh herbs, at their peak of flavor, to the waiting guests.

The influence on design was significant. Food presentation reflected the esthetic sensibility, but not the small portions, of nouvelle cuisine. In gourmet restaurants nationwide, American chefs combined ingredients in ways that no European chef would dream of and then paired plates with food in artful arrangements of form, color, and texture.

In more casual eating places, the kitchen also gained stature, often moving to the front of the house so that patrons could watch the cooks at work. This new direction infiltrated all types of restaurants, from Italian to Mexican to American. What better way for people to know what they were eating than to watch it being prepared? All manner of kitchen references—dessert displays, woodburning pizza ovens, rotisseries, theatrically lit grill stations—became hallmarks of restaurant design in the 1980s.

DECORATIVE AND FASHION TRENDS

The 1970s had fern-bar restaurants, plasticized fast food restaurants, stuffy hotel restaurants, slick contemporary restaurants, and a host of instant-history theme restaurants. Few establishments reflected avant-garde design treatments. In fact, fashion and furnishing trends often took years to influence restaurant interiors.

In the 1980s, everything changed. The trend started slowly, with an overall lighter look and a clean esthetic hand: Neon replaced hanging plants, bentwood cafe chairs supplanted molded plastic seating, and walls were stripped bare of theme memorabilia. An increasing variety of design and architectural firms began taking on restaurant commissions. Restaurant reviews described the décor as well as the food. Cookie cutter was out, fashion was in, and a new generation of restaurantgoers avidly sought out the most stylish new places. By 1987, restaurant design had burst out of its prescribed genres and was itself setting trends.

No single style prevailed. The 1950s diner came back into vogue, art deco influences were seen in restaurant furniture and accessories, and the decorative embellishments of postmodernism manifested themselves in restaurant interiors. Even the geometric shapes and bright colors characteristic of the high-design style known as Memphis, filtered into restaurants. Theme didn't die, but it often became more subtle and more complex, with evocative references rather than stock clichés. Many restaurant designs took themselves very seriously, but others reflected humor and whimsy. Theatrical lighting helped to create dramatic stage sets, and hard-surfaced materials contributed to the loud noise levels that were associated with the see-and-be-seen gathering place. Murals and other commissioned artwork individualized interiors. Color was newly appreciated as a design tool. Intricate color schemes, ranging from muted pastel hues to bold primary accents, formed the decorative shell of many 1980s restaurants, and along with the new palette came a variety of new light sources that made the colors come alive and helped customers see their surroundings as never before.

In general, the gap between fashion and restaurant design became smaller. Style was crucial, but the restaurateur had many choices: Just as one person's wardrobe might contain many different styles of clothing, any given American city sported many different styles of restaurant design. Like fashion, restaurants often reflected a kind of mix-and-match mentality.

ARCHITECTURAL DIRECTIONS

Over the past few decades, growing numbers of architects began to design restaurants. Their influence was evident in interiors whose décor was formed by the interior architecture: restaurants where materials, form, color, space, and light took the place of decoration. The building itself became important, and often surface coverings were stripped away to reveal the building structure, be it ventilation ductwork in the ceiling or structural columns. Some architects created buildings within buildings, using architectural objects instead of applied decoration to break up space and create visual interest. Many solutions were metaphorical as well as functional, in an effort to stimulate people's perceptions. Straightforward architectural treatments, such as the use of levels to define different seating areas, became commonplace in restaurant interiors.

By 1987, the architectural influence had been felt in restaurants nationwide. Emerging directions, however, indicated a new sensuality and playfulness. The California architect Frank Gehry, for instance, designed the restaurant Rebecca's with such elements as a gigantic glowing octopus dangling from the ceiling. Elsewhere, building walls were stripped down to their rough-textured, unfinished state. Rough, natural materials such as concrete, stone, and wood, plus all sorts of metals, dominated the new architectural toolbox.

CHANGING LIFESTYLES

Restaurants are barometers of social change. They mirror more than fashion; observing an urban gathering place can teach a lot about a certain segment of youth culture, for example. Here, grazing has hit the scene. People don't want to get filled up with a heavy (and fattening) meal; rather, they want to snack and socialize. What this means in design terms is big bars—where, because of a variety of reasons, alcoholic consumption is lessened in importance—that serve food, have open areas with enough aisle space for patrons to move around, and reflect high noise and light levels to spark the action.

Changing lifestyles have also resulted in a new breed of single diner who is courted by restaurants that serve food at a bar or counter. As the well-documented rise of two-income families continues, so will the take-out and delivery sections of restaurants—and provisions should be made in the front- and back-of-the-house design for these services.

TRENDS FOR THE 1990S

Many of these directions will continue right into the 1990s. No doubt this decade will bring some surprises as well. The following predictions are based on our observations and interviews with restaurateurs and designers. They represent just a few educated guesses about the near future.

The American love of food will continue to grow stronger. In connection with this, open cooking areas and other kitchen references will remain popular in the front of the house, and intimate settings that focus on food will regain popularity.

The French *sous vide*—the in-house prepared, vacuum-packaged fare—may supplant the current a la carte system in many restaurant kitchens. Such individual-portion vacuum packaging can help boost kitchen productivity, especially at a time when labor shortages are plaguing restaurateurs in many areas of the country. In terms of space planning and equipment, this trend means a need for added refrigeration, vacuum-packaging equipment, and rethermalization systems that can bring these precooked foods up to serving temperatures.

The central hot cooking island station, common to European kitchens, may become popular in the United States as well.

Fabrication areas will reappear in kitchens. More operators will install such items as fish files to meet the growing demand for fresh fish and seafood.

Restaurant architects and designers will retain increasing numbers of artists and craftspeople to design special pieces for restaurants.

A back-to-basics philosophy will pervade

both front- and back-of-the-house design in restaurants with limited FF&E budgets. Although equipment manufacturers are now adding sophisticated, on-board self-diagnostics to many types of equipment, there will be a driving force to keep kitchen equipment simple. Affordability will be an important factor in both front- and back-of-the-house design.

The design of all food services—cafeterias, hotel restaurants, and independent restaurants alike—will become increasingly interchangeable with each other.

Historic architecture will provide some of the most popular and dramatic restaurant interiors.

The see-and-be-seen gathering place will continue to be popular with young people, but there will also be a new wave of smaller, quieter restaurants.

The double-sided drivethrough will become increasingly popular, especially on the fast food scene.

Humor and fun will be evident in restaurant interiors.

Good restaurant design will integrate architecture, graphics, and food to form a functional whole that works from front to back. Every element of the interior, from the restroom to the butter plate, will be part of the design scheme.

In summary, restaurant design in the 1990s will be more diverse than ever. Competition on all levels should help to spur original design. At the very least, consumers won't be bored.

INDEX

For ease of reference, restaurant names are printed in *italics*.